SMALL AND LARGE TOGETHER

Volume 56, Sage Library of Social Research

SAGE LIBRARY OF SOCIAL RESEARCH

SMALL AND LARGE TOGETHER
Governing the Metropolis

Howard W. Hallman

Volume 56
SAGE LIBRARY OF
SOCIAL RESEARCH

 SAGE PUBLICATIONS   Beverly Hills   London

For information address:

SAGE PUBLICATIONS, INC.
275 South Beverly Drive
Beverly Hills, California 90212

SAGE PUBLICATIONS LTD
28 Banner Street
London EC1Y 8QE

Printed in the United States of America

Library of Congress Cataloging in Publication Data

Hallman, Howard W
    Small and large together.

    (Sage library of social research v. 56)
    Bibliography: p. 289
    Includes index.
    1. Metropolitan government–United States.
I. Title.
JS422.H28   352'.0094'0973   77-15428
ISBN 0-8039-0898-9
ISBN 0-8039-0899-7 pbk.

FIRST PRINTING

CONTENTS

To Beth and Joy

PREFACE

Where I Come From

Like all social science, this book reflects the author's values and personal experiences. Therefore, let me tell a little about my background so that the reader may place my ideas in better perspective.

My first professional work in a metropolitan area was in the 1950s with the Philadelphia Housing Association, a citizen organization, where I was assigned to give staff services to a couple of citizen housing and planning groups in the suburbs. The focus was on the need for county planning, subdivision control, creek valley preservation, and low-rent housing. With a political science background, I was also interested in local governmental organization and got involved in a project which led to a regional citizen research and action organization.

But more and more, I was drawn into the problems of the central city and such programs as housing code enforcement, urban renewal, and public housing. Next I moved to New Haven, where my work was entirely focused on the inner city, first neighborhood rehabilitation and then human resource programs, and I only vaguely paid attention to the metropolitan scene. After coming to Washington in 1965, I dealt mainly with employment programs, the Community Action Program, and then community corporations in low-income areas.

In 1969 I organized the Center for Governmental Studies, a small non-profit organization, and a lot of our research focused on neighborhood decentralization. When I examined the feasibility of neighborhood government, I cast around for analogous situations and decided that small suburban municipalities have similarities. When I thought about what neighborhood governments might do, I had to think about what they couldn't do, and this led to an examination of the division of functional responsibilities among jurisdictions of various sizes. I realized that neighborhoods can't act alone, and ultimately my book on this subject bore the title *Neighborhood Government in a Metropolitan Setting* (1974).

So through this circuitous route, I returned to an interest in governmental organization for metropolitan areas, looking from the small outward to the large. This obviously gives me a different perspective from those who have concentrated upon land use planning, transportation, water quality, and other matters which cause them to think a lot about areawide solutions.

Acknowledgements

Because I haven't been a regular sojourner in metropolitan studies, I am deeply appreciative of the output of those who have been. I should like to mention particularly Victor Jones, John C. Bollens, Henry J. Schmandt, and Joseph F. Zimmerman, whose works over many years have been an invaluable resource to me. Numerous reports issued by the Advisory Commission on Intergovernmental Relations (ACIR) have been a gold mine of information, and the five-volume study of substate regionalism, headed by David B. Walker and Carl Stenberg, I have used like an encyclopedia. The National Municipal League's monthly *National Civic Review* has been quite useful, and so also a classic published by the league, Paul Studenski's 1930 book, *The Government of Metropolitan Areas*.

During the period I was writing this book, I had the privilege of serving as a member of a panel of the National Academy of Public Administration for the "neighborhood-oriented metropolitan government" project. Panel discussions and field trips gave me an opportunity to try out some of my ideas, and I am certain that through osmosis I have absorbed other panelists' ideas and now pass them on as my own. Panel members were York Willbern (chairman), George L. Brown, John J. Callahan, Alan K. Campbell, Edward P. Curtis, Jr., John M. DeGrove, Idamae Garrott, Arthur Naftalin, Elinor Ostrom, and E. Robert Turner. Charles R. Warren was staff director.

Charles Warren and Albert Richter of ACIR read the entire manuscript, and selected portions were reviewed by William Brussat, Richard Hartman, Milton Kotler, Norton Long, Elinor Ostrom, Vincent Ostrom, John Thomas, and York Willbern. Their comments were quite helpful in making the final revisions. Many other people whose published works I draw upon are indicated in the footnotes. Beth Hallman assisted in statistical analysis.

Naturally, I take full responsibility for the views stated.

Washington, D.C.   *Howard W. Hallman*
July 1977

PART I

HOW IT NOW IS

Chapter 1

METROPOLITAN PROBLEMS

Cataclysmic riots tore apart numerous American cities during the summer of 1967, the fifth straight year of such happenings and the worst. To understand why this came about and what could be done to prevent recurrence, the National Advisory Commission on Civil Disorder labored hard for eight months and in March 1968 issued its report. "This is our basic conclusion," the commission exclaimed. "Our Nation is moving toward two societies, one black, one white—separate and unequal" (1968:1).

This finding is the most disturbing view of metropolitan problems heard during the last ten years. But this isn't the only metropolitan problem perceived. Service deficiencies, fiscal disparity, unwise development, environmental hazards, administrative chaos, loss of sense of community are other concerns frequently expressed. Some of these relate to governmental structure, which is the primary focus of this book, but others less so.

These varied problems have been documented many times over in the reports of government commissions during the past ten years. Each study commission brings a particular perspective to the task, but among them a number of common themes emerge. This can be seen through a sampling of four reports in addition to the one from the Commission on Civil Disorder. They include the report of the National Commission on Urban Problems (1968) and one by the Commission on Population Growth and the American Future (1972). Of more recent origin are the *1976 Report on National*

Growth and Development, issued by President Gerald R. Ford's Domestic
Council, and a summarization of many years of study by the Advisory
Commission on Intergovernmental Relations (ACIR) in a report entitled
Improving Urban America: A Challenge to Federalism (1976A).

UNPLANNED GROWTH

According to these several reports, metropolitan areas as now governmentally constituted aren't well equipped to cope with population growth,
the development of vacant land by housing, commercial, and industrial uses,
and the expansion of public facilities. The urban sprawl characteristic of the
thirty year period following World War II vividly demonstrates this. Even
though metropolitan growth is slowing down in some areas, other areas,
particularly in the South and West, continue to expand, and all around the
country growth is occurring in counties outside metropolitan areas but within
the commuting and economic orbit.

"Missing," the Commission on Population Growth observed (1972:60), "is
the effective force seeking comprehensive solutions to comprehensive problems from a metropolitan-wide perspective." Another is the fragmentation of
building regulations, documented by the Commission on Urban Problems
(1968:xi): thousands of little kingdoms for building codes; zoning distorted
by economic considerations from its mission to serve as a guide to orderly
development. These factors, along with rising land costs, have forced up
housing prices beyond the means of low- and moderate-income households,
thus exacerbating the physical separation of economic classes.

INADEQUACIES IN SERVICE DELIVERY

Some governmental services aren't delivered well because units of the
proper scale don't exist. According to the 1976 National Growth Report, the
proliferation of governmental units has created parochialism and resulted in
wasteful duplication (1976:139). This suggests the need for areawide organization of service delivery systems. Yet, a recurring secondary theme is that
for certain services the units are too large and neighborhood decentralization
is needed, as both the Commission on Civil Disorder and the Commission on
Urban Problems advocated. Underlying the service delivery problem is the
mismatch of responsibility for administration and the fiscal capacity to
support services.

FISCAL DISPARITY

The latter relates to fiscal disparity, that is, the uneven availability of
revenues to support public services. The root of the problem, ACIR claims
(1976A:3), is that the national government has the most elastic and produc-

tive revenues, but solutions to urban problems must be handled mostly by state and local governments with less responsive revenue systems. Similar disparity exists between needs and resources of governmental units within metropolitan areas. It is particularly noticeable where an older central city hasn't expanded its territory to encompass newer outlying commercial and industrial areas. The concentration of people with low income and high service demands within the central city adds to the difficulty.

RACIAL AND SOCIAL SEPARATION

This social division between poor people and minority groups in the central city and more affluent households in the suburbs underlies many of the problems of service delivery and fiscal disparity. And the desire of many people to maintain this pattern of population distribution strongly influences how controls over development are used. "The result of all this," says ACIR (1976A:5), "has been to forge a white, middle- and high-income wall around the increasingly black and poor inner city." Thus, the dramatic finding of the Commission on Civil Disorder in 1968 still prevails. And future trends are bleak, the 1976 National Growth Report predicts, for quite likely, "social and economic disparities between the central city and suburb will persist with the central city taking in and retaining the poorest population, and the suburbs generally absorbing the more affluent population" (1976:31). Thus, attitudes and actions dealing with race and social class are pervasive factors in metropolitan problems.

LESSENING OF CITIZEN CONFIDENCE

Among the most disadvantaged people confidence in government is low because of the conditions in which they live. But others who are more affluent also display lack of confidence in the ability to get things done. Official corruption is a factor in some places, but so too is the structure of government, so complex that accomplishments are hard to attain, and in many instances government is so distant that people feel out of touch. Specialization and professionalism of public services and the vast scale of city and urban county government seem to have diminished the capacity for neighborhood action and self-help activities. The absence of both neighborhood and metropolitan governmental institutions makes it difficult to develop citizenship opportunities for the smallest and largest communities of the metropolis.

UNCLEAR PUBLIC OFFICIAL ACCOUNTABILITY

The irony of problems arising both because of the proliferation of many small units and the scale of large units appears in the issue of public official accountability. It is hard to trace the pattern of responsibility among numerous special districts, townships, small municipalities, independent school districts, cities, counties, and multijurisdictional agencies. But where consolidation occurs or a central city or an urban county serves a large population, bigness may cause separation of citizen and official and accountability thus diminishes at this larger scale.

ROLE OF STRUCTURAL SOLUTIONS

This is a small sampling of metropolitan problems, but enough to set the scene. Many of them aren't solvable by changes in the structural pattern of local government in metropolitan areas or by modifications in the fiscal arrangements of the larger federal system. For some of them relate to people's attitudes, some to how people use economic and political power, some to the class structure of our society. But the way government is organized within metropolitan areas and the relationship of this pattern to state and national government can make a difference by giving metropolitan inhabitants the institutional mechanisms they need to handle their problems. Thus, this book concentrates on structural and fiscal solutions not because they alone are a panacea but because they have an important contribution to make.

Chapter 2

SOME DEFINITIONS AND A FEW STATISTICS

Before moving on, it might be useful to put forth some definitions so that the terms used in this book are clear. Also, presentation of a few statistics outlining the growth and present size of metropolitan America and its local governments can help place the topic in perspective.

What is a Metropolitan Area?

To begin with, what is a metropolitan area? In general terms a metropolitan area is a city and the surrounding developed and developing territory. It is a metropolis functioning as a labor market and retail trade area regardless of governmental boundaries. It usually has cultural institutions serving the whole area. People have a sense of identity with the area, and if asked while a thousand miles from home where they come from, they will commonly give the name of the central city even if they live in the suburbs.

Government statisticians, though, want more precision than this general concept, so they have concocted something called the *Standard Metropolitan Statistical Area,* or SMSA as it is known in the trade (OMB, 1975). Except in New England, an SMSA is a county or a group of counties containing at least one city of 50,000 or more inhabitants, or "twin cities" with a combined population of at least that amount. In New England, where counties are minor entities, cities and towns are combined into SMSAs. In 1976 there were 272 SMSAs in the United States and four more in Puerto Rico.

In recent years the persons in the U.S. Office of Management and Budget (OMB) who define SMSA boundaries have kept adding more and more fringe counties to various SMSAs. The result might be justified by technical statistical definitions, but in practical concerns of local government operations, which is the interest of this book, quite a few SMSAs with two or more counties encompass a territory far beyond the central core and principal suburban area where urban services are required. Therefore, this book draws in the operational definition and will later describe what will simply be called *single-county metropolises,* smaller in size than SMSAs in many instances. However, SMSAs will be used for most comparative statistical analysis because that is the data base available.

Because some metropolitan areas have grown together, OMB has also defined 13 *Standard Consolidated Statistical Areas* (SCSAs) consisting of two or more SMSAs. Again, this book uses these statistics but changes the terminology when other combinations of areas are considered in discussion of governmental organization. Thus, the term *metropolitan region* will be utilized to describe two or more metropolitan areas together and also some very large free-standing SMSAs. And a nonmetropolitan multicounty area will be referred to as a *town-and-country district.*

One other census definition should be noted, the *urbanized area.* This is generally smaller than an SMSA and consists of the central city, or twin cities, and the surrounding closely settled territory. It excludes rural residents within the same county, and in many instances the urbanized area of a multicounty SMSA is found only in the core county.

Growth of Metropolitan Areas

POPULATION

The U.S. Bureau of the Census first provided data on metropolitan areas in the 1910 census and found that 29.4 percent of the total U.S. population lived in 44 districts with a central city of 100,000 or more and adjacent territory. These districts had grown 33.8 percent during the preceding ten years compared to a 16.4 percent growth rate for the rest of the country.

In every decade of this century up to 1970, metropolitan growth has exceeded the growth rate of nonmetropolitan areas. But this trend changed in the seventies, for from 1970 to 1975 metropolitan areas grew at a slower rate than the remainder of the nation. Even so, the proportion of the population living in metropolitan areas increased from 68.7 percent in 1970 to 73.2 percent in 1974. Because the vast majority of metropolitan areas continued to grow, several new SMSAs were added to the list, and some additional counties were tacked on to some previously existing SMSAs.

As the population now stands, nearly three out of four Americans live in metropolitan areas, reversing the proportionate distribution of 1900 when only one out of four were metropolitan residents. This means that a substantial majority of the people are directly affected by the governmental structure of metropolitan areas, and they will continue to be in the foreseeable future.

NUMBER OF AREAS

As metropolitan population has grown so also has the number of localities which can be considered metropolitan areas. Using today's concept of a central city with at least 50,000 as the core of a metropolitan area, we find that in 1800 only New York City had that many inhabitants. Ten cities had reached that threshold by 1850 and 78 by 1900.

The 1910 census was more conservative and required at least 200,000 population for the central city of a "metropolitan district" but also provided data for cities of 100,000 and more and their adjacent territory, coming up with 44 areas. The 1930 census used 50,000 as the core but set a 100,000 minimum for the metropolitan population, and so defined 96 such districts. The 1950 census adopted a definition of Standard Metropolitan Areas somewhat like the current one and identified 222 SMAs. The latest refinement by the Office of Management and Budget lists 272 SMSAs in 1976. Although changing definitions prevent exact comparisons, nearly half of contemporary metropolitan areas reached the qualifying size in the last 30 years as a product of post-World War II growth.

For this book, the universe is 272 metropolitan areas containing approximately three-quarters of the U.S. population.

Governmental Units in Metropolitan Areas

NUMBER OF UNITS

The metropolitan areas of the United States contain 22,185 local governmental units out of a total of 78,269 such units in the whole nation. This is the count for 1972 when the last census of governments was conducted and when the number of SMSAs was 264. Since then, there has been a net increase of eight SMSAs, some SMSAs have been expanded in territory, a few new units of local government created, some consolidated (particularly school districts), but the basic situation probably hasn't changed greatly since the 1972 census of governments.

Table 2.1: Types of Governmental Units in SMSAs (1972)

Types of Units	Number	
General government		9,373
Counties	444	
Municipalities	5,467	
Townships (including New England towns)	3,462	
Special districts		8,054
With property taxing power	4,344	
Without property taxing power	3,710	
School units		5,275
Independent school districts	4,758	
Dependent school systems*	517	
Total units of local government (excluding dependent school systems)		22,185

*A dependent school system operates as a subunit of local general government and doesn't have independent taxing power.
Source: U.S. Bureau of the Census, 1973: Table 17.

The breakdown of the 22,185 governmental units in metropolitan areas as of 1972 is shown in Table 2.1. Of these, 42.3 percent are units of general governments, including counties (2.0 percent), municipalities (24.7 percent), and townships (15.6 percent); 21.4 percent are independent school districts and 36.3 percent are special districts. There are also many other subordinate agencies of local general government which the U.S. Census Bureau doesn't consider to be separate governmental units.

Later chapters present more detailed information about these several types of governmental jurisdictions, but these are enough statistics for now to give a sense of the situation.

GOVERNMENTAL PLURALISM

What we find is a highly pluralistic local government in metropolitan areas. As the next part of the book reveals, it became that way through historical evolution, occurring mainly through pragmatic responses to changing conditions arising along with metropolitan growth. But here and there major structural changes, purposefully conceived, have been achieved.

As we saw in the previous chapter, several national commissions have felt that this multiplicity of governments causes problems for metropolitan areas. None of them, though, believe that completely unified government is achievable or desirable for all metropolitan areas. Some change is needed, they said, but governmental pluralism is likely to remain. I concur. The key questions are how many governments and what kinds, who does what and who pays the bill, and how do the various parts relate to one another and to the whole.

But before getting to these questions, we need to know more about what now exists and how it came into being. Those are the topics of Part II.

PART II

RESPONSES, PAST AND PRESENT

Chapter 3

ADAPTATION OF LOCAL GENERAL GOVERNMENT

It is easy to focus upon metropolitan problems and to forget that in truth metropolitan areas do function as human habitats with considerable effectiveness. Safe drinking water reaches almost every home. Sewage disappears out of sight and smell is usually eliminated. Garbage and trash are taken away. Houses are built, and schools and hospitals, too. People move around, and many journey quite a way to work and shopping. Children have places to play, and people in need get social services. Although American metropolises don't function perfectly—for many inequities exist and numerous problems remain unsolved—they do keep going and do satisfy a wide variety of human needs.

The fact that a metropolis, with its concentration of population and its conglomerated land uses, can function at all is a tribute to the adaptability of governmental institutions to this new form of sprawling settlement. Adaptation it has been primarily: the gradual evolution of old forms, hesitant beginnings with new forms followed by slow development, none of it particularly planned, just happening as circumstances require. To be sure, some new institutions have emerged and now and then major reforms have occurred. But the predominant process has been adaptation.

As in the past, so in the future, adaptation will likely be the primary method for dealing with problems of metropolitan governance. Although I and others of reformist persuasion favor some major institutional changes, we must recognize that reform is the exception, not the rule. Therefore, it is useful to understand the various ways we Americans have adapted our governmental system to the conditions of metropolitan life. Then we can build upon this knowledge as we make further changes, minor and major.

Historical Influences

If we are to comprehend the pattern of government now found in metropolitan America, we need a sense of historical development. Ironically, an understanding of governmental systems designed earlier for rural areas is particularly important.

At the time of the American Revolution four patterns of rural government existed in the 13 colonies, and they all had roots in seventeenth century English government which divided the land into counties subdivided by parishes. Virginia tried both but settlement was too scattered for parishes to take hold, so only counties survived, governed by courts of justices appointed by colonial governors and generally dominated by the landed gentry. Similar arrangements developed in the other colonies from Maryland southward. By contrast, New Englanders formed towns encompassing centers of settlements and the surrounding rural area—the parish idea—and they governed them with town meetings; only later were counties superimposed, primarily as judicial districts. New York tried each approach and ended up with a compromise whereby elected town selectmen joined with city representatives to form the county board of supervisors of considerable size; the towns and counties were of approximately equal power. New Jersey had a similar arrangement. Pennsylvania went its own way and formed counties like the southern colonies but established elected boards of commissioners with three members to run them; at first there were no townships, but later they were created and assigned some minor administrative chores but not as much authority as New York's towns (Duncombe, 1966:18-22; Wager, 1950:5-8).

When settlement moved westward, the new states tended to adopt the form of rural government to which most settlers were accustomed, except that the New England form wasn't reproduced anywhere. Thus, Michigan, Wisconsin, and parts of Illinois followed New York by creating a balance between counties and towns or townships and had large county governing boards elected by districts. Pennsylvania influenced the rest of the north central states as far west as the Dakotas, Nebraska, and Kansas, where small-size county boards were dominant and townships fairly weak. And the Virginia approach with an elected county court and no townships spread in the South, except that in Louisiana they called them parishes because their boundaries approximated former Spanish ecclesiastical districts. Then, the western states produced a fifth form, using the small, elected county board of the Pennsylvania model but not forming townships, in this respect following the South. Alaska established vast administrative units called boroughs, but they are similar to counties in their responsibilities.

Municipal government has its separate history, also derived from England, in this case the model of corporate status granted by the crown. In America the grantor of municipal charters was the proprietor (such as William Penn) or the colonial governor, evolving to the colonial council, then the state legislature after independence, and finally to general state law. Municipalities thus came into existence to serve population concentrations at specific places but in territory also served by counties. Municipalities and townships were considered to be the local government, and the counties were seen more as administrative agents of state government.

In New England the general practice was for cities and towns to be separate, though today exceptions occur where incorporated villages in Vermont and a few small boroughs and cities in Connecticut exist within town boundaries. In New York and another six states, villages are also contained within towns or townships but cities are completely separate. All municipalities in Indiana operate in areas also served by townships, but in the remaining 11 township states there isn't any overlap. And of course the matter doesn't arise in the twenty-nine states without townships.

When the U.S. Bureau of the Census made its count of governments in 1972, there were 264 SMSAs containing 444 counties, 5,467 municipalities, and 3,462 townships. Thus, a lot of units of local government designed originally to serve rural areas have been drawn into the metropolis, not all at once but over the years in a gradually adaptive process.

Incremental Expansion of Cities

As urban centers gained population, settlement began to tumble beyond the bounds of city limits. This produced an elementary structural problem: the inability of one government to serve all metropolitan residents. The most obvious response was expansion of city boundaries to encompass the outlying settlements.

Many cities have followed this course in their history, and the fringe residents have often welcomed and sometimes pleaded for inclusion in order to gain city services. Although city expansion doesn't happen very often now with the older cities, particularly the larger ones, smaller cities and relatively young urban centers (those gaining metropolitan status within the last forty years) are still enlarging their borders. This happens particularly where state law favors city expansion.

ANNEXATION

Annexation of unincorporated land is the primary means for incremental growth. Through this process a city expands its territory to take in developed, developing, and potentially developable land beyond the previous city limit.

In the early years of this nation, each city was chartered individually by the state legislature, and to annex more land, it had to ask for a special act of the legislature. After a while this changed to general state laws delegating annexation powers to the cities. Over the years many states added a requirement for a local vote. Around the turn of the century Virginia brought the courts into the act, and within the past twenty years six states have provided a role for administrative commissions. Thus, there are now five basic methods for determining annexation: state, municipal, popular vote, judicial, and administrative (ACIR, 1974A:84-86; also see Sengstock, 1960 and National League of Cities, 1966).

A legislative decision is required in the New England states, and because the towns are fairly sacrosanct, annexation rarely happens. The Georgia and Florida legislatures have retained this power as one option and occasionally exercise it, but not often. The other states have largely delegated annexation authority to cities, the judiciary, or an administrative body.

Three-fifths of the states require a vote prior to annexation. As a minimum, residents or property owners of the area proposed to be annexed vote on the matter; sometimes voters of the annexing city are involved, and in a few cases also voters of the jurisdiction faced with the loss of territory. In contrast, a small number of states give city council virtually unilateral powers to decide about annexation of unincorporated territory; home rule cities in North Carolina, Missouri, Oklahoma, and Texas have particularly wide latitude.

Commencing in 1902 in Virginia, ad hoc annexation courts, composed of three circuit judges, reviewed all annexation proposals and determined whether all technical requirements were met and whether the annexing city was more capable of providing urban services than the county from which the land would be taken (for in Virginia cities and counties are territorially independent). However, in 1971 the Virginia legislature clamped a partial moratorium on annexation as a reaction to a controversial case in the Richmond area and in response to pressure from urban counties, and the 1977 session extended the moratorium another ten years.

Elsewhere, Alaska, Minnesota, Iowa, and Michigan have state boundary commissions to review proposed annexations, and Washington, Oregon, and California have local commissions for this purpose (more about them later in the chapter).

MUNICIPAL MERGER

A second and less common way for the central city to grow is through merger with suburban municipalities. It is really more like absorption because the personnel and public facilities of the smaller municipality are amalgamated into the larger system.

Thus, between 1868 and 1874 citizens in the towns of Roxbury, Dorchester, Charlestown, Brighton, and West Roxbury, desirous of a better water supply, voted to become part of Boston, and Hyde Park joined in 1911. Los Angeles aggressively used water politics to get nine previously independent cities to merge during its peak period of expansion from 1909 to 1927. Among other major cities in this period, Cleveland absorbed eleven small municipalities, Chicago fifteen, Denver thirteen, and Seattle fourteen (Studenski, 1930:74). On a smaller scale, Norwalk, Connecticut became a city in 1913 through the merger of four towns, and in the same year the twin cities of Winston and Salem in North Carolina became one. The village of Eastwood became part of Syracuse, New York in 1926. Between 1950 and 1972 Lincoln, Nebraska absorbed five municipalities. Here and there are some other cases, but municipal merger has never been a major movement.

BROADENING POWERS

As cities expanded their territory, they gradually enlarged their powers and number of employees. For instance, two functions we now take for granted, police and fire protection, were not handled by municipal government in the early days of this nation. Benjamin Franklin organized the first voluntary fire brigade in Philadelphia in 1739, but it was nearly a century before the first paid public fire department was set up in Boston in 1837. A year later Boston hired the first publicly paid, day police force.

Lent D. Upson traced the expansion of governmental power in Detroit, beginning with the granting of city status by the territorial legislature in 1823. With 1,500 inhabitants the city was responsible for 23 activities, including legislation and general administration; tax assessment and collection; enforcement of local ordinances; maintenance of a few public buildings, some unpaved streets, and the public market; control of weights and measures; and a modicum of fire prevention. By 1840 the activities had increased to 36 and included street and sidewalk construction, sewerage, and water supply. Elementary education was added in 1842, street lighting in 1850, a high school in 1858, a prison in 1861, an organized police patrol and a library in 1865, and organized fire fighting in 1867 so that by 1870 the city government was involved in 59 separate activities. The number grew steadily thereafter, reaching 132 in 1900 and then expanding rapidly in the next 30 years until Detroit managed 306 distinct governmental activities in 1930 (1931:11-21).

Similar broadening of local governmental powers and activities has occurred through the country during the past 150 years.

EXTRATERRITORIAL POWERS

Cities have also tried to cope with growth through the use of extraterritorial powers. One of the first was the right to acquire land outside city limits for public purposes, and in some states cities have evoked the power of eminent domain to condemn land for certain kinds of facilities. Acquisition of sites for reservoirs, intake plants, and treatment facilities for water supply was one of the first usages of this power and has been the most frequent. Cities have also constructed sewage disposal plants outside city limits at spots with a suitable drainage outlet. They have built airports beyond the city's borders and have extended major highways as far as ten miles from the city. Other city facilities built beyond the corporate limits are cemeteries, hospitals, penal institutions, workhouses, wharves, markets, slaughterhouses, storage buildings for explosives, playgrounds, quarries, animal shelters, zoological gardens, and parks (Sengstok, 1962:60).

Provision of services to nonresidents is another use of extraterritorial power. Water supply is the most common example in the form of retail sale to individual uses (also, cities have contractual agreements for whole distribution to suburban municipalities for resale to their inhabitants). Linkage to the city's sewerage system happens less frequently but does sometimes occur. Fire protection may also be provided, but this is more often a reciprocal arrangement of mutual aid. A city policy academy and a firefighter training center may take in suburban enrollees, and the health department might provide some technical services to outlying public health units. Direct services where personnel are a major factor, such as police, street maintenance, and recreation, are less likely to be extended, though in some places the independent city school district may reach into the suburbs.

In some instances, cities exercise extraterritorial police power, such as health quarantine, abatement of nuisances arising outside the city, regulation of slaughterhouses both for environmental effects and for quality of the product intended for sale within the city, inspection of dairies within the city's "milkshed," regulation of cemeteries. But such power is used sparingly (Sengstok, 1962:52-53).

In 33 states municipalities have authority for subdivision control for distances of one-half to six miles beyond city limits, and in 21 states municipalities may adopt extraterritorial zoning regulations. Four states give municipalities power to apply their building code for one to five miles outside the city (Federal Insurance Administration, 1976:32). Among the strongest of such controls are those in Texas where the municipal annexation law gives cities an extraterritorial jurisdiction ranging from five miles for cities over 100,000 to one-half mile for cities of less than 5,000. Within this area, the city has the presumptive right of annexation, can prevent incorporation of a new municipality, and can exercise subdivision control. The extraterritorial zone expands with the city, and Houston has used this device aggressively by annexing along highways and railroads to vastly extend its extraterritorial jurisdiction.

These varieties of extraterritorial powers have helped some cities to cope with problems of metropolitan growth. But with rare exception where they have acted as a prelude to annexation, they haven't produced governmental unity. Instead, they are useful stop-gap measures and devices of adaptation, performing in an arena of governmental pluralism.

CENTRAL CITY'S SHARE OF URBAN POPULATION

Some cities have succeeded better than others in using annexation and municipal merger to absorb the growing metropolitan population. If we use the urbanized area—the census concept of the closely settled territory—as an approximation of the "real city" which requires urban services, we find that of the 248 urbanized areas tabulated in 1970, about one out of five (21 percent) had more than 90 percent of the inhabitants residing in the central city. Cities in the South, Southwest, and Midwest do best in holding onto the urban population. The leader is Texas where 11 cities take in more than 90 percent of the urbanized area's inhabitants; for, as we have noted, Texas cities have powers to annex unilaterally and to prevent suburban incorporation near city limits. The Northeast, where strong towns and municipalities surround the cities, has very few cities containing most of the urbanized population. The same is true for the three Pacific coast states, for there residents of any territory proposed for annexation must give their consent, and they have the fairly easy options of suburban incorporation or formation of special districts.

Thus, incremental growth through annexation and the prevention of suburban incorporation does offer a potential for achieving something close to one municipal government for the "real city," at least for the smaller cities which have recently moved into a metropolitan status. This depends upon the existing pattern of local government and the existence of favorable state laws. But most of the larger metropolises have lost this opportunity and require more drastic measures if they want to achieve unified government. This is the subject of Chapter 7.

Growth of Suburban Governments

The establishment of numerous suburban governmental units has been another major adaptive response to metropolitan growth. It is a long-standing phenomenon, starting modestly in the early 1800s, becoming quite apparent around some eastern cities by 1850, steadily expanding the rest of the century, burgeoning in the 1920s, and exploding in the years since World War II.

Suburban government, though, is not of one kind. It consists of small-area, general-purpose governments in the forms of incorporated municipalities, townships, and New England towns. In addition, once rural-oriented counties have become major deliverers of urban services, and there are also small-area special districts (considered in the next chapter).

MUNICIPAL INCORPORATION

The oldest suburban municipalities—known variously as cities, boroughs, towns, villages—didn't originate as suburbs but rather as independent towns across the river from a larger settlement or at a distance of five, ten, or more miles from the city. In bygone days, they had their separate identities, their own governments and schools, their shopping areas and places of work. But through no desire of theirs the metropolis spread out, touched, and encircled them. Many remained as independent suburban governments, but some lost their political identity when consolidation ended their separate existence.

A second group were suburbs from the beginning. They bordered the central city, or they were close by, located along streetcar lines, railroads, or highways which commuters use. On the one hand, where the central city couldn't expand legally except through a special act of the legislature or wouldn't grow voluntarily where it had the power, suburban incorporation provided a means for getting needed municipal services. On the other hand, if the city was aggressive in its use of annexation, suburban incorporation was a defensive maneuver for those who didn't want to be part of the central city for reasons economic, social, or political. In either case, the desire for a separate identity, to do one's own thing, was a motivating factor.

ENLARGEMENT OF TOWNSHIP POWERS

In New England, though, suburban municipalities didn't have to be incorporated because towns already existed. As ancient as cities and as sacred, the towns were able to expand their powers as service demands increased. For services which can be handily administered within small areas, they could do about as well as the central city. It was the larger-scale services, particularly reaching out to the hinterlands for water supply, that did in the six towns Boston absorbed. But when other bodies were created to handle these areawide services—the Metropolitan District Commission for the Boston area (see Chapter 4)—the towns could have their cake of independence and enjoy the benefits of large-scale operations without joining the city.

In the mid-Atlantic states and the midwestern states which copied the New York model, the once-rural townships took on new functions. The Pennsylvania legislature, for example, created two classes of townships in 1899. First class townships had a population density of at least 300 per square mile, and their powers became as broad as those of cities and boroughs; even the rural second class townships eventually gained wider authority, and now they have the right to draw up home rule charters like all other categories of municipalities. New Jersey's townships also got new strength, and so did towns in New York and Wisconsin, and townships in Michigan.

But the states following the original Pennsylvania model didn't keep up with the Quaker state in township modernization. So most townships are fairly weak creatures in Ohio, Indiana, Illinois, Minnesota, North Dakota, South Dakota, and Kansas, though here and there some have become stronger, such as a few in Ohio. Townships exist in Washington only in Spokane County, have been eliminated in Missouri's and Nebraska's metro-politan areas, and have atrophied in Iowa to minor administrative subdivisions of the counties.

NUMBER OF SUBURBAN UNITS

General-purpose suburban governments abound in those states with two local forms, municipalities and townships. But in states without townships, suburban governments are usually fewer. Altogether the 1972 census of governments enumerated 8,588 general-purpose local units in the suburbs of the 264 SMSAs; of these, 5,126 were municipalities and 3,462 were town-ships. Two-thirds of them were under 5,000 in population, though in terms of metropolitan population the small suburban units contained less than ten percent of the total. In contrast, 54 percent of the people lived in places over 50,000, including the central city and the larger suburban municipalities and townships.

RESTRICTIONS ON INCORPORATION

Over the years municipal incorporation has become more difficult in many states as the legislatures acted to prevent organization of unviable units. As of 1974, 41 states had standards for municipal incorporation, mostly dealing with minimum population, area, and property value in order to prevent establishment of fiscally unsound units. A handful of states have taken another step by requiring specific services to be supplied by the new munici-palities (ACIR, 1976A:163).

Nine states have laws to prevent the incorporation of new municipalities within the vicinity of existing cities. They are Idaho, Wyoming, Arizona, New Mexico, Texas, Nebraska, Ohio, North Carolina, and Georgia. In Arizona, for example, no new municipality may be formed within three miles of a city or town of less than 5,000 or within six miles of a city over 5,000 unless the governing body of that city gives its consent or unless that city doesn't respond favorably to a petition of annexation from the unincorporated fringe area. The laws in the other eight states differ in details but all have the same intent (Bollens and Schmandt, 1970:294).

Although the extraterritorial jurisdiction of Texas cities applies to municipal incorporation, it doesn't prevent incorporation beyond the limits of this power and sometimes suburban municipalities are established as a defense against the city's unilateral annexation powers. The same pattern of defensive incorporation also occurs in Oklahoma, and between 1967 and 1972 over 30 percent of all municipal incorporations in the United States occurred in these two states at a time when their cities were aggressively using their annexation powers.

BOUNDARY REVIEW AND APPROVAL

During the last eighteen years, seven states have established boundary commissions for the purpose of reviewing all proposals for annexation, municipal incorporation, and the formation of special service districts. Alaska, Minnesota, Iowa, and Michigan have statewide commissions, and Washington, Oregon, and California provide for local commissions. In California each local agency commission (LAFCO) has jurisdiction over a whole county, and all but one county has one. In Oregon and Washington boundary commissions are mandated for the major urban areas, and the one around Portland encompasses four counties; they are also permitted in rural areas, but none have formed. The Minnesota Municipal Commission is charged with defining spheres of influence for all municipalities, and the local agency formation commissions have this task in California (ACIR, 1974A:86-91; ACIR 1976A, 167-170).

ACIR has concluded (1976A:170) that "fairly significant achievements have been chalked up by these boundary commissions." Although not many annexation proposals have been turned down, the various boundary commissions have shaped them to their basic standards. During its first ten years the Minnesota boundary commission drastically reduced the rate of new municipal incorporations and doubled the average size of new units. The local commissions in California have eliminated defensive incorporations and slowed formation of new units. No municipal incorporations occurred in areas served after local boundary commissions were formed in Washington and Oregon.

Strengthened County Government

All states except Rhode Island and Connecticut have functioning counties, though they don't amount to much in the rest of New England. In the other 44 states, counties are of growing importance, and in them 90 percent of the SMSAs are located.

However, not all the territory of these SMSAs is covered by functioning counties. Washington, D.C. has no county government, and Baltimore, St.

Louis, and Columbus, Georgia are located outside any county area. Five cities—Lexington, Denver, San Francisco, Anchorage, and Honolulu—are legally designated as city-counties but operate primarily as cities, and the Metropolitan Government of Nashville and Davidson County constitutes a similar consolidation. Six other cities have remnants of county offices within a mostly consolidated government, including New York (five counties), Philadelphia, Jacksonville, Indianapolis, New Orleans, and Baton Rouge (Census, 1973:14).

When these cities and the New England areas are subtracted from the total SMSA population, we find that 82 percent of the SMSA inhabitants in 1970 were living in functioning counties. Because counties are taking on new roles, county government has become quite significant to metropolitan America.

EVOLUTION

This wasn't always so, for counties were once considered to be mainly administrative districts of the states, and only gradually during the nineteenth century did state officials cease to appoint county officers. In law they were treated as quasi-municipal corporations, thus differentiated from cities. A typical expression of this viewpoint was an 1857 Ohio supreme court ruling:

A municipal corporation proper is created mainly for the interest, advantage, and convenience of the locality, and its people; a county organization is created almost exclusively with a view to the policy of the state at large, for purposes of finance, of education, of provision for the poor, of military organization, and of the means of travel and transport, and especially for the general administration of justice. With scarcely an exception, all the powers and functions of the county organization have a direct and exclusive reference to the general policy of the state, and are, in fact, but a branch of the general administration of that policy *(Commissioners of Hamilton County v. Mighels,* 7 Ohio St. 109,118-119; quoted in Duncombe, 1966:13).

In keeping with this philosophy, counties' main functions throughout the last century were assessment, tax collection, elections, recording legal papers, county roads, school operations in some states and a county superintendent of separate school districts in others, relief, charitable institutions, courts, and the sheriff for law enforcement in rural areas. And they were also a fundamental organizational unit for political parties.

As the twentieth century began, the impact of metropolitan growth was starting to reach beyond city limits, particularly in the East and Midwest, and this had its impact upon counties. By the 1920s suburbanization was in full flower, and this led to pressures for counties to perform more urban-type services. Parks, libraries, airports, hospitals, health services, and utility systems were some of the new functions counties undertook. At the same time the governmental reform movement, which had earlier pressed for a merit system for the federal civil service and for spoils-free city government, turned its attention to county government. As a result, some counties began to get home rule charters to replace the plural executive of the county board with an appointed manager or elected executive, and to institute merit civil service (Duncombe, 1966:28-31).

MODERN URBAN COUNTY

By now many counties, though not all, have evolved into up-to-date instruments of government (Jones, Gansel, and Howe, 1972). Their old functions have been modernized, such as extensive use of data processing for assessment and record keeping and the conversion of the rural sheriff's office into an urban police force. And many new functions, once handled mainly by cities, have been added. Not every urban county performs all municipal services but a sizable proportion do. More than half of the counties in metropolitan areas are now involved in mental health, subdivision control, libraries, animal control, and solid waste disposal. Forty to fifty percent of the counties handle industrial development, fire protection, hospitals, water and air pollution control, solid waste disposal, and airports (Lawrence and DeGrove, 1976).

With all these new functions, the nineteenth century notion of a county as merely an administrative branch of the state has long passed, and the legal designation as a quasi-municipal corporation has lost its meaning. Pennsylvania recognized this in a 1968 constitutional revision which gave counties status as municipalities, and statutes and practices of other states have had this effect, too, especially for the 66 counties which have adopted their own charters (Zeller, 1975:33).

Using either home rule authority or general state law, many counties have reorganized. By 1974, 557 of the 3,101 counties in the United States had altered the traditional commission or board form of government. One hundred counties over 50,000 in population had appointed chief administrators (Brown, 1975:34). Thirty-seven counties in metropolitan areas had established the position of elected county executive, and 12 consolidated city/counties were headed by a strong mayor (Zeller, 1975:31).

DIVERSITY OF COUNTIES

We should realize, though, that the counties within metropolitan areas aren't all alike, for they differ in size, character, and powers. By size the SMSA counties in 1970 fell into three main groups, as follows:

County population	Percentage of SMSA counties
Under 100,000	38
100,000 to 250,000	32
Over 250,000	29

Out of a total of 444 counties in SMSAs outside New England, 73 counties on the fringe were under 50,000, but 16 counties were over a million, including three strictly suburban counties without a central city.

In terms of character, a few counties have consolidated with the city, and others encompass the central city and independent suburbs. Many others are entirely suburban or a mixture of suburbs and rural areas. Some counties falling within the SMSA definition have a fairly low population density and are hardly even suburban in the conventional sense but rather house commuters living in small towns, highly scattered developments, and estates, thus drawing the county into the metropolitan orbit. Certain counties constitute the entire metropolitan area while others are but one of several counties composing the metropolis. (Chapter 15 analyzes these variations in greater detail.)

The powers exercised by counties vary considerably, too. Counties in the South and West have been stronger historically than those in the East and Midwest, and many have become heavily involved in municipal services for suburbanites living in unincorporated areas. But some eastern and midwestern counties have also become strong entities, and in the states where townships are weak, the counties within metropolitan areas are also providing urban services for persons residing outside municipalities. Beyond these broad distinctions, there are differences from state to state, and even within the same state one county might be handling more functions than others. Diversity is the rule.

Composite of Local General Governments

Thus, our metropolitan areas have (a) municipalities (cities, boroughs, villages), (b) towns and townships, and (c) counties as their units of local general government. Since cities and townships for the most part fall within counties, we can identify two layers: (1) municipalities and townships serving the smaller areas and (2) counties serving a larger territory.

WHERE PEOPLE LIVE

Looking at the municipal and township layer, we can differentiate between the central city and the suburbs. In the suburbs, municipalities and strong townships are quite similar in terms of their powers while rural-type townships do very little and are more like the unincorporated areas in states without townships.

Therefore, we can divide municipal and township government of metropolitan areas into three types of governmental subareas: (a) central cities, (b) strong suburban governments, consisting of municipalities and strong townships, and (c) weak suburban governments, consisting of rural townships and unincorporated territory outside both municipal and township boundaries. Eliminating duplication in the few states where some territory is served by both municipalities and townships, we find that in 1970 45 percent of metropolitan dwellers lived in the central cities and 39 percent in suburban units with strong government, as shown in Table 3.1. The remaining 16 percent resided in suburban areas with relatively weak or no small-area government though most of them probably received municipal-type services from the county or special districts.

In terms of size, 54.0 percent of the metropolitan population in 1970 lived within the jurisdiction of a municipality or township with 50,000 or more inhabitants, 20.9 percent in places in the 10,000 to 50,000 range and 11.7 percent in units under 10,000, as shown in Table 3.2. The remaining 13.4 percent of the metropolitan population lived outside any municipality or township and had only the county as local general government.

Table 3.1: Place of Residence of Metropolitan Population (1970)

Place of Residence		1970 Population (in millions)	Percentages
Total: 264 SMSAs*		143.3	100
Central cities		64.8	45
Strong suburban government		55.1	38
Municipalities	38.8		
Strong townships outside municipalities	16.3		
Weak suburban government		23.4	16
Rural townships outside municipalities	4.2		
Unincorporated territory outside townships	19.2		

*1972 definition of SMSAs
Source: U.S. Bureau of the Census, 1975. Tables 1 and 3.

Table 3.2: Population of General-Purpose Governments in SMSAs, by Size
            (1970)

Population Group	Population (in millions)	Percentages
In a municipality or township		
50,000 and more	77.4	54.0
25,000 to 49,000	13.7	9.5
10,000 to 24,999	16.3	11.4
5,000 to 9,999	7.7	5.4
Less than 5,000	9.0	6.3
	124.1	86.6
Not in a municipality or township	19.2	13.4
Total	143.3	100.0

Source: U.S. Bureau of the Census, 1975: Tables 1 & 3.

TWO LAYERS

In addition to persons living in a county but outside any municipality or township, some other metropolitan residents have only one local general government to serve them: those residing in a consolidated or separated city/county, in the District of Columbia, in Virginia where cities and counties are mutually independent, and in New England without functioning counties. This adds up to one-third of the metropolitan population with a single layer of local general government. (In addition, there may be special districts and regional councils, the subject of later chapters, but these aren't general-purpose governments.)

Conversely, two-thirds of the metropolitan population live under two layers of local general government: county and municipality or township. Moreover, there are some cases where a second layer is found in a mostly one-layer situation, such as the consolidated city/counties which have excluded a few small municipalities from unification, a few Connecticut towns containing "boroughs," and some Virginia counties having "towns" with minor powers.

And there are three layers of local general government in some metropolitan areas, mostly in the suburbs. This is the case with villages in New York, which remain as part of the town although cities and towns don't overlap. Also in Michigan, villages, towns, and counties provide three layers. All municipalities in Indiana and some small ones (villages mostly) in Ohio, Illinois, and Kansas operate within territory served by townships, but township government does very little in these states. And the Metropolitan Council of Minnesota's Twin Cities area is taking on the character of a general government, thus providing a unique triple-layer pattern, as Chapter 8 will elaborate. So three layers can be found, but not often.

Thus, two-layer local general government is the most common situation for metropolitan areas in the United States. In a way, it is a kind of local federalism, the product of over 350 years of historical development on this continent. But we must be careful with the analogy of federalism when talking about local government in metropolitan areas as now organized. The layers aren't nearly as distinct as the states and national government in the larger American federal system. And missing almost everywhere is an area-wide general-purpose government concentrating on metropolitan matters. Nevertheless, the idea of local federalism holds a key to understanding the present arrangement and charting the course for structural improvements. We will return to this idea in Chapter 11 when we explore the theoretical foundation for future reform.

PROBLEMS

If we look at this structure of local general government in metropolitan areas in terms of the major problems enumerated in Chapter 1, we find that some of them are endemic but there are some counterbalancing advantages. To a considerable extent the numerous municipalities and townships rely upon a local tax base which is spread unevenly around the metropolis, and this produces fiscal disparities and results in service inadequacies. Yet, with a variety of small units, there are opportunities to adapt services to local needs.

Since land use control is usually in the hands of cities and townships, most metropolitan areas haven't had an effective overall mechanism for managing growth, and the way localities have utilized zoning laws has contributed to separation of economic groups, excluding low- and moderate-income people from some areas with the byproduct of racial segregation. But local influence over land use, if not abused, can help strengthen neighborhoods. Most counties, as broader geographic juris-dictions, have been slow to act on crucial planning issues and may not even have the power to do so, but where they do, they add a valuable dimension.

On the one hand, where there are small units, residents know their local officials and hold them accountable, and this can bolster confidence in their local government. But on the other hand, the pattern of many, many local governmental units, plus numerous special districts (which the next chapter discusses), makes public official accountability unclear by clouding who is responsible for broader, areawide functions with a resultant effect of lowered citizen confidence. In sum, the pattern of local general government in metropolitan areas as it now functions has some assets but it is also a source of metropolitan problems.

Chapter 4

CREATION OF NEW TYPES OF UNITS

With the country blanketed with local general government, two layers thick in most places, one would assume that this was enough. But not so. For we Americans love to set up organizations, as Alexis de Tocqueville discovered in the 1830s (n.d., Book I:204):

> In no country in the world has the principle of association been more successfully used, or more unsparingly applied to a multitude of different objects, than in America. Beside the permanent associations which are established by law under the names of townships, cities, and counties, a vast number of others are formed and maintained by the agency of private individuals.

So it isn't surprising that when public education spread across the nation as a new governmental function during the nineteenth century, it was often assigned to new units created for this purpose. And in the growing metropolitan areas when existing governments seemed unwilling or unable to meet certain service needs, local people and state officials set up special districts to handle new tasks. There were other reasons, but the American penchant for new organizations was a factor.

School Districts

Public education is a major governmental activity carried out in metropolitan areas and is usually handled by an independent school district, though sometimes the school system is part of local general government. In many jurisdictions it is the function absorbing the greatest share of the local property tax dollar.

ORIGINS

The historical roots of public education in the United States go back to the New England colonies where Massachusetts took the lead with a 1642 law ordering that children be taught to read and be instructed in religion and then a 1647 law requiring towns to establish schools. Inhabitants of the middle colonies were also interested in education for the whole populace but relied more on private and parochial schools. In the southern colonies tutoring and private schools served the well-to-do, and apprenticeship training and pauper schools were offered to the lower classes (Kandel, 1955:979).

As settlement spread in New England, persons living away from town centers wanted control of their own local schools, and Connecticut in 1766 and Massachusetts in 1789 obliged by authorizing the election of local school boards which could levy taxes and select teachers. During the next century as public education spread across the nation, this independent school district became a model for the western states, but in the mid-South school departments were established as part of city and county government. States passed compulsory attendance laws and took on a supervisory role over local school systems even though actual operations were under local control (Bollens, 1957:191).

As the public school movement advanced, educators came to believe that small school districts were educationally deficient. In 1869 Massachusetts instituted school consolidation and in 1882 returned control of schools from independent districts to town governments. The consolidation idea spread, was applied intermittently in a number of states, and began to get considerable attention in the 1930s (Bollens, 1957:198-200). In 1942 there were 108,579 independent school districts in the United States, by far the most numerous type of governmental unit. But during the next 30 years school consolidation swept the nation, and by 1972 the total fell to 15,781 school districts, the most remarkable change in local governmental organization in this era. It occurred because the states' primacy over local education had long ago been established and the state legislatures either mandated consolidation or backed state education departments which brought it about; sometimes the process was sweetened by financial incentives through state aid. Rural areas were most affected except in New England with its town system and in the South, which tended to have county school systems already, but school consolidation came to metropolitan areas as well. For instance, independent school districts in the 264 SMSAs covered in the 1972 census of governments dropped from 5,421 in 1967 to 4,758 in 1972, a decrease of 12 percent, and the downward trend has continued since.

PRESENT STATUS

Nevertheless, there remain many independent school districts in metropolitan areas, accounting for 21 percent of all local governmental units in SMSAs in 1972. These are public school systems which have their own governing boards and taxing power. In the census definition, they contrast with dependent school systems which lack fiscal autonomy and operate as an agency of a county, city, or town even though most of them have elected boards. Dependent school systems constituted 10 percent of all public school systems in SMSAs in 1972, but they contained 25 percent of the enrollment because the schools in quite a few big cities are part of municipal government.

Most of the 517 dependent school systems of SMSAs are found in ten states: Maine, Massachusetts, Rhode Island, Connecticut, Maryland, Virginia, North Carolina, Tennessee, Alaska, and Hawaii. Among these states, the state government itself handles education in Hawaii, and counties are in charge of the schools in Maryland and North Carolina, though in the latter school operations in the large cities are assigned to local administrative boards. Both counties and cities are involved in education in Virginia and Tennessee, and schools are part of city and town government in the New England states mentioned. The Municipality of Anchorage handles education, and so does the District of Columbia.

In the other states the general pattern is for all or almost all of the schools to be run by independent units. School districts have boundaries coinciding with county lines throughout Florida and West Virginia. This is partially so in 11 other southern and western states, though in some of these states the independent school districts serving central cities observe municipal boundaries. But in the majority of states, independent school districts frequently cross municipal and township boundaries but almost never extend beyond the county line except for some joint districts handling upper levels of education. Elected school boards are the dominant pattern for the independent school districts, but some are appointed by the mayor, city council, or county officials.

Metropolitan-wide school systems are rare in the United States but can be found in single-county metropolitan areas in Florida, some other southern states, and a few consolidated city/counties elsewhere. For the most part, though, metropolitan school organization is as pluralistic as municipal organization.

Special Districts

Another governmental structure created by Americans is the special district.

GENERAL DESCRIPTION

Definition. ACIR describes special districts as "limited purpose governmental units which exist as corporate entities and which have substantial fiscal and administrative independence from general purpose local government" (1973A:20). They usually handle only one function—fire protection, water supply, sewerage, to cite the three most common ones in metropolitan areas—though a small proportion of them take on two or more functions. Some have elected governing boards, others appointive, but in either case the governing board has substantial decision-making authority. Specialization and separateness from general-purpose government are the salient characteristics of special districts.

Historically, special districts have been formed to carry out assignments which general-purpose government couldn't or wouldn't undertake within its existing legal authority or structure. ACIR cites these claims for their use (1973A:21): "(1) fiscal self-sufficiency, (2) emphasis on technical specialization, (3) efficiency, and (4) geographic flexibility." Fiscal self-sufficiency stems from an ability to obtain their own revenues—from bonds, grants, user charges, and special assessments, and for many of them, independent property tax authority. They can undertake specialized activities and perform them efficiently. They can set up natural local service areas (such as drainage areas) without regard to municipal boundaries and include unincorporated territory, and they can serve many jurisdictions, even the whole metropolis, when more far-reaching metropolitan reorganization is unattainable.

What they do. There were 8,054 special districts within SMSAs in 1972, and they constitute 36 percent of all governmental units in metropolitan areas, making them the most numerous type of local government. Some 4,344 of them, or slightly more than half, had property taxing authority. One out of four was coterminous with a county, municipality, or township while the others had their own district boundaries.

The special districts found in metropolitan areas vary widely in what they do, as Table 4.1 shows, encompassing many functions which municipalities and counties often handle directly. The bulk of them aren't large operations, for only 10 percent of those reporting employment patterns have more than 20 employees, and more than half have none at all, underscoring their role as a fiscal device or, as is the case with fire districts, their use of volunteers. But a few special districts are metropolitan in scope and are vast undertakings with huge staffs.

Many of the special districts without property taxing authority are basically adjuncts of county, municipal, and township governments and independent school districts. The ones which can levy a property tax are more truly independent governmental units with their own separate existence. Three-fourths of the special districts with property taxing authority are found

Table 4.1: Special Districts in SMSAs by Major Functions (1972)

Function		Number
Single-function districts		*7,492*
Fire protection		1,547
Natural resources		1,371
Drainage	449	
Soil conservation	423	
Irrigation, water conservation	272	
Flood control	135	
Other and composite functions	92	
Utilities		939
Water supply	888	
Transit	31	
Electric power	13	
Gas supply	7	
Sewerage		866
Housing and urban renewal		731
School buildings		619
Parks and recreation		378
Cemetaries		157
Hospitals		153
Highways		151
Libraries		148
Health		103
Other		329
Multifunction districts		*562*
Sewerage and water supply		396
Natural resources and water supply		44
Other		122
Total, all special districts		8,054

Source: U.S. Bureau of the Census, 1973: Table 15.

in seven states—Washington, Oregon, California, Colorado, Nebraska, Illinois, and New York, and another dozen states have most of the remainder.

METROPOLITAN DISTRICTS

One group of special districts serves all or a substantial part of the metropolitan area. As such they are an invention designed to cope with problems which existing structures couldn't solve.

Historical beginnings. The earliest ones arose in the Philadelphia area, which was the first place where independent suburban units formed adjacent to the city. From 1790 to 1854 when city/county consolidation occurred, special authorities serving city and suburbs were established to handle prisons, poor relief, port development, public health, police, and education. In the

New York area between 1857 and 1866 metropolitan districts were set up for
police, fire, and sanitation, but because of opposition from the cities encompassed they were abolished in 1870 and operating responsibility was redivided
among the local jurisdictions until the consolidation of 1898 (Studenski,
1930:257-259).

The Massachusetts legislature set up metropolitan bodies in the form of
state agencies for sewers (1889), parks (1893), and water (1895). These three
became united as the Massachusetts Metropolitan District Commission in
1919 (Studenski, 1930:260-264,274). In 1869 the Illinois legislature created
three large park districts to serve parts of Chicago and its suburbs, and over
the years 19 smaller ones were added until they were all consolidated in 1934
as the Chicago Park District, a unit now coterminous with but independent of
the city of Chicago (Bollens, 1957:132-138). Going well beyond city limits is
a body now known as the Metropolitan Sanitary District of Greater Chicago,
which began in 1889 and expanded its territory as the metropolis grew
(Bollens, 1957:74-77). And likewise as other urban centers grew big, they set
up metropolitan districts responsive to areawide problems, especially water
supply, sewerage, large parks, ports, airports, and transit.

Contemporary situation. Of the 8,054 special districts within SMSAs in
1972, 604 were multicounty districts and another 447 were countywide for a
sum of 1,051. Thus, about one-eighth of the special districts are fairly broad
in geographic scope, though perhaps less than a couple of hundred cover all or
substantially all of a metropolitan area. They fall into several categories.

A handful are *multistate.* The most gigantic is the Port of New York
Authority which operates extensive port facilities, truck and rail terminals,
six airports, six interstate bridges and tunnels, the twin-building World Trade
Center, and a variety of other enterprises related to trade and transportation.
Other multistate metropolitan districts include the Delaware River Port
Authority (Philadelphia area), the Washington Metropolitan Transit Author-
ity (national capitol area), the Bi-State Development District (port and mass
transit for the St. Louis area), and the St. Louis Metropolitan Airport
Authority.

Some other metropolitan districts are *multifunctional.* Water supply and
sewerage systems are the responsibility of the Hartford County Metropolitan
District in Connecticut and the East Bay Municipal Utility District in California. The Municipality of Metropolitan Seattle is a special district handling
transit and sewage disposal. And the long-time operating Metropolitan District Commission of the Boston area in 1952 added refuse disposal to its
other assignments of water supply, sewage, and metropolitan parks.

Most of the metropolitan districts deal with *single functions.* Of numerous
possible examples, one case for each major function covered can serve as an
illustration:

Sewerage system—Milwaukee Metropolitan Sewer District

Water supply—San Diego County Water Authority

Electricity—Omaha Public Power District

Transit—Regional Transportation District (Denver area)

Bridge—Golden Gate Bridge and Highway District

Airport—Raleigh-Durham Airport Authority

Port—Port of Portland (Oregon)

Parks—Cleveland Metropolitan Park District

Library—Fort Wayne-Allen County Library District

All of these involve the central city and suburbs, though not always the entire metropolitan area.

In addition there are *submetropolitan* districts taking in substantial sections of the suburbs. For example, the Washington Suburban Sanitary Commission handles water and sewers for two large Maryland counties next to the District of Columbia. Suburban counties in Pennsylvania around Philadelphia have sewer authorities as do many northern New Jersey counties. The East Bay Regional Park District serves part of its metropolitan region in northern California.

The functions undertaken by metropolitan special districts have several features in common. Almost all are capital intensive and by their nature they serve the whole metropolis, some of them uniquely so, such as transit, port, airport, metropolitan parks, and the central library. The flow of traffic, commerce, and water cuts across municipal and county boundaries, making areawide organization a necessity. Economical operation and equitable cost sharing favor metropolitan administration, and since a general-purpose metropolitan government isn't available in any of these places, the creation of a metropolitan special district was the most viable option. Again, invention and adaptation got the job done.

However, it is also important to note what metropolitan districts don't do. Except for short periods in Philadelphia (1850-1854) and New York (1857-1870), there have been no metropolitan police forces though some metropolitan bodies have security forces for their own operations, such as the park police of the Boston area's Metropolitan District Commission and security officers of the Port of New York Authority, but they lack general jurisdiction. Fire protection (except for briefly in New York and today at airports), public housing, social services, street maintenance, assessment, school operations, and other kinds of personnel-intensive services haven't been undertaken by metropolitan districts. Moreover, for every function now handled by metropolitan districts there are city, county, and joint-power agencies administering that function on a metropolitan basis under the auspices of local general government.

LOCAL SERVICE DISTRICTS

The biggest special district operations are areawide in scope, but the most numerous variety are those providing localized services. They too were formed to carry out activities which local general government couldn't because it wasn't organized in a particular suburban area or lacked the power to undertake a specific activity. The alternatives of municipal incorporation and broadening local powers might have been chosen, but they weren't.

Growth. The usage of local service special districts can be traced back to eighteenth century New England, where residents of distinct districts within towns were empowered to undertake certain tasks on their own apart from town government (ACIR, 1976A:101). Although statistics aren't available to trace their historical development, the growth of local service special districts is mostly a product of this century, especially since the 1930s. In that decade New Deal programs encouraged the formation of soil conservation and other natural resource districts in rural areas and housing authorities in cities, and the legislatures in a number of states made the use of special districts a viable alternative to suburban incorporation. The 1942 census of governments recorded 1,097 special districts in the 140 metropolitan areas defined for that period. In 1952 there were 2,598 special districts for the 168 SMAs, and the number shot up to the 8,054 found in 264 SMSAs in 1972. In the latest count, more than 90 percent were dedicated to local service, and most of these handled a single function (93 percent of all special districts).

Functions. Table 4.1 has revealed what these functions are. Fire protection leads the way, followed by water supply and sewage, with these services rendered mainly in the suburbs. Of the multifunction special districts, sewage and water supply are the most common combinations. Fourth and fifth on the list of special district activities are housing and urban renewal and school buildings. Housing and renewal authorities are mostly in central cities, and school building authorities are usually coterminous with school districts. But three out of four special districts in SMSAs have boundaries which don't coincide with a county, city, or township. Of the 6,042 noncoterminous special districts in 1972, 604 were multicounty and 5,428 involved smaller areas. Thus, two-thirds of the special districts are small, noncoterminous units, primarily handling a single function.

These local service districts have different reasons for being. Fire districts, for example, derive from volunteer fire companies in rural areas and the suburbs and were once financed by voluntary contributions; they continue as independent units even after they are tax supported and pay their fire fighters. The ones for natural resources, sewerage, and water supply take in

Table 4.2:   Number of Governmental Units in SMSA by Population Size
            (1972)

1970 population of SMSA	Total SMSAs	Number of Governmental Units in SMSA				
		1-25	26-50	51-100	100-200	251 & more
50,000 to 100,000	27	19	7	1	—	—
100,000 to 250,000	110	45	39	18	8	—
250,000 to 500,000	61	7	15	21	18	—
500,000 to 1,000,000	33	4	5	11	13	—
1,000,000 and more	33	—	4	3	13	13
Total	264	75	70	54	52	13

Source: U.S. Bureau of the Census, 1973: Table 19.

drainage basins determined by land contours rather than the man-made
boundaries of political subdivisions. Housing and urban renewal authorities
respond to a preference of federal agencies for this form at the time of
organization. School building authorities tend to constitute a special fiscal
arrangement to finance school construction, and they usually have no operating staff. The other varieties reflect the need to have a particular task carried
out when existing local general government lacked the authority or willingness to undertake the function.

Multi-purpose districts. A handful of local service districts are organized
under state statutes authorizing the district to administer a number of
services. In his 1961 study of special districts, John Bollens called them
"junior city urban fringe districts" because their potential powers were
broader than most special districts though fewer than a regular municipality.
He found units of this sort in California, Colorado, Michigan, Connecticut,
and South Carolina (1957:106-114). The 1972 census of governments also
identifies some broadly empowered "suburban and consolidated improvement districts" in Arkansas, and some units called "villages" in Montgomery
County, Maryland but considered by the Census Bureau to be special districts, not full municipalities.

In all their varieties, special districts are very much part of the scene of
governmental organization in metropolitan areas.

Volume of Local Governmental Units

When we add up all the governmental units found in metropolitan areas,
we find that municipalities, towns and townships, counties, school districts,
and special districts come together in different combinations in particular
areas. We will look into these differences in greater depth in Chapter 15 when

we develop a typology of metropolitan areas, but for now let us note the differences in the number of local units per SMSA. This is shown in Table 4.2.

UNITS PER SMSA

At one end of the spectrum are 75 SMSAs with 25 or fewer governmental units. If we cut that even finer, we find 35 SMSAs with 12 or less units, mostly areas under 250,000 in population but a few larger ones where some consolidation has occurred. The simplest structure at the time of the 1972 census of governments was the Honolulu SMSA with a consolidated city/ county government, three soil conservation districts, and state government in charge of education. Now the Municipality of Anchorage is the simplest because in 1975 one borough and three municipalities consolidated into a single unit, which also takes care of education, and there are no special districts. Of the other SMSAs with very few units, some are one-county areas in states without townships and sparse use of special districts, and some are in New England or Virginia where a city and several towns or a few independent cities and counties make up the SMSA.

At the other extreme are 13 SMSAs with 251 or more units, and four of these have over 500 units. All 13 are areas over one million in population. The Chicago SMSA is the leader with 1,172 units consisting of six counties, 256 municipalities, 113 townships, 327 school districts, and 470 special districts of which 402 have property taxing authority.

Nearly half of the SMSAs under 250,000 have 25 or fewer governmental units while three-fifths of those over a half million have more than 100 units. So governmental multiplicity is partly a matter of population size, but not completely. It also relates to the pattern of government established by state law. States with the fewest units of local government per SMSA include Hawaii, Alaska, Nevada, New Mexico, Mississippi, Georgia, North Carolina, Virginia, Connecticut, New Hampshire, and Maine. States with the most units of local government per SMSA are Washington, Oregon, California, Colorado, Nebraska, North Dakota, Minnesota, Illinois, Indiana, Ohio, Pennsylvania, New Jersey, and New York. Because SMSAs tend to be smaller in several of the states in the first group and larger in the second, the total population variable is a factor. But the use of townships in the mid-Atlantic and midwestern states and an abundance of special districts, particularly in the West, are also major determinants of the multiplicity of governmental units in particular metropolitan areas.

PROBLEMS

In many ways the existence of independent school districts and special districts has compounded the difficulties caused by the large number of local general governmental units, as outlined at the end of the previous chapter, but in some other ways they contribute to solutions. They greatly add to the confusion of public official accountability with its side effects of lower citizen confidence. But when special districts do their tasks well, they may improve service delivery. Their specialization makes it more difficult to coordinate interrelated functions, including those which enable the metropolis to respond to growth, but some of the metropolitan districts serve as a needed areawide vehicle which the local general government structure doesn't provide.

To the extent that independent school districts rely upon property taxes, they experience the same fiscal disparities as municipalities and townships. Where local service districts charge directly for services rendered, the beneficiaries pay for what they get, and while differences in personal income levels may have an impact, it isn't quite the same fiscal disparity as the uneven property tax base produces. Where local service districts and independent school systems make possible exclusive enclaves, they increase social and racial separation, but where metropolitan districts provide service equality through the metropolis, they diminish some of the effects of separation.

So, the creation of special districts solves some problems but makes some other problems worse.

Chapter 5

INVENTION OF NEW MECHANISMS

Simultaneously with the growth of special districts, we have also invented a number of legal and administrative mechanisms to make existing local general governments function better in metropolitan areas without changing the basic structure. This has been a product of American pragmatism.

Speaking of reform attempts of the past 50 years, Henry J. Schmandt remarks (1974:149):

> With a few notable exceptions, these efforts have brought about no fundamental change in the basic political structure of urban areas. Modifications of incremental nature have occurred, such as the creation of special districts and the consolidation of certain functions, but these have been designed to accommodate in minimal fashion the most pressing service needs of the area without altering the character of the system. The principal method of adaptation in this process has been intergovernmental volunteerism, one of the most influential concepts in the political history of the nation's metropolitan communities since the early decades of this century.

A major expression of this volunteerism has been several forms of inter-local cooperation. This chapter looks at two of them, intergovernmental agreements and transfers of functions, saving until Chapter 6 a third type, councils of governments and other confederated organizations. The present chapter also reviews some fiscal devices invented to pass revenues from one level of government to another without changing the basic structure.

Practice first, theory second is the American approach. So, after this highly pluralistic governmental system has evolved for metropolitan areas, we are seeing the emergence of a theory to support the arrangements that adaptation has produced. This chapter ends with a review of one such theory, and I present my own ideas on theory in Chapter 11.

Intergovernmental Agreements

Numerous cities, towns, townships, and counties within metropolitan areas have worked out agreements among themselves for the purposes of (a) helping each other on special occasions, (b) one unit providing regular services to another, and (c) undertaking joint endeavors.

MUTUAL AID

Among the simplest cooperative arrangements is a mutual aid agreement. This might be a matter of information sharing or an agreement to help one another in emergency situations.

Police departments within a metropolitan area often cooperate by sharing information in criminal investigations, by helping out in hot pursuit of a fleeing suspect, and on occasion by joining forces to cope with civil disorder. For example, the police departments in the Washington, D.C. area have established radio and teletype networks and an areawide computerized police information system.

Fire departments also support one another, often accomplished through written agreements. However, even without advance agreements, jurisdictions assist one another in emergencies, as happened in Detroit during the 1967 riot when fifty-six pieces of fire equipment were brought in from suburban communities.

Civil defense and disaster preparedness plans in metropolitan areas are often built around mutual support. Health departments share information about communicable diseases.

CONTRACT SERVICES

Interlocal agreements are also used to arrange for one jurisdiction to provide ongoing services to inhabitants of another unit. Joseph F. Zimmerman (1974:30) indicates they are popular because they enable a locality to obtain a service it couldn't produce itself, or at least not as cheaply. They have flexibility both in duration and territory served, allowing a contracting unit to terminate the service at the end of a set period or on notice if it chooses and also to expand the service area when appropriate. And service agreements are politically feasible because they don't require changes in the basic governmental structure.

Forty-two states have enacted a general statute authorizing local governments to enter into interlocal agreements. Thirty of them permit cooperation with local jurisdictions in other states, and Michigan extends this opportunity across the Canadian border. However, the majority of states qualify the general authority by restricting it to functions which local governments are currently empowered to undertake. Beyond these general statutes, many states also have laws allowing service contracts for specific functions (Zimmerman, 1974:31).

In a 1972 nationwide survey conducted for ACIR, Zimmerman found that 63 percent of all reporting municipalities had service agreements. The county was the most common service provider, but for second choice central cities turned to state government while suburban municipalities relied upon the central city. Both city and suburbs also had service agreements with school districts and special districts. On the giving side, 78 percent of the central cities provided services to another government, but only 39 percent of the suburban units did so. In a separate 1971 survey of counties, ACIR found that 48 percent of the responding counties over 50,000 population supplied services on a contract basis (1974:36, 45-46).

The returns from the survey of municipalities (including nonmetropolitan cities) revealed that service agreements involved 76 kinds of governmental activities. The top five activities were jails and detention homes, police training, street lighting, refuse collection, and libraries. Interesting to note is that some of these services are the same ones for which local-service special districts are commonly organized, suggesting the interchangeability of the two approaches. But others aren't. Police, particularly, is a governmental function rarely consigned to a special district but suitable for a contract agreement between two units of local general government. Fire protection is first among the special districts but eighteenth on the list of service agreements in the ACIR survey, though another study of service agreements in five states found it to be the most popular (Stoner, 1967:15).

In its county survey, ACIR found that one-third of all counties reporting provided contract services. Jail and detention centers, police protection, and roads and highways were the most frequent services furnished.

PACKAGE OF SERVICES

Most commonly a service agreement deals with a single activity. However, 22 percent of the central cities in metropolitan areas and 16 percent of the suburban municipalities covered in the Zimmerman-ACIR survey receive a package of services from another jurisdiction. And it works the other way, too, for another 23 percent of the central cities provide service packages, and 11 percent of the suburban units put together a group of services for another unit (Zimmerman, 1974:37).

The greatest provider of service packages is Los Angeles County, which since early in this century has had service agreements with municipalities. The number of individual agreements had grown to 400 by 1954 when the package idea went into use with the new suburban city of Lakewood. The crucial ingredients were the willingness of the county sheriff's department to supply police services under contract for the first time, and the willingness of residents to delegate law enforcement while acquiring control over land use and development. To the contract package the county added other services it had been delivering in unincorporated areas. A further incentive was a state law allowing sales tax rebates to the city of collection. Residents of other unincorporated areas liked the idea, and between 1954 and 1965 there were 31 other incorporations, all but three contracting for police services (Sonenblum, Kirlin, and Ries, 1975:31; also see Crouch and Dinerman, 1963:199-206; and Warren, 1966:141-180).

To get a new contract city going, county staff assisted the city council by providing drafts of resolutions and ordinances covering emergencies and public safety and by presenting a list of services currently handled by the county and special districts. The city council then chose which services it wanted to handle directly and which to contract. For the latter, a five year renewal contract was signed by the city and county officials.

All seventy-eight cities in Los Angeles County, including the city of Los Angeles, have service agreements with the county. They all contract for election services, most contract for health services and emergency ambulances, and slightly more than half for libraries. The thirty-one contract cities, as the newer group are called, usually include in the package such matters as law enforcement, fire protection, street maintenance, engineering services, building inspection, and animal control, but rarely parks and recreation. Most of the forty-seven cities with the fewest service agreements spend less than one percent of their budget on contract services, but the contract cities on the average allocate one-third of the city budget to contracts (Sonenblum et al, 1975:28).

Contract services in Los Angeles County are financed in three ways. Some are self-financed through user fees, such as building inspection fees and dog licenses (for animal control). Property taxes in special tax districts provide funds for services closely tied to a locality, such as fire protection, libraries, street lighting, and sewer maintenance. And the municipality is billed directly for such general services as police, engineering, planning, street maintenance, and elections. For this third group, the county auditor-controller annually establishes the rate for each service based upon actual costs, both direct and indirect.

Some of the bloom has faded from the Lakewood plan because as contract prices have risen to cover full costs, the differential between direct operations and contract services isn't very great. A recent study, for instance, found that law enforcement productivity is about the same for a municipal police department and the county sheriff's department, but the latter provides a lower level of service and therefore a lesser financial burden for the contract cities (Sonenblum et al, 1975:50). Contract cities opt for lower costs and continue to use the sheriff's department, though from time to time one of them takes back some other service or arranges for a private contract.

JOINT FACILITIES AND SERVICES

Another kind of interlocal agreement brings together two or more governmental units to construct and operate a joint facility or to provide a joint service. The earliest ones, going back to the nineteenth century, were for waterworks and bridges. Looking at the contemporary situation, an ACIR survey found that 40 percent of the metropolitan central cities responding were involved in joint construction or leasing agreements and 22 percent of the suburban municipalities. Sanitary landfill operations were particularly popular for joint facility agreements. Sewage treatment plans, airports, and hospitals were built and operated in this manner, and there were also some cases of joint leasing of equipment and the loan of personnel or equipment (1974A:41).

Even more cities have joint service agreements: 35 percent of all those reporting (including nonmetropolitan cities) but 62 percent of the central cities and 39 percent of the suburban units. Also 57 percent of the counties over 50,000 were involved in joint service agreements. Among the cities the ranking of services with joint agreements placed sewage disposal, fire service, and recreation at the head of the list (Zimmerman, 1974:41, 46). All of these activities also had high ranking in the previous list of services provided to municipalities under contract, but in a different order. Furthermore, there were many more service contracts than joint service agreements.

Both kinds of joint agreements—facilities and services—ran into difficulties in allocating costs equitably between the participating jurisdictions. Zimmerman reports that "A significant number of joint agreements have been terminated because of disputes over the apportionment of costs" (1974:43).

Again, the western states make most use of joint service agreements. This is a long-standing practice in California under the Joint Exercise of Powers Act of 1921. This act permits a county, city, school district, special district, public corporation, state government, and any federal agency operating in California to enter into an agreement for the exercise of joint powers. In Los Angeles County several major sewerage systems are administered in this manner, so is the coliseum and a metropolitan traffic commission, and in the 1960s the community action agency was set up by the city, county, and school district under a joint powers agreement. The Association of Bay Area Governments in the San Francisco Bay region is a joint powers agency, and there are many others throughout California (Crouch and Dinerman, 1963:112, 401).

OTHER MEANS OF COOPERATION

In addition to these formal methods of interlocal cooperation, public officials from various local jurisdictions keep in contact by telephone, in meetings, and through correspondence. Such communication is a routine part of their workaday world. In addition, other channels are open to them. For instance, in a study of the Davenport, Iowa-Rock Island and Moline, Illinois area, H. Paul Friesma found contacts among local officials occurring in the following order of frequency (1971:91): in the course of work (the most), municipal and professional organizations, personal friendships, social organizations, business and work associations, and political parties (the least). He also identified several indirect processes involving influential individuals, interest groups, corporations and industrial firms, newspeople, and municipal consultants.

Transfer of Functions

Another kind of adjustment made within the framework of the established structure of local government in metropolitan areas is the transfer of functions from one unit to another. Most often responsibility is transferred from a municipality to the county or state, or to a special district, but sometimes the opposite occurs.

In reporting on a 1975 survey of functional transfers conducted for ACIR, Joseph Zimmerman indicates three principal reasons for this occurrence (1976:3-4). First is a conviction that certain services can be best provided by a unit serving a larger area than a municipality. Second, the failure to achieve metropolitan government has led people to look to the county or state government for the performance of areawide services. Third, the growing fiscal problems of central cities has produced an interest in shifting responsibilities to a unit with a broader tax base. At the same time, county modernization has made that venerable institution more attractive as a major deliverer of urban services.

SOURCES OF AUTHORITY

Functional transfers are made from a municipality to some other jurisdiction, such as the county, with or without specific state authorization. Ten states have constitutional or statutory authorization, but in the other states transfers may take place without it whenever the jurisdiction taking on the service already has authorization to handle it. Voter approval is required in five of the states with constitutional or statutory provisions: Vermont, New York, Pennsylvania, Ohio, and Florida. But voter participation isn't necessary in the other five states: Virginia, Michigan, Illinois, California, and Alaska (Zimmerman, 1976:9).

Almost always the transfer is voluntary, though sometimes the state legislature has mandated a transfer or set up a special authority to take over an activity previously handled locally. Among the functions absorbed by one or more states are public welfare, public health, population control, local courts, property tax assessment, building codes, coastal zone management, and regulation of surface mining (Zimmerman, 1976:20).

SERVICES TRANSFERRED

Of the 3,319 cities responding to ACIR's 1975 survey, about one out of three (31 percent) indicated that they had transferred one or more functions between 1965 and 1975. However, 51 percent of the central cities (and 81 percent of those over half a million) had transferred functions compared to 30 percent of suburban cities and 30 percent of nonmetropolitan municipalities. Zimmerman indicates (1976:28):

> A partial explanation for this finding is the fact that many central city institutions and facilities—hospitals, airports, marine ports, major ports, major parks, libraries, museums, and zoos—are utilized by suburbanites, and the city has been able to convince the county, or arrange for the formation of a regional special district, to take over an institution or facility in order to enlarge the tax base for its support, thereby reducing benefit overspill. A growing financial crisis—the product of several developments—has impelled central cities to investigate the possibility of the upward shift of responsibility for an expensive facility which serves the region.

Of the transferring cities, 66 percent gave up only one function, 22 percent two functions, and 16 percent three or more (Zimmerman, 1976:29). Central cities transferred an average of 2.6 functions compared to 1.5 functions for suburban and nonmetropolitan cities. In some cases the transfer may have entailed an entire function, such as shifting the city health department to the county, but it more likely was one activity or subfunction, such as police communications or training, not the complete law enforcement responsibility, or refuse disposal, but not collection.

Central cities most frequently transferred activities within the public health and law enforcement functions followed by social services, transportation, and planning. Among suburban cities (which as a group had proportionately fewer transfers), sewage and solid waste responsibilities were the functions most often transferred.

At the receiving end, 56 percent of the transfers went from municipalities to county government, 19 percent to special districts, 14 percent to the state, 7 percent to other municipalities, and 4 percent to councils of governments (Zimmerman, 1976:37). The largest number of transfers to counties were for solid waste collection and disposal, followed by public health, law enforcement, and taxation and assessment. Social services was the function most frequently transferred to state government; sewage collection and treatment was the number one transfer to special districts; and planning to councils of governments. The largest groups of transfers from one municipality to another related to sewage, water, and solid waste.

In addition to taking on functions by transfers from other municipalities, some cities assume new responsibilities which have been previously handled by private firms (13 percent of those reporting), the county (5 percent), and the state (3 percent). Public transportation has been taken over from bankrupt private companies, and cities have started sanitary landfill operations, once handled privately, because of state requirements. The new functions taken on by cities from these several sources rank in the following order of frequency: solid waste, public health, transportation, public works, law enforcement, water supply, and fire protection (Zimmerman, 1976:57-61).

Fiscal Devices

Another way to adapt the local governmental structure of metropolitan areas is to keep functional assignments where they are but to shift around financial responsibilities. To do this requires increased intergovernmental funding, and this, in fact, has happened.

At the beginning of this century when the metropolitan age was still in its youth, each governmental level—national, state, and local—largely took in revenues from its own sources and spent the money directly. But this has changed remarkably in the last 75 years. Thus, in 1975, federal aid amounted to 16 percent of federal general expenditures, and state aid to local government (including schools) was 42 percent of state expenditures (ACIR, 1976B:9, 15). This was accomplished through a variety of grant-in-aid and revenue sharing programs.

At the receiving end, 49 percent of local school budgets came from intergovernmental sources in 1975 and 43 percent of the funds of local general government. Of the latter, three-eighths came from federal aid (including federal money passed through the states) and five-eighths from state revenue sources.

In addition, there are ways to move around revenues within metropolitan areas, as we shall see in a moment. So altogether quite a number of devices have been invented to deal with metropolitan fiscal disparities without rearranging the structure of local government.

STATE GRANTS AND SHARED REVENUE

Education. Education was the first major locally run function to benefit from sizable amounts of state financial assistance. But even at that, the local property tax was the major source of school financing until a generation ago, and still today it produces almost half of local school district revenues on a national average.

Because assessed valuation of property varies greatly among local school districts, substantial inequities have arisen. School consolidation has reduced some of the disparities by creating larger districts with more balanced tax bases, but it hasn't eliminated fiscal inequality altogether because short of statewide consolidation (which only Hawaii has accomplished), there remains a considerable spread between the richest and poorest school districts.

This leaves intergovernmental financing as the other main tool available, a practice of increasing significance. By far the largest amount comes from state aid, though federal grants and some interlocal transfers are also involved. From state to state the formulas used for distributing education funds vary widely, but the states increasingly are making efforts to achieve greater fiscal equity among local school districts, in part spurred by court rulings (for a summary of recent cases, see ACIR, 1976A:49). Most states have taken the first step toward equalization by utilizing aid formulas based upon need, as determined by local resources and enrollment (perhaps also taking into consideration the presence of disadvantaged pupils). Some states have mandated a minimum level of support and have guaranteed state aid to cover the shortfall where a standard local tax rate won't produce enough revenue. A few states have added a "recapture" provision so that if a rich school district raises more than the standard amount per pupil at a given tax rate, the surplus goes into a state equalization fund. These various devices keep local districts intact and use the state's revenue and regulatory authority to reduce fiscal disparities (ACIR, 1976A:47).

Revenue sharing. The same kind of unevenness of local revenue sources found for school districts prevails among the townships, municipalities, and counties of metropolitan areas. To overcome this difficulty, the states have devised a number of fiscal mechanisms, many of them designed specifically to augment revenues from sources beyond the property tax. Thus, the states authorize new locally collected taxes (income and retail sales among others), and some states share taxes with local units on the basis of origin of the tax payment, such as with taxes on natural resources, business licenses, financial institutions, cigarettes, general sales, and some other items. About half the states allow local governments to piggyback a local sales tax on top of the state sales tax; the money is collected by the state and the locality's share is returned. Piggybacking also occurs for a local personal income tax, gasoline tax, and several other taxes. About one-fourth of the states share one or more taxes on a needs-based formula, such as state taxes on sales, income, intangibles, cigarettes, and motor fuel. Where a local government grants property tax relief to elderly persons, the state might offer a reimbursement (ACIR, 1974D:74-81).

State grants. In addition there are a wide number of state grants to local general governments in different program areas. In second place after education is public welfare (but this varies among the states because welfare isn't a local function everywhere), highway funds are third, and various other program activities also receive state assistance (ACIR, 1974D:63). Some of the programs are originated by the states, and some are federal programs channeled through state agencies with state funds sometimes added. A number of states also "buy in" to programs funded directly by federal agencies to local governments by contributing a substantial part of the required local matching share.

FEDERAL AID

Federal aid is also an important factor for local governmental financing, producing about one-sixth of the total of local general revenue. Its significance stems from the federal government's ability to tap the national economy and to introduce needs factors into distribution formulas.

Federal grants. There are over 500 federal grant programs with a 1976 budget of $59 billion. Of the total amount, 76 percent went for specific-purpose grants (categorical programs), 12 percent for block grants and other broad-based aid, and 12 percent for revenue sharing and other general-purpose assistance (OMB, 1977:276). Eighty-five grant and revenue sharing programs went to local governments directly or through the states.

Revenue sharing. General revenue sharing authorized by the State and Local Fiscal Assistance Act of 1972 is the latest form of federal aid to local and state governments. It goes only to general units, including incorporated villages, townships, cities, and counties but not to school districts or special districts. The distribution formula takes into account population, general tax effort, and relative per capita tax income, and this has a redistributive effect. But the law lessens this by setting a minimum and a maximum share which any local government within a state may receive, and the result is that some central cities don't get as much as they would without this restriction and some more prosperous jurisdictions get more.

LOCAL REVENUE SHARING

Local government has its own methods of passing some of the fiscal burden for services to persons outside its jurisdiction.

User fees. The oldest method is the user fee, and it applies to residents and nonresidents alike. This might be for a commodity supplied (water), a service rendered (hospital), or an opportunity offered (admission to a facility). In a sense, the service agreement represents the institutionalization of this idea by collecting a wholesale fee from the contracting government and including overhead and capital costs as part of the contract price.

Commuter tax. Levying of a personal income tax upon all persons working in the city is another means of gaining revenue from nonresidents. Charleston, South Carolina had such a tax in the early nineteenth century but later dropped it. In 1939 Philadelphia was the first city in our era to put a municipal income tax into effect (ACIR, 1970). By 1976, 56 cities over 50,000 were using this tax, and all but Washington, D.C. and Baltimore applied it to commuters, though in some cases at a lesser rate for residents (ACIR, 1977A:225-229). Thus, the local income tax extends the fiscal reach of the municipality, an asset particularly valuable to central cities which are hard pressed to match service demands with revenue sources.

Metropolitan tax-base sharing. Minnesota in 1971 pioneered another technique for mitigating metropolitan fiscal disparity. This was done by pooling 40 percent of the growth of the commercial-industrial tax base of the seven-county Twin Cities metropolitan area. The 300 independent taxing units in the area share in the property taxes raised from this base, and their shares are determined on the basis of market value of all real property per capita within each jurisdiction. The lower the market value per capita, the bigger the share. It took a while for legal challenges to get resolved and administrative procedures to be worked out, and the first revenues from this source were distributed in 1976. Shared valuation amounted to 8.6 percent of the total commercial and industrial valuation of the metropolitan area. Minneapolis and St. Paul gained and so did 18 out of 39 other municipalities over 9,000, indicating the redistributive effect of this approach.

ANALYSIS OF FISCAL DEVICES

These several kinds of fiscal devices have in common an intent to introduce greater equity into the funding of services within metropolitan areas. Thus, they deal with the concern about fiscal disparity which all the governmental commissions reviewed in Chapter 1 worried about, and they help overcome problems stemming from concentration of low-income people in the central city and some poorer suburban municipalities. They haven't eliminated all inequities by a long shot, but they are pointed in the right direction.

Likewise, interlocal service agreements and transfer of functions attempt to lessen some of the service deficiencies which plague metropolitan areas. If they do that, citizen confidence can be increased. However, when services are supplied by another government under contract and funds come from an outside source separate from spending authority, public official accountability may be a little blurred. None of these devices do much to guide growth, though the Minnesota tax-base sharing plan helps by reducing harmful competition for commercial and industrial uses. Yet on the whole, the inventions are helpful and seem to solve more problems than they create.

The Case for Multiplicity

RECAPITULATION

To recapitulate the last three chapters, we Americans have adapted local general government in metropolitan areas through the incremental expansion of cities both in power and territory, by the growth of suburban government, and through the strengthening of county government. We have created new types of special-purpose units, including school districts, metropolitan districts, and local-service special districts. We have invented new mechanisms, such as interlocal agreements, transfer of functions, and various fiscal devices. We have produced this multiplicity of approaches not out of any particular theory, for as a people we aren't highly theoretical or ideological, but more because of necessity, and we are pragmatic and try to be practical.

Quite a few scholars and practitioners believe that our creation is a mishmash of fragmented, dangerously proliferated governments, and they argue for unification or structured federation, as we shall see in Chapters 7 and 8. But there are others who find what we have isn't all that bad compared to possible alternatives. One group who feels this way is the voters who defeat referendum proposals on metropolitan reorganization. Another group consists of some scholars who look at the positive values of governmental pluralism. York Willbern, for one, finds that individuals and groups are mostly able to satisfy their varying needs and wants through a "pluralistic political marketplace" (1964:124). Norton Long observes that the unplanned metropolitan polity may be closer to oligopoly than free market competition. "What we have," he continues (1962:158), "is a number of institutions, public and private, sharing a common territory, making demands on each other, cooperating, hindering, damaging, and helping in an interdependent set of relations with no overall government exercising control." Although both Willbern and Long might wish for some kind of effective governmental mechanism to give expression to the metropolitan political community, they find a multiplicity of local governments quite acceptable.

PUBLIC CHOICE THEORY

This line of thought has had its fullest development by some scholars who have developed what they call "public choice theory." The public choice approach applies economic reasoning to public sector problems (for example, see Tiebout, 1956; Warren, 1966; Bish, 1971; and V. and E. Ostrom, 1971).

A recent articulation of this approach came in a book by Robert L. Bish and Vincent Ostrom (1974). The authors start with an assumption that all individuals are motivated by self-interest but have different preferences. Some of the goods and services people want can be best provided under private market arrangements, but others require governmental actions. In the private sector, willingness to pay the price indicates consumer preference. In the public sector, the choice of the public goods and services can be expressed through voting, lobbying, and other expressions of opinion. "Citizen demands can be more precisely indicated in smaller units rather than larger political units, and in political units undertaking fewer rather than more numerous public functions." But it wouldn't be easy for citizens to articulate preference to a single small unit for each public service. "The optimal situation is more likely to be one in which each of several units performs multiple services" (1974:24).

On the supply side, Bish and Ostrom conceive of government as a natural monopoly, and like all monopolies it has little incentive to operate efficiently, to innovate or reduce costs, or to be responsive to consumer demands. As with private monopoly, the adverse effects of monopoly in the public sector can be alleviated by rivalry and competition. "If ample fragmentation of authority and overlapping jurisdictions exist," they insist, "sufficient competition may be engendered to stimulate a more responsive and efficient public economy in metropolitan areas" (1974:30).

Several ways are available to use competition to counter monopolistic behavior. Elections provide political competition. Furthermore, people can "vote with their feet" by moving to a governmental jurisdiction which has the level and mix of services and tax payments they want if there are enough local units to allow a choice. They can arrange for alternative producers of public goods and services, obtained through private arrangements or from overlapping governments, and if there is ample overlap, competition can occur among different public agencies. (The Los Angeles metropolitan area best epitomizes the arrangement they favor.)

Both small jurisdictions and large ones are needed, according to Bish and Ostrom (1974:1-2):

> Different public goods and services are most efficiently provided under different organizational arrangements. Services which involve proportionately large expenditures for physical facilities may be provided most efficiently by large organizations. Economies in such services can often be realized by serving large populations and large areas.

> Other services, such as education and police, are provided in person-to-person situations. These services are both more difficult to manage and highly sensitive to individual preferences and localized conditions. Diseconomies are likely to accrue when these services are organized on a large scale.

> A governmental system of multiple, overlapping jurisdictions can take advantage of diverse economies of scale for different public services. A public economy composed of multiple jurisdictions is likely to be more efficient and responsive than a public economy organized as a single area-wide monopoly.

Thus, public choice theory provides a philosophical underpinning for the multiplicity of governmental units of metropolitan areas and for the various legal and informal relationships which exist among them.

BRIEF COMMENTARY

As the title of my book indicates, I am very sympathetic with the notion of small and large jurisdictions, each doing what it can do best. What bothers me about public choice theory is its view of people mainly as consumers and government primarily as a service provider. Missing is an outlook of people as citizens and government as an institution which helps achieve a sense of wholeness in community life. Thus, not only is it a question of at what scale a particular service can be most efficiently produced but it also is a matter of what geographic areas best serve as the locus for providing a sense of community. There might be communities of several sizes just as there are areas of different scale for services: the neighborhood community, the city community, the suburban county community, the metropolitan community. Each such community size would have a cluster of services under a general government rather than having so many separate, specialized units, which public choice theorists seem to favor.

A second concern I have about public choice theory is something which also disturbs me about market theory for the private economy. In actuality the "haves" benefit the most and the "have-nots" and "have-littles" continue in their lowly condition. Thus, the rich can set themselves in nice suburban

Chapter 6

CONFEDERATION

Multiplicity of local governments in metropolitan areas we have, but not everybody is pleased with this arrangement. For many years, numerous scholars, civic leaders, and public officials have been disturbed about the situation, especially the absence of an areawide instrumentality for dealing with problems of the metropolis as a whole. Some have proposed unification and others have advocated federation, and sometimes these schemes have been carried out, as we shall see in the two chapters following this one. But since these alternatives haven't gained widespread application, persons desirous of an areawide approach have developed other responses.

As a start, they devised metropolitan planning bodies encompassing multiple local jurisdictions, and later they formed councils bringing together representatives of local governments to work for joint solutions to common problems. Since 1965 these two thrusts have drawn together in many areas, producing what can properly be called a metropolitan confederation. It is now the predominant form of organization found in the metropolitan areas of the United States.

The Case for Confederation

Like multiplicity, the confederated approach evolved without much of an underlying theory. Even this term to describe the phenomenon has only recently had much usage.

Confederation is a political science concept of governments uniting for common purposes but with the member governments themselves retaining their independence and supremacy. Thus, after the American Revolution from 1781 to 1789 the United States functioned under the Articles of Confederation, which clearly specified: "Each state retains its sovereignty, freedom, and independence, and every power, jurisdiction and right, which is not by this confederation expressly delegated to the United States, in Congress assembled." But after eight years this was replaced by our present federal constitution in which both the national government and the states have independent sources of authority.

Applying the concept to metropolitan areas, we find that councils of governments (COGs) are confederations and so are regional planning commissions (RPCs) when a majority of the governing board is composed of representatives of local governments. The Advisory Commission on Intergovernmental Relations refers to these units as "regional councils," and its study of substate regionalism made the case for what ACIR calls "regional confederalism."

Regional confederalism, then, is a largely voluntary interlocal compact or covenant to promote common interest without the individual member units subordinating any of their essential powers or autonomy to the areawide body. Confederal arrangements such as COG's and RPC's serve as catalysts in encouraging members to act jointly to meet areawide needs or implement comprehensive or functional plans. They cannot bind their members or non-members to policy decisions nor compel them to take implementing action. COG's and RPC's are not units of government in the legal sense, since as a rule they lack the power to tax or exercise powers. Their powers are mainly advisory, and their services or assistance to members are usually limited to "software" functions such as planning, technical assistance, and joint purchasing (1973A:51).

Let us look at the two principal species of confederation—regional planning commissions and councils of governments—how they developed, and how they have emerged in the 1970s as regional councils.

Early Regional Planning Commissions

City planning as we know it today came to American cities in the early twentieth century. Hartford, Connecticut was the first to have an official planning commission—in 1907—and other cities followed suit during the next 20 years until by 1927 390 city planning commissions were functioning (Scott, 1969:78, 249).

In the same period agencies to undertake larger scale metropolitan planning were also set up, commencing with the Boston Metropolitan Improvement Commission of 1902. The first metropolitan county planning commission was established in 1922 by the Los Angeles County Board of Supervisors, and during the twenties a private organization called the Committee on Regional Plan of New York and its Environs produced a plan for a vast bistate region of 5,500 square miles. Elsewhere metropolitan planning proceeded under both public and private sponsorship. The New Deal used public works and relief programs to give regional planning a boost, and by 1937 there were over 500 metropolitan multicounty and county planning agencies, about three-fifths of them with official status. As the decade ended, regional planning commissions or private associations were operating in and around 20 major metropolises (ACIR, 1973A:53-55).

The need to cope with urban development on a scale far exceeding the bounds of the central city produced this interest in regional planning. As a result, regional planning commissions became the first widespread expression of voluntary intergovernmental cooperation at the metropolitan level.

AFTER WORLD WAR II

This interest in regional planning continued during World War II, and in 1943 and 1944 private regional planning councils were set up in the Boston, Pittsburgh, Cincinnati, St. Louis, Kansas City, and San Francisco areas. Typically they involved leaders from business, labor, and local government. In the years immediately after the war, government-based voluntary regional planning bodies were established for areas of Lane County, Oregon (Eugene), Reno, Detroit, Atlanta, and northern Virginia in the national capital area. In 1945 the Michigan legislature authorized creation of regional planning commissions, and ten other states adopted similar legislation in the next two years. By 1950 official regional planning commissions were functioning in twenty metropolitan areas (ACIR, 1973B:55-59).

Regional planning commissions continued to grow in number during the 1950s. They got a substantial boost when Section 701 of the Housing Act of 1954 authorized 50-50 matching funds for metropolitan planning conducted by official state and regional planning agencies. This was reinforced by the passage of the Interstate Highway and Defense Act of 1956, which stimulated metropolitan transportation planning, most notably in the Penn-Jersey Transportation Study in the Philadelphia area and then in the Seattle-Tacoma, Minneapolis-St. Paul, Milwaukee, and Boston areas. By the end of 1963, all but three states, all rural, had authorization for metropolitan planning.

Initially the states were content to pass enabling legislation and leave it up to local officials whether to organize. Connecticut was the first state to provide assertive leadership for this purpose when in 1958 the Connecticut

Development Commission demarcated regional planning areas and set about establishing regional planning commissions and providing them assistance. Georgia took similar initiative beginning in 1961, and in the following years, Massachusetts, New York, Pennsylvania, Tennessee, Wisconsin, and California joined in (ACIR, 1973A:226).

A study of the effectiveness of metropolitan planning conducted by the Joint Center for Urban Studies of MIT and Harvard in the midsixties concluded that the agencies had insufficient legal power to participate in development decisions, lacked clear statutory direction, and had uncertain budgets. This left them unequipped to have much effect on patterns of metropolitan growth (ACIR, 1974A:63).

To be more effective, regional planning commissions, particularly those serving multiple jurisdictions, would need more power, but this was hard to come by because counties and cities were reluctant to give up their controls over land use and the states weren't eager to delegate state power to metropolitan agencies. Nevertheless, changes have occurred in metropolitan planning during the last dozen years. This has happened as regional planning commissions have merged their destiny with another form of voluntary intergovernmental cooperation—councils of governments.

The First Councils of Governments

EARLY EXAMPLES

Councils of governments (COGs) are "multi-functional voluntary regional associations of elected officials or of local governments represented by their elected officials. The governing body of a COG is composed predominantly of the chief elected officials of the member political jurisdictions, and at least part of its funds comes from local public sources" (ACIR, 1973A:50).

In 1960 five organizations met this definition, some others were in the gestation stage, and by 1965 several more had been born. The oldest was the Supervisors Inter-County Committee, set up by six counties in the Detroit region in 1954. Second was the Metropolitan Regional Conference for the tristate New York region (1956), and third was the Puget Sound Governmental Conference for the Seattle-Tacoma area (1957). Other metropolitan areas served by these early COGs included Utica-Rome, Philadelphia, Washington, Atlanta, Salem (Oregon), San Francisco-Oakland, and Los Angeles. However, by 1965 the one in the Utica-Rome area had collapsed, and the one around New York City was virtually defunct.

The basic membership of these initial COGs consisted of municipal and county officials representing member governments, with some variations such as inclusion of state legislators in metropolitan Washington and the governor and a school superintendent in Oregon. Communications was a major activity as the COGs got going, and often these local officials within the same metropolitan area had never met one another before. Planning and development were the major program interests, and they tried to link the various city and county planning efforts and regional studies, especially transportation. The possibilities of cooperative services were another activity some of them undertook. The member governments contributed funds so that the COG could hire staff and some COGs got private contributions, but budgets were small. It was a period of testing, and the participating local governments didn't want to move too far too fast.

Looking back on this first decade of experience with COGs, the Advisory Commission on Intergovernmental Relations observed:

> Common weaknesses in these COG's included their heavy fiscal dependence upon member local governments and in some instances their primary reliance on private sector support. Regional organizations serving interstate metropolitan areas encountered the severest jurisdictional problems. The issues dividing COG membership and causing nonparticipation included inequitable systems of assessing dues; differences between central city and suburban perspectives on problems; dominance by single, large jurisdictions; and conflicts over race, economic development, transportation, and fiscal resources (1973A:69-70).

IMPACT OF FEDERAL LEGISLATION

"Locally initiated, locally financed, locally governed" describes the COGs organized up to 1965. But this has since changed because federal funds have flowed to COGs and federal legislation has carved out a new role for them.

The icebreaker was the Housing and Urban Development Act of 1965, which added a provision to Section 701 making organizations of locally elected officials in metropolitan areas eligible for federal funds. The same act started a new program for water and sewer facilities with a requirement for conformance to areawide planning. This same idea of areawide planning had been expressed in a 1961 program for open space grants, a 1962 highway act, and a 1964 mass transportation program, so federal programs were offering a new legitimacy to metropolitan planning.

In 1965 one federal act called for the establishment of local development districts in Appalachia and another act provided for economic development districts elsewhere. The latter in particular took on COG-like characteristics because they included county and city officials along with other interests. Although many of these new districts were outside metropolitan areas, some of them encompassed metropolitan centers. They joined regional planning commissions and councils of governments as species of regional councils.

In the next year, Section 204 of the Demonstration Cities and Metro-politan Development Act of 1966 established a project notification and review system whereby applicants for certain federal aid programs were required to submit their applications to a metropolitan or regional planning organization for review and comment as to its consistency with areawide comprehensive planning.

Two years later Title IV of the Intergovernmental Cooperation Act of 1968 gave this effort a further boost by calling upon the president to establish rules and regulations to assure that the review of federal assistance applications take into account national, regional, state, and local viewpoints and the objectives of state, regional, and local comprehensive planning. Insofar as possible, planning of individual federal programs, such as highway, urban renewal, and open space, was to be coordinated and made part of local and areawide development planning.

In implementing this requirement in Circular A-95, the Bureau of the Budget combined it with the previous project notification and review system, extended the system to nonmetropolitan areas and state clearinghouses, and broadened the program coverage. By the spring of 1977, approximately 95 percent of the U.S. population was in areas where A-95 review was functioning.

SUBSTATE DISTRICTS

These several federal acts and implementing regulations gave state govern-ment the responsibility for delineating substate districts. By 1976, 44 states had demarcated a total of 530 districts, the majority of them in town-and-country areas. Most, but not all, of the substate district organizations serve as A-95 clearinghouses (where they don't, a county agency fulfills this function).

Regional Councils in the 1970s

Given a place in the sun by federal law and regulation and provided operating money by federal grants, councils of governments grew rapidly after 1965. Their number passed 100 in 1968, and in 1976 there were 559 regional councils of the three species with local elected officials comprising a majority of the governing body, 195 of them in metropolitan areas (National Association of Regional Councils, 1976). What was once a neat distinction between regional planning commissions, economic development districts, and councils of governments has now blurred, for areawide units of each species handle the A-95 review-and-comment process, COGs are heavily into metro-politan planning, regional planning commissions have broadened their clear-inghouse role, and economic development districts have moved well beyond their initial function. Moreover, some agencies are simultaneously a COG and an RPC or a COG and an economic development district. Thus, the generic term "regional council" is used to refer to all multijurisdictional organizations controlled by local elected officials, regardless of original form.

CHARACTERISTICS

In its monumental study of substate regionalism, the Advisory Commission on Intergovernmental Relations reported on a 1972 survey it conducted with the cooperation of the National Association of Regional Councils (1973A:79-80). Questionnaires went to 705 regional councils and other A-95 clearinghouses and 312 replied, 45 percent of them covering all or part of an SMSA. Because regional councils are about the same now as they were in 1972, this survey still gives a fairly accurate picture.

On the average the regional councils surveyed had membership from 5 counties, 19 municipalities, 8 school districts, and 10 special districts, but there was a wide range among them. For the majority, voting was based upon one government, one vote, but 11 percent had adopted a formula of weighted votes in proportion to population of the member governments, some had a combination of weighted and nonweighted voting, and others diluted the votes of special districts. Two-thirds of the regional councils got more than half of their money from federal sources, of which Section 701 led the way. Typically local governments put up more than the state governments (1973A:80-82, 88-89).

The work program of the regional councils was heavily weighted toward physical planning. More than half of them had adopted plans or policies for water and sewers, land use, open space and recreation, transportation, solid waste, and economic development. Using terminology developed by Oliver P. Williams (1971), ACIR calls these "systems maintenance activities" as compared with "life-style" matters, such as pollution, housing, education, urban renewal, police, and zoning. The latter are heavily value-laden and therefore highly controversial, but some of the federal programs are moving regional councils into these kinds of problems (1973A:96).

NOTEWORTHY EXAMPLES

Several examples of noteworthy councils of governments can illustrate more precisely what they do, and some of their tribulations.

San Francisco Bay. Local officials in the San Francisco Bay area set up the Association of Bay Area Governments (ABAG) in 1961 to provide a forum for discussion and study of metropolitan problems and their solutions, and also to prevent the state government from establishing a regional planning authority, which seemed a possibility at the time. Created under California's Joint Exercise of Powers Act, ABAG now has a membership of 85 out of 93 cities and seven out of nine counties in the Bay area, and 25 special districts, regional agencies, and other governmental bodies are nonvoting members. Representatives from each member jurisdiction participate in a general assembly, which gathers at least once a year. A 36-member executive committee meets monthly, and 15 policy committees and task forces work on functional topics. ABAG's 1976/77 budget is $3.6 million (excluding pass-through funds), of which $2.8 million comes from federal sources. The state puts in about $100,000, and the remainder is local funds, mostly dues from member cities and counties. The staff numbers 110.

Comprehensive regional planning is ABAG's primary emphasis. In 1970 it completed a comprehensive regional plan with a land use emphasis, and it has done major studies related to open space, ocean coastline, airports, water, sewerage, and drainage. The current work plan emphasizes planning for air quality, environmental management (particularly water quality and solid waste), allocation of low- and moderate-income housing, and human services (emergency medical and local organization of human service delivery). ABAG has an interest in transportation policies, but the Metropolitan Transportation Commission is the official planning body in this field. And there are some other regional agencies and planning bodies, particularly in the human services area. Even so, ABAG is into many concerns as the A-95 areawide clearinghouse, and as such it reviewed more than 1,000 local applications for federal funds in 1975. (For more on ABAG, see Jones, 1973 and 1974.)

Atlanta. In 1947 the Georgia legislature formed a two-county Metropolitan Planning Commission for the Atlanta area and in 1960 expanded it to five counties. Four years later the Metropolitan Atlanta Council of Local Governments came into being, and in subsequent years independent regional bodies for health planning, transportation, and rapid transit. In 1971 the legislature combined all but the latter into the Atlanta Regional Commission (ARC), keeping the Metropolitan Atlanta Rapid Transit Authority (MARTA) as a separate operating agency (McArthur, 1973A:37-42).

The Atlanta Regional Commission now has 16 public members and 15 members at large. Public members include the chairmen of the boards of county commissioners from the seven participating counties, the mayor and a city council member from Atlanta, and a mayor from each county, elected by the other mayors. The members at large come from districts of approximately equal population and are elected by the public members. The staff of 100 handles a $3 million budget (1976), about half a million from local appropriations, a little over $100,000 from the state, and most of the rest from federal funds.

In 1975 ARC adopted a major regional development plan, intended to serve as a policy framework, particularly for land use and transportation systems. To go with it are about 20 sets of policy statements or guidelines on such matters as airports, water and sewers, criminal justice, hospitals, and family planning services. A significant document is the regional improvements program, updated regularly to indicate plans for capital improvements. But like the other COGs, the Atlanta Regional Commission depends upon local governments, special authorities like MARTA, and state agencies like the highway department to implement its plans, though it can influence some of the implementation through the A-95 review-and-comment process.

Kansas City. Taking on the challenge of an interstate metropolis is the Mid-America Regional Council of the Kansas City area. In 1957 civic leadership had promoted a Mo-Kan Metropolitan Development Compact and had gotten an enabling act passed by the Kansas legislature, but not in Missouri; another try in 1965 met the same fate (Murphy, 1970:206). For highway planning each state set up a separate apparatus for its part of the metropolitan area in 1964, but pressure from federal agencies produced a new bi-state Metropolitan Planning Commission (Metroplan) in 1966 to serve seven counties. Local officials wanted greater involvement in implementation of the plans which were being developed, so they formed the Mid-America Council of Governments in 1967. At first this COG was served by the Metroplan staff but later got its own, and the two organizations drifted apart. In 1972, though, they came back together by merging into a new Mid-America Regional Council (MARC) with an eighth county added.

As now organized, MARC is governed by a thirty-member council: four from Kansas City (Missouri), three each from the largest four counties, two each from the four smallest counties, and two each from Kansas City (Kansas), Independence (Missouri), and Overland Park (Kansas). There are also fifteen nonvoting members on the board representing other organizations and state officials and agencies. It has a staff of one hundred twenty-seven, and a 1976 budget of over $4 million, with $210,000 from local contributions and most of the rest from federal funds. As a planning agency it deals with transit and transportation, housing, solid waste disposal, emergency rescue, land use, resource recovery, the elderly, human resources, air and water quality, and population and employment projections. Emergency rescue and programs for the elderly are particularly large programs of a nonphysical nature. MARC also serves as a clearinghouse agency for A-95 review.

INTRAMURAL CONTENTION

As officials from counties, central cities, suburban municipalities, and other local jurisdictions get together in regional councils, their relationships aren't always harmonious. Disputes break out and sometimes seriously disrupt and occasionally tear asunder the regional council. Three cases can serve as illustrations.

Puget Sound. The Puget Sound Governmental Conference in the Seattle-Tacoma area got going in 1957 under a state law authorizing counties to form regional planning commissions. So the original membership consisted of the three county commissioners from each of the four participating counties. When the law was changed in 1957 to allow municipal participation, mayors from three central cities became members and some other municipal officials were added later. In 1961 the conference took charge of the regional transportation study, and this became its major focus for several years (ACIR, 1973A:65).

Like many COGs, the Puget Sound Governmental Conference expanded its program during the 1960s. Mass transportation, land use planning, manpower, health, and other human service programs all became part of its agenda. By 1975 its budget was $1.6 million, it had thirty-three member cities, three Indian tribes, and the four counties, and its executive board had seventeen members representing the various governmental units. In that year the name changed to the Puget Sound Council of Governments, but the organization began to unravel. One county had quit paying its dues because of disillusionment with regionalism, and some other county officials were disgruntled. To cope with this dissatisfaction, subregional committees were organized for each county and delegated some of the planning and A-95 responsibilities, but this didn't satisfy all the dissenters and three counties withdrew completely. During 1976 a negotiating group of city and county officials worked to put the COG back together. This produced an executive committee of twenty-two members, half from counties and half from cities. There would be subregional planning organizations with power to handle A-95 review on subregional issues. The memorandum of understanding outlined a process for determining what issues are regional and what subregional, for this was the heart of the dispute. With this done, the Puget Sound Council of Governments became functional again in the fall of 1976.

Cleveland-Akron. Conflict within the seven-county Northeast Ohio Areawide Coordinating Agency of the Cleveland-Akron area became so bad in 1971 that Cleveland withdrew because it felt its interests were ignored. The U.S. Department of Housing and Urban Development (HUD) decertified the agency as an areawide planning organization eligible for federal funds. Compromises were worked out to give Cleveland more votes, though not the equivalent of one person, one vote. HUD recertified, then decertified again because of internal personnel difficulties. After two years of back-and-forth negotiations, the agency was put back together and recertified but with a smaller area because the Akron area got its own A-95 agency (ACIR, 1973A:83-86).

San Diego. The Comprehensive Planning Organization of the San Diego Region has been torn by strong disagreements between elected officials from the City of San Diego and San Diego County over transportation systems, airport location, and manpower programs. The governing board consists of a representative from the county and each of the thirteen municipalities. Each member has one vote except when a member and two seconders request a weighted vote; then the central city's vote is worth forty units, the county's is thirty units, and the twelve suburban municipalities share thirty units; in this way neither the city nor the county dominates, a factor which has kept the organization going despite the disputes.

Elsewhere. Here and there in other metropolitan areas a fringe county or a central city has seceded from the COG, temporarily or permanently, due to dissatisfaction, but when the whole nation is considered, these are exceptions. The overwhelming pattern is voluntary cooperation of cities and counties in regional councils, which are still primarily advisory in their authority.

OTHER AREAWIDE BODIES

While the regional councils have emerged as instruments for the A-95 review process and for land use planning through federal encouragement, other federal programs have promoted areawide planning in their particular fields. As of 1976 there were twenty programs of this sort, dealing with such matters as urban development, rural development, economic development, economic opportunities, open space, transportation, water, health, solid waste, air pollution, manpower, and law enforcement (ACIR, 1976A:106; also see 1973A:168). Some of these efforts come under the jurisdiction of multifunctional regional councils, but others are handled by single-purpose functional agencies; and a particular program might be administered one way in some states, and another way in others. Many of the single-purpose, areawide agencies have their own district boundaries, often differing from the boundaries of other regional bodies. As a result, a fairly complex pattern of regional agencies is developing in many states.

In terms of authority over federal programs, the regional councils and most of the other areawide bodies have only an advisory role—"review-and-comment" is how it is described in OMB Circular A-95. But in recent years federal programs for water quality and transportation have extended this to "review-and-approval" authority. Under Section 208 of the 1972 amendments to the Federal Water Pollution Control Act, the states may designate areawide planning agencies or may retain complete control over the program. Under the Federal-Aid Highway Act of 1973 and the National Mass Transportation Assistance Act of 1974, states are supposed to designate metropolitan planning organizations. These respective areawide and metropolitan bodies draw up plans, decide upon local programs which various agencies will carry out, and allocate funds, subject to state and federal review.

In many metropolitan areas, the regional council has been designated to handle water quality and/or transportation planning, but in other areas, some other metropolitan agency has gained the assignment. Where the latter has occurred, the specialized agency has greater direct influence upon land use decisions than most regional councils whose comprehensive land use planning is only advisory in nature because transportation and water quality management strongly affect the pattern of growth. This strengthening of the metropolitan role in these two fields represents the latest evolutionary step in trying to develop areawide mechanisms. (For more on the federal role in this, see Chapter 10, p. 136.)

Analysis

ACIR'S EVALUATION

Looking at the broad picture of regional councils in 1973, the Advisory Commission on Intergovernmental Relations concluded that six basic challenges confront them (1973A:109).

Increasing pressure from central cities for proportionate representation.

The dependence upon federal funds which displaces local goals and priorities with federal ones and also changes the voluntary nature of membership.

Lack of machinery for handling central city-suburb and intersuburban conflict as the program moves into controversial social and life-style subjects.

Lack of power to implement plans directly or to compel local governmental units to carry them out.

Even though a consensus is emerging to perform certain urban functions on an areawide basis, only a handful of regional councils have been able to assume operational responsibilities for public services and programs.

The feudalistic attitudes of program specialists and the general public's opposition to metropolitan government remain as barriers to expanded action.

ACIR was particularly disturbed by the growing number of areawide organizations handling a single function, either as a coordinating body or an operating agency. The commission felt that functional specialization and the overlapping boundaries of diverse districts were unnecessarily adding to the complexity of local government.

UMBRELLA MULTIJURISDICTIONAL ORGANIZATIONS (UMJOs) PROPOSED

To counteract this trend, the Commission advocated greater use of "umbrella multijurisdictional organizations" (UMJOs). (This was a term originally used in recommendations coming from some national associations of local and state officials.) As ACIR saw it, an UMJO would be "a comprehensive and functional planning, coordinating, programming, servicing, and implementing body—in short, a regional council with some meaningful, but limited authority" (1973A:372). It would become the preferred instrumentality for all federally assisted districting programs. Functioning under the policy control of representatives of cities and counties, an UMJO would be assigned a decisive policy-guiding role for regional special districts and authorities, but wouldn't get into operations. ACIR also recommended that an UMJO have special review authority over state agency actions having a regional impact and also over local government actions having a multi-jurisdictional impact. An UMJO would be funded from a combination of federal, state, and local sources on a regular basis. In this manner, ACIR wants to build upon the experience of existing regional councils and make them something more. This something would still be a confederation, but one with more power delegated to the areawide organization.

STRENGTHS AND WEAKNESSES OF METROPOLITAN CONFEDERATION

My own view on regional councils relates to what I see as the strengths and weaknesses of the confederation approach. Regional councils are a useful development because they advance interlocal cooperation and help adapt local government to the conditions of metropolitan areas. They have created a forum for local elected officials to meet, share information, exchange ideas, bargain, and come up with cooperative solutions to common problems. The regional staff brings together personnel from various jurisdictions to work out common data bases, trade reports, and develop technical recommendations of mutual interest. In these ways the regional councils are facilitators of intergovernmental volunteerism.

As planning vehicles most of them are failures according to my concept of what planning is. As I see it, true planning is part of decision-making and is inextricably linked to implementation. Planning is used to develop facts, analyze problems, formulate alternative courses, weigh and narrow choices, and propose specific actions. Unless these steps result in decisions and implementation measures, the process isn't really planning but rather study, report writing, map drawing, and daydreaming. By this test, most regional councils do very little real planning because they don't make decisions on zoning and other land use controls, capital and operating budgets, allocation of state and federal grants, and program operations. The A-95 process in particular is devoid of a decision-making element because the regional councils don't control the federal funds for the projects they are commenting on and federal agencies seem to pay little heed to their comments.

Two exceptions occur with regards to federal transportation and water control programs where regional councils (or some other areawide organization) has authority to allocate federal funds to local projects. These decisions make planning real and elevate the regional councils to a new status as an instrumentality of areawide government.

But this raises a problem of accountability, and this goes to the heart of my concern about ACIR's UMJO proposal. Regional councils are composed of elected officials from various local governments, sometimes with the addition of citizen members appointed by them. In their metropolitan role, these officials are called upon to make decisions on matters in which their individual jurisdictions have a vested interest. While this can lead to what ACIR (1973A:143) calls the politics of negotiation, it can also result in mutual "backscratching" which distracts participants from looking for the larger metropolitan view. Furthermore, since their dominant role is with the local jurisdiction, these officials aren't very clearly accountable to the people through an electoral process for their areawide decisions. Conversely the people don't have direct representation into metropolitan decision-making. This may tend to lessen citizen confidence in areawide planning and implementation processes.

As to other metropolitan problems, regional councils only have a modest potential for dealing with unplanned growth as long as they lack authority over implementation measures. Their tools for improving service delivery are mainly persuasion and the encouragement of interlocal cooperation, both helpful actions but relatively weak in impact. They can do very little about fiscal disparity except work on the state legislature and take equity into consideration when they comment on federal grant allocations. On social disparity, a few regional councils have worked out fair-share housing agreements calling for voluntary dispersal of low- and moderate-income housing around the metropolitan area; this helps, but the absence of metropolitan land use controls makes it a precarious process dependent wholly on local acceptance.

These are real limitations, but they shouldn't detract from the useful role regional councils play in facilitating communications and interlocal cooperation.

Chapter 7

UNIFICATION

As a product of adaptive evolution, metropolitan areas have gained numerous governments, complexly related to one another. Far too many, some reformers insist. The entire settled area of the metropolis and its developing fringe is a single economic and social community, they argue, and therefore it should have one government. Confederation to them is an inadequate solution because it leaves the multitudinous units in place and doesn't create an areawide government with strength. Their solution is unification.

The Case for Unification

FROM THE PAST

Almost as long as the United States has had cities over 50,000, the case for unification has been heard. In this century one of the strongest cases for unification was made by Paul Studenski in a pioneering report on metropolitan government, prepared for the National Municipal League (1930:29):

> Whatever the reasons for the great number of political divisions, they do not provide an ideal political organization for metropolitan regions. They tend to divert the attention of the inhabitants from the fact that they are members of one large community and lead them to act as

members of separate units. They result in great variation in municipal regulations in force in different sections of the metropolitan area, and in the standards of the services maintained, in sectional treatment of problems which are essentially metropolitan, in radical inequalities in the tax resources of the several political divisions, and in jurisdictional conflicts. . . . It is difficult under these conditions to bring about concerted action throughout the metropolitan area. Consequently it is often well-nigh impossible to solve effectively municipal problems common to all.

While recognizing the existence of local communities, Studenski maintained "it is necessary that the localities be integrated in such a manner as will enable the whole region to function as a political unit" (1930:41).

In the 1930s William Anderson began counting the units of local government in the United States, and he concluded that there were too many of inadequate size, resulting in inefficiencies and diseconomy. He recognized the need for holding government responsible to the voters but thought that this could be accomplished with fewer units. Instead of the 165,000 local units existing in 1941, he proposed a reduction to approximately 17,800: 200 city/counties of at least 50,000 each, 2,100 rural and part-rural counties, 15,000 incorporated places including the larger New England towns, and 500 miscellaneous units (1949:38-46).

CED'S 1966 PROPOSAL

Studenski's interest in metropolitan consolidation and Anderson's concern for an excessive number of governmental units were picked by a committee of the Committee on Economic Development (CED) in the 1960s. Marion B. Folsom of Eastman Kodak Company served as chairman of the committee, and Robert F. Steadman was staff director.

In a 1966 report entitled *Modernizing Local Government*, CED concluded that there are deep-rooted and extensive weaknesses in local government throughout the United States, both within and outside metropolitan areas. Six inadequacies were particularly noted: very few units large enough to apply modern methods; overlapping layers of local government; ineffective popular control; weak policy-making mechanisms; antiquated administrative organizations; and lack of personnel with knowledge of modern technology (1966:11, 13). CED's study committee developed recommendations to respond to all of these problems, including reducing the number of local governments in the United States by at least 80 percent and by severely curtailing the number of overlapping layers.

As to the situation in metropolitan areas, the 1966 CED report had this to say (1966:44):

The bewildering multiplicity of small, piecemeal, duplicative, over-lapping local jurisdictions cannot cope with the staggering difficulties encountered in managing modern urban affairs. The fiscal effects of duplicative suburban separatism create great difficulty in provisions of costly central city services benefiting the whole urbanized area. If local governments are to function effectively in metropolitan areas, they must have sufficient size and authority to plan, administer, and provide financial support for solutions to area-wide problems.

To eliminate these kinds of problems, CED advocated as much unification as feasible. In one-county metropolitan areas, a reconstituted county govern-ment, possibly achieved through city-county consolidation, would be used as the basic framework for handling areawide problems. For multicounty areas within a single state, county lines might be redrawn to produce a single metropolitan county for each area; if that isn't feasible, then multicounty federations. In New England, towns should be consolidated or closely fed-erated to create metropolitan governments. For interstate metropolitan areas, county cooperation should be created across state lines. But at the same time within large metropolitan areas, "neighborhood districts should be created—each with a small council to assist city and county governments in adapting services to neighborhood needs" (1966:44-47).

Thus, consolidation was the basic course favored by CED in 1966. It is an approach advocated by reformers in quite a number of metropolitan areas but achieved in only a few localities.

Metropolitan Consolidation

The most far-reaching proposals for unification call for the consolidation of all governmental units within the metropolitan area into a single govern-ment. Mostly this approach has been proposed for single-county metropolitan areas, and sometimes achieved by the consolidation of the central city and the county. If the suburban municipalities and special districts are amal-gamated, unification is complete and a single metropolitan government is achieved. Sometimes, though, a few county offices remain intact and some municipal units and special districts continue to function so that consolida-tion falls a little short of total unification.

NINETEENTH AND EARLY TWENTIETH CENTURIES

Four major city/county consolidations took place in the 19th century: Boston (1821), Philadelphia (1854), New Orleans (1870), and New York (1874 and 1898). Intermediate steps of consolidation occurred in New Orleans and New York prior to the final merger. Boston absorbed six suburban towns after consolidation and New Orleans annexed some additional land, but not the other two.

In all four places, city/county consolidation was accomplished by the state legislatures, not by a vote of local residents. The same is true for the next one to occur, consolidation of the city of Honolulu and Honolulu County in 1909 by action of the territorial legislature.

During this same period four acts of city/county separation also happened: Baltimore (1851), San Francisco (1856), St. Louis (1876), and Denver (1901). Since these cities then took over county functions, the product was unified government. San Francisco and St. Louis expanded their boundaries considerably before separation and encompassed for the time the total urbanized area, and these borders haven't changed since. Denver added a little land, Baltimore none at all at the time of separation, but both expanded later, taking territory from the county they had once been a part of, that way keeping up with metropolitan growth for a while.

But except for Honolulu, which takes in all of Oahu Island, time ran out on all of these city/county consolidations and separations as unified metropolitan governments because unceasing metropolitan growth eventually went beyond the enlarged boundaries. For example, by the 1880s railroad and streetcar suburbs began springing up around Philadelphia and by the 1920s suburban expansion was in full flower. Similarly the Boston area grew well beyond the city even with the six added towns. Baltimore's annexation efforts kept up with the growth for a while but not after 1920. Only Denver among the consolidated cities took in most of the urbanized population as late as 1940 only to see post-World War II expansion burgeon in its three suburban counties. Although serving forty years or more as a unified metropolitan government, as some of them did, isn't a bad record, once again it must be pointed out that structural solutions tend to be temporary.

SINCE WORLD WAR II

During the first half of this century the idea of city/county consolidation was talked about in numerous places around the United States. Among them, according to Victor Jones, were Virginia's Tidewater region, Durham, Atlanta, Macon, Miami, Birmingham, Cleveland, Minneapolis, Fort Worth, Houston, Salt Lake City, Seattle, and Portland, Oregon (1953:544). But nothing came of it in any of these places. However, county/county consolidation occurred twice: Jones County, Tennessee merged into Hamilton County (Chattanooga) in 1919; and Campbell and Milton Counties, Georgia consolidated with Fulton County (Atlanta) in 1932.

Baton Rouge and East Baton Rouge Parish broke the drought by partially consolidating in 1949. Since then the floodtide of suburban growth outside the central city has produced a renewed interest in the possibility of metropolitan reorganization in other areas. Since 1945, reorganization proposals have come to a vote forty-eight times in thirty-three metropolitan areas (through 1976). Six of the proposals arose in subareas of two SMSAs in the Virginia Tidewater region and will be taken up in the next section. Three proposals related to some kind of federated arrangement, and Chapter 8 considers them. The other thirty-nine called for city/county consolidation and involved twenty-eight different counties (since some of them came to a vote twice in the same area). The voters gave their approval in six of them. (Also during the same period, three out of nine proposals for city/county consolidation in nonmetropolitan areas gained voter approval.)

The six metropolitan counties where city/county consolidation has been voted in are the following: Baton Rouge-East Baton Rouge, Louisiana (approved in 1947); Nashville-Davidson County, Tennessee (1962); Jacksonville-Duval County, Florida (1967); Columbus-Muscogee County, Georgia (1970); Lexington-Fayette County, Kentucky (1972); and Anchorage-Greater Anchorage Area Borough, Alaska (1975). In addition, the state legislature brought about city/county consolidation in Indianapolis-Marion County, Indiana in 1969. The Nevada legislature in 1975 provided for consolidation of Las Vegas and Clark County, but before it could take place, the state supreme court ruled against the measure on the grounds that it was special legislation and had a faulty pattern of representation on the intended eleven-member county commission (Grose, 1976:569-570).

Six of these seven cases of city/county consolidation encompass the "real city" in terms of the present pattern of urban development (although the U.S. Office of Management and Budget adds other counties to the SMSA for all but Anchorage). Only for Columbus, with Phenix City, Alabama directly across the Chattahoochee River, does the urbanized area extend out of the core county.

CASE HISTORIES

Baton Rouge. When consolidation occurred in Baton Rouge, Louisiana, the locality wasn't large enough to be considered a metropolitan area, but it is now. Consolidation was made possible by a 1946 state constitutional amendment permitting preparation of a home rule charter for East Baton Rouge parish. Two-thirds of the nine-member charter board favored city/county consolidation, and the proposed charter required only a single, parishwide majority, which it got in a 1947 vote. The product was actually partial consolidation, for both the city and parish governments were retained as were two small municipalities. The seven members of the city council are joined by two other persons elected from the rural area to form the parish council. The mayor-president presides over both councils and acts as chief administrator of both governments. Some departments are unified but not all of them, and city and parish budgets are separate. The parish is divided into three zones—urban, industrial, and rural, and different services and tax rates apply in each zone (Bollens and Schmandt, 1970:299-300; also see Havard and Croty, 1964).

Nashville-Davidson. In the early 1950s metropolitan growth was sprawling beyond Nashville city limits into unincorporated portions of Davidson County, Tennessee. Local leadership rejected halfway measures and after six years' effort got a state constitutional amendment and enabling legislation for city/county consolidation. A merger plan went on the ballot in 1958, carried the city, but lost in the suburbs, thus lacking the necessary dual majority. Immediately the Nashville city council embarked upon a vigorous annexation campaign and levied a motor vehicle tax aimed at communters. Resentment against the city government caused by these measures and strong campaigning by county political forces produced the necessary majorities when consolidation came up for a vote again in 1962, and the county leadership took charge of the enlarged city (McArthur, 1973B:26-35; also see Booth, 1963; Coomer and Tyer, 1974; Elazar, 1961; Grant, 1965; Hawkins, 1966; and Rodgers and Lipsey, 1974).

The Metropolitan Government of Nashville and Davidson, as the consolidated unit is officially called, is governed by a mayor and a council of forty members, thirty-five selected from single member districts and five chosen at large. The county as a whole is considered a general services district (GSD), and there is also an urban service district (USD), which at first was only the area of the former city but has since expanded. All residents pay a GSD tax to cover most services, and USD residents pay an additional tax because they receive fire protection, street lighting, street cleaning, and refuse collection. At one time water and sewer services were covered by the urban service district tax, but now they are on a user charge basis, which some residents living outside the USD also pay. Six suburban municipalities existing in 1962 remain and provide a few services, and their residents pay only the GSD tax.

Jacksonville. Most of the post-World War II boom in Duval County, Florida occurred in unincorporated areas surrounding Jacksonville, but neither the county government nor any other structure was properly equipped to provide the needed urban services. The city's tax rate soared because of an inadequate tax base compared to need, and its sewerage system was obsolete. The countywide school district ran into financial difficulties because low assessment ratios in the suburbs returned insufficient revenue, and the school system became so bad that all the high schools lost accreditation (DeGrove, 1973A:17-25; also see Martin, 1968; and Mogulof, 1972).

The first attempt to resolve this crisis was through massive annexation, but bids in 1963 and 1964 lost when suburban residents voted against it. Civic leadership turned to the possibility of consolidation and got the state legislature to authorize a study commission. This body sent back to the legislature a proposal for a single government for the county except for several special authorities. The legislature made some modifications, including giving four, small existing municipalities the option to join or remain independent. During this period a grand jury indicted a number of local officials for corrupt practices, and this reinforced the desire for change. The plan went before the voters in August 1967 and gained a strong majority in both the central city and suburbs. The people in the small municipalities approved the charter but exercised their option to remain in existence.

The consolidated city of Jacksonville is governed by a nineteen-member city council with fourteen elected by districts and five at large and by a mayor, who is in charge of most operating departments. The voters also elect the sheriff, tax assessor, tax collector, supervisor of elections, and county clerk, all former county officers. Several authorities (electric, port, two hospitals) and several boards (school, area planning, and civil service) remain with semiindependent status but are subject to budget, purchasing, and personnel controls of the city. A general service district covers the entire city/county and provides most services, and five urban service districts function to provide street lighting, garbage collection, street cleaning, and debt service within the old city and the four other municipalities. However, the latter also have continued their own police and fire services even though the residents pay for such services from the consolidated city as part of the general service district tax.

Indianapolis. Although some annexation occurred in Indianapolis during the period of postwar expansion, the primary response to metropolitan growth was for the state legislature to create functional authorities and taxing districts, one by one, for sewers and sanitation, libraries, health and hospitals, public housing, planning, airports, parks and recreation, and mass transportation. Some of these used the Marion County boundaries, but others took in areas smaller than the whole county but larger than the city. The central city gradually lost control over more and more functions, but the county government remained a weak institution (Willbern, 1973:48-73).

In a state where party politics are ever-present in local government, the Democrats swept most state and local offices in Marion County in 1964. They tried to strengthen the mayor's control of the numerous boards but mostly failed to get legislative enactment. The political tide turned in 1968, Republicans gained control of these offices, and their leaders succeeded in getting the legislature to enact a city/county consolidation measure known as "Unigov." Since home rule is unknown in Indiana, no vote of the local electorate was required or permitted.

The product was substantial though not complete merger of the city and county under the policy control of a twenty-nine-member city/county council (twenty-five from single-member districts and four at large) and a mayor. However, both the City of Indianapolis and Marion County remain as legal entities. Some county offices continue, including seven elected officials; the eleven school districts were unchanged; several authorities and boards were preserved; four incorporated municipalities were excluded; and a number of small towns were included but given special status. Nevertheless, the consolidated government has substantial budgetary authority and its metropolitan development commission is a strong planning agency. To go with Unigov the legislature passed a bill known as "Minigov" in 1972 to set up community councils but weakened the measure in 1973. However, the city/county council balked by refusing to establish boundaries, and Minigov never went into effect.

York Willbern describes the governmental arrangement in Indianapolis-Marion County as nine different service and taxation areas, appearing as "a set of concentric circles of increasing size (although they are obviously not circular in shape), each associated with a function or group of functions" (1973:61): (1) center township handling poor relief; (2) the Indianapolis school district (surrounded by ten other school districts); (3) the fire service district with boundaries equivalent to the old central city; (4) the police service district, which is slightly larger to encompass some industrial land; (5) the sanitation district, substantially greater than the police service district; (6) the housing authority going five miles beyond the old city limits; (7) the consolidated city which covers all the county except the four excluded municipalities; (8) the library district which excludes only two municipalities; and (9) the county itself which is used as the territorial and financial basis for health and hospitals, parks and recreation, planning and zoning, airports, and the traditional county functions.

Columbus, Georgia. A prelude to the consolidation of Columbus, Georgia, and Muscogee County was the merger of the health departments into one countywide department in 1940 and the consolidation of the school system in 1950. Then in 1960 the city more than doubled its size through annexation, though it still didn't encompass all the developed area outside Fort Benning, a major military base within the county. So in 1961 a citizens committee began exploring the possibility of city/county consolidation and came to an affirmative conclusion. With the endorsement of a majority of the city and county commissions, the state legislature passed enabling legislation to put the issue to a vote. In a 1962 referendum the idea failed both in the city and in the county. Four years later civic leaders renewed their effort. They got permissive state constitutional amendments passed in 1966, authorization for a charter commission from the legislature in 1967, approval of the voters in 1968 to create this commission, and more enabling legislation in 1969. The same session of the state legislature authorized a local vote on another substantial annexation measure, and by the end of 1969 Columbus had added most of the remaining population of the county outside the military base as another step toward complete consolidation (Chamber of Commerce of the United States, 1971:1-7).

The vote for city/county consolidation occurred in May 1970 and carried by wide margins in both the city and the whole county, with city residents participating in both votes (as they had done previously on annexation and the first consolidation proposal). The new government consists of a mayor and ten council members, four chosen from districts and six at large; there is also an appointed city manager. The county sheriff remained, but he transferred all patrol units to the police department and retained a criminal investigative unit. The school district is independent but otherwise there is complete functional merger. The consolidated government has three urban service districts with successive lesser tax reflecting different kinds of services: the old central city prior to the 1969 annexation, the area annexed in 1969, and the rest of the county, which is largely undeveloped. In addition, tiny Bibb City (population 712) remains separate, receives no fire or police protection, public works, paving, or storm drainage from the consolidated government, and it is considered a general service district with a smaller tax rate.

Lexington. Over the years Lexington, Kentucky made many small annexations so that by 1970 the city boundaries were extremely jagged but yet omitted quite a lot of developed territory (Lyons, 1973:143-145). In the face of this situation, the state legislature in 1970 authorized city/county consolidation, and a local commission went to work. By the time the proposal came to a vote in 1972, a court order had been issued to permit Lexington to annex all the built-up area beginning in 1975, and for fringe-area residents, merger was a more attractive solution. With this background, the voters approved city/county consolidation by more than two to one in November 1972. The merged government went into effect in 1974 with a fifteen-member council (twelve by districts, three at large), a mayor, and a chief administrative officer, but seventeen elective county officers remained even though they became a part of the amalgamated government. Like the other consolidations, the new charter provided for a general service district and an urban service district and also permitted the establishment of partial urban services districts with the tax rate adjusted to the lesser service level. Even after consolidation took place, a small band of opponents maintained their antipathy, and in 1975 they made an unsuccessful attempt to place the question of demerger on the ballot (Chi, 1975:474-476).

Anchorage. When Alaska achieved statehood in 1959, the legislature divided the state into vast county-like boroughs with limited powers and also granted home rule to cities. After a while, state leaders concluded that this

pattern contained redundancies, and the legislature enacted a law permitting
cities and boroughs to consolidate upon voter approval. This came about in
Juneau (1969) and Sitka (1971). Twice the issues came before the Anchorage
electorate (1970 and 1971), gained approval in the city, but lost in the
borough outside the city. Finally city/borough consolidation achieved the
needed dual majority in September 1975. Two small cities were also merged,
for their residents didn't have an option of staying out. The consolidated
government is known as the Municipality of Anchorage.

The Assembly, as the governing body is called, has eleven members elected
from six districts—two from each of five districts and one from the other
district. The mayor is elected at large, and he appoints a manager with
assembly concurrence. The public school system is part of the municipality
and is run by a seven-member school board elected at large. There may be
service areas with individual tax rates, and upon consolidation the former
cities took on this status. Other service areas previously functioning in the
borough were continued as were some community councils with advisory
powers which the former borough assembly had authorized. All of these
special units are attached to the municipality, and there are no special
districts with independent authority. This means that unification is total in
Anchorage.

Partial Consolidation

In addition to these cases where all or most of the urbanized area is
encompassed within a unified government, there are some instances where
partial consolidation has occurred to unify parts of a metropolitan area. And
there are some cases where certain functions have been consolidated on a
metropolitan basis even though the structure of general government hasn't
changed.

FUNCTIONAL CONSOLIDATION

To take up the latter first, functional consolidation looks at the process of
transfer of functions, as described in Chapter 5, from the topside. When the
city transfers its public health activities to the county health department, a
metropolitan unit is created for public health. Where all the municipalities
utilized a central police communications system run by the county, functional consolidation has occurred for police communications though not for
the entire law enforcement function.

We saw earlier how establishment of a county health department and a
county school system came before complete consolidation of Columbus and
Muscogee County. The Indianapolis area gained a number of authorities and

metropolitan districts prior to city/county consolidation, and not all of them were fully incorporated into the new government.

The governments of Charlotte, North Carolina and Mecklenburg County have drawn closer together over the years by entering into agreements under which the county has assumed full responsibility for funding and administering libraries (1940), public schools (1960), health services (1964), hospitals (1968), and jails (1970). Jointly funded programs administered by either the city or county include veterans services (1949), civil defense (1953), planning (1954), tax collection (1958), community relations (1969), intergovernmental programs (1969), purchasing (1969), manpower planning (1970), water and sewers (1972) (ACIR, 1974A:42). The political leadership thought the two jurisdictions were ready for complete consolidation, but the electorate voted against it in 1971 (DeGrove, 1973B:3-4). Since then Charlotte has embarked upon an aggressive annexation program, which it can accomplish without a vote in the annexed territory, and the city is spreading out to cover most of the urbanized area. Quite likely another attempt at city/county consolidation will occur in the future.

Many other places, particularly single-county metropolitan areas, rely upon functional consolidation to achieve partial unification even if the central city and county don't merge completely.

SUBMETROPOLITAN CONSOLIDATION

Since 1952, the Tidewater region of Virginia has experienced six mergers of counties, cities, and towns. The region contains two SMSAs, Newport News-Hampton and Norfolk-Virginia Beach-Portsmouth, located north and south of the harbor known as Hampton Roads, and each merger involved only a portion of either SMSA. Indeed, avoidance of areawide government was a major objective. As DeGrove has reported (ACIR, 1973B:4): "The consolidation resulted, rather, from a political self-defense effort by the counties and smaller cities to avoid capture or total encirclement by the larger cities in the area, especially Norfolk, Portsmouth, and Newport News."

As a result, the SMSA north of Hampton Roads contains two major cities, Newport News and Hampton, the small inland city of Williamsburg, and four low-density counties. The SMSA on the south side of the harbor now has five cities: Norfolk, Virginia Beach, Portsmouth, Chesapeake, and Suffolk plus one small county. So even though complete metropolitan consolidation hasn't occurred in Tidewater Virginia and has in fact been avoided, each SMSA contains only six units of local general government, all of viable size.

SPECIAL DISTRICT MERGERS

No other state presently has a judicial or administrative mechanism playing the strong role the special courts in Virginia do in bringing about municipal and county mergers. However, in some of the states with boundary commissions (described in Chapter 3) these bodies are sometimes involved in bringing about consolidation of special districts.

In Oregon, the Portland Metropolitan Area Boundary Commission specifically plays this role, and as a result, it has helped reduce the number of independent governmental units in the three-county area from 279 in 1969 (excluding school districts) to 142 in 1975. The most notable change was the reduction of lighting districts from 116 to 6. Eighteen sanitary districts were eliminated, leaving three in existence; 17 of those were dissolved due to the organization of a unified sewerage agency in one county through previous initiative. In the six year period, two new cities were incorporated through proceedings started before the commission was formed, bringing the total to 39 for the metropolitan area. The Boundary Commission hasn't attempted to merge municipalities.

Analysis

CITY/COUNTY CONSOLIDATION

Origins. In reviewing the politics of city/county consolidation, Vincent L. Marando has reported that the community problems stimulating most of these efforts were of a noncrisis nature, such as duplication of functions, too many administrative agencies, and a lack of long-range planning. Action usually wasn't brought about by more serious problems, such as lack of adequate water and sewer facilities, inequitable city-county tax base, blight and congestion, and air and water pollution. An exception was Jacksonville-Duval County where discreditation of the public schools and criminal indictments of local officials led to proposals for governmental reorganization. "City/county consolidations," he concluded, "do not spring from the desires of a broad base of the population. The benefits of consolidate government appear too abstract or too long range for the more immediate interests of the voter. More specific and direct benefits need to be attached to consolidation to meet the concerns of residents, particularly those concerned with higher taxes" (1975:78-81).

Adjustments. All of the areawide consolidations except for Anchorage made accommodations with existing offices, boards, or municipalities and stopped short of complete consolidation and an entirely new design for local government. Baton Rouge set up both city and parish councils. Jacksonville, Indianapolis, Columbus, and Lexington retained some county offices. Nashville-Davidson County, Jacksonville, Indianapolis, and Columbus excluded from one to six municipalities from merger. Separate authorities remained in Jacksonville and Indianapolis.

The consolidated city/counties commonly utilized two or more service and taxing districts in order to relate property taxes to level of services rendered. Usually this is a general service district for the entire area and an urban service district for the built-up portion which receives more intensive services, but some have two or three urban service districts and Indianapolis has a complex of nine concentric service layers.

A long process. As the previous narration indicated, city/county consolidation is a long and complicated process. Since the city and the county emanate from state powers under different sets of constitutional provisions and statutes, the state legislature has to set up the conditions under which consolidation can occur and this might even necessitate a constitutional amendment to be adopted by the voters of the entire state. Drawing up a proposed charter, working out local compromises, possibly going back to the legislature, conducting a campaign, maybe having a second go-round after the initial defeat, all of these steps stretch over months and years. Then new officials must be elected and go through a period of departmental consolidation before the new government is reorganized and fully operational. It isn't a course to embark upon lightly.

Value. But it may be worth it. As John M. DeGrove has written about the two mergers occurring in the South during the 1960s (1973B:43):

> Some ten years of experience in Nashville and almost three years in Jacksonville support the thesis that consolidation, where it can be accomplished, has great merit. Economies of scale can be identified, but perhaps most impressive has been the extension of critical urban services to all sections of the metropolitan areas, supported by a fiscal system that promotes an equitable distribution of the tax burden.

This observation can properly be applied to the other mergers. All of them have improved service delivery and given the localities greater capacity to cope with metropolitan growth. A countywide tax base produces greater fiscal equity, and the use of general and urban service districts permits adjustment of tax rates to service levels. These improvements thus respond positively to three of the problems highlighted in Chapter 1.

Citizen involvement. Public official responsibility comes into better focus under consolidation and this may help build citizen confidence. Yet, the suspicion people have toward centralization—as strongly evidenced by the numerous defeats of consolidation proposals around the country—isn't entirely allayed by the effectiveness of the new city/county governments. Some of them try to deal with this by having a large council, mostly elected by districts. The Minigov proposal in Indianapolis also had this purpose, but council blocked it as a competing form of representation. Elsewhere some efforts of greater citizen involvement at the neighborhood level are beginning to show, but most of these places aren't as advanced as some unconsolidated central cities described in Chapter 9, which deals with neighborhood decentralization.

Race. On the matter of racial and social separation, the record is mixed. In some places, the increased proportion of black population in the central city motivated some people to push for city/county consolidation in order to assure retention of white control. Yet, blacks might have inherited a city on the edge of bankruptcy. For the most part, the city councils have been districted to give blacks a fair chance to be elected, and the biracial councils are in a better position to work on metropolitan racial problems than a metropolis divided into a radically mixed central city and mostly all-white suburbs.

Chapter 8

FEDERATION

Other persons concerned about metropolitan governmental organization favor a strong areawide government, but they see the need to have small units as well. So they favor a federation with two levels of government, areawide and local. As we saw in Chapter 3, two layers are common, though without an areawide government in multicounty areas. Federation would achieve this and would produce a more formal two- (or three-) level structure with a rearrangement of functional responsibilities.

The Case for Federation

VIEWS OF SCHOLARS

As he made the case for an areawide approach, so also Paul Studenski in his 1930 report explained the need to deal with both the local and the metropolitan levels (1930:41):

> We have seen that the modern metropolitan region is composed of local communities each with its own personality and a measure of peculiar needs. Yet, side by side with the locality needs, exist the broader metropolitan interests which the component cities, towns, and villages, acting as independent organs of local government, can never serve.

What he referred to as a "federated region" or "federated city" would be a form responsibe to these two levels of action. The constituent municipalities wouldn't be completely merged but would continue to exist as separate entities, exercising a degree of local control within their boundaries, just as the metropolitan body would deal with areawide matters. Powers would be distributed between the whole and the parts, and each would have its own legislative body and administrative officers (1930:367).

Victor Jones, another scholar of metropolitan governance, has advocated carrying the federation idea a step further by reorganizing the municipal level into "more compact and homogeneous boroughs." This might be achieved by combining small suburban municipalities into some larger "borough units" and by dividing the central city into several boroughs. The product, Jones maintains, would be a "more rational distribution of functions as between the metropolitan and borough governments." (1953:590).

CED'S 1970 PROPOSAL

The Committee for Economic Development used this idea as the central theme of its 1970 report, *Reshaping Government in Metropolitan Areas.* This report, developed by a committee chaired by Phillip M. Klutznick of the Urban Investment and Development Co. and assisted by Alan K. Campbell of Syracuse University serving as staff director, came to conclusions differing from the consolidation of the 1966 CED report. Said CED in 1970:

> All metropolitan areas are affected to a greater or lesser extent by conflicting forces of centralization and decentralization. The inter-dependence of activities within metropolitan areas requires area-wide institutions for some functions or parts of functions of government. Just as clear is the need for units of government small enough to enable the recipients of government services to have some voice and control over their quality and quantity (1970:18).

Continuing its case, CED asserted:

> To gain the advantages of both centralization and decentralization, we recommend as an ultimate solution a governmental system of two levels. Some functions should be assigned in their entirety to the area-wide government, others to the local level, but most will be assigned to each level (1970:19).

In single-county metropolitan areas, CED would use a reconstituted county government as the basic framework for areawide government, but where the metropolis spreads over several counties or towns, a new juris-diction would be needed to embrace the whole territory. The local level of government would consist of "community districts" with boundaries worked out to correspond with perceptions of community identity. In the process the existing central city would go out of existence with some of its functions transferred to the metropolitan government and some taken on by the community districts. The division of functional responsibility greatly concerned CED, and the report had specific recommendations to make for the sharing of power over functions (1970:51-56). This is a subject we will get into in depth in Chapter 13.

Plans for Federation

IN THE PAST

The idea of federated metropolitan government is not new in the United States. Something like it existed from 1836 to 1852 when New Orleans was divided into three cities but with an overall council. Since then federation has been proposed repeatedly, starting with an 1896 proposal from a metropolitan study commission for the Boston area (inspired by a two-tier arrangement which emerged in London, England in 1888), but the Massachusetts legislature rejected the idea.

In this century the federation approach has popped up with some frequency. Versions got on the ballot in Alameda County (Oakland), California in 1921 and Allegheny County (Pittsburgh), Pennsylvania in 1929. The Alameda proposal carried Oakland but lost countywide. The countywide vote in Allegheny was favorable, but a requirement for a two-thirds affirmative vote in a majority of the one hundred twenty-two municipalities wasn't met. Second attempts were made during the 1930s in the Boston area and in Alameda and Allegheny counties, but to no avail.

In that same era talk occurred about a federation involving San Francisco and San Mateo County, but nothing came of it. A similar effort to combine St. Louis and St. Louis County into a federated government was thwarted in 1930 by electoral disapproval, and so was a 1959 proposal for a multipurpose metropolitan service authority, in effect a form of federation (and a consolidation proposal of 1962 also lost). An attempt to convert Cuyahoga County, Ohio into a metropolitan government while retaining Cleveland and other municipalities was blocked by the state legislature in 1929; county charter proposals lost at the polls in 1936 and 1950, and a new scheme for a metropolitan county, which would express the federation idea, went down to defeat in a 1959 referendum. A study board in Dade County (Miami), Florida came up with a federation scheme in 1955, but the state legislature changed it to only a partial federation, as explained later in this chapter.

RECENT PROPOSALS

Although no complete federation proposal has come before an electorate or state legislature in the United States between 1959 and 1976, the idea is still alive and has indeed been receiving increased attention since the publication of the 1970 CED report (see for example, League of Women Voters, 1974).

In two instances charter-writing bodies put a trace of the federation idea into proposals which predominantly represented city/county consolidation. This occurred in Sacramento County, California and Salt Lake County, Utah. Both proposals called for consolidation of the central city, county, and all special districts within the county and allowed small cities to join if they chose. In Sacramento County, community councils would be established within the urban area of the county and would have whatever advisory and operating powers the county board of supervisors selected from a list of possibilities enumerated in the charter. Salt Lake County would have fifteen community councils with only an advisory role; the city/county council would consist of the community council chairpersons, and the consolidated government would hold all the power. Voters turned down the Sacramento proposal in November 1974, and a majority of the electorate of Salt Lake County voted "no" in March 1975, in both cases apparently because of opposition to consolidation, which was the major thrust. (The defeated 1962 proposal for consolidation in the St. Louis area also provided for "borough councils," basically with advisory powers in what was otherwise a vast centralization of authority.)

NATIONAL ACADEMY PROJECT

More relevant to the federation idea is a demonstration project of the National Academy of Public Administration (NAPA), financed by funds from the U.S. Department of Housing and Urban Development. Dubbed the "neighborhood-oriented metropolitan government project," it was consciously designed to apply CED's two-tier government proposal. For the first round (1972-74) a NAPA panel selected the Rochester, New York area and the Tampa Bay, Florida area as sites for study and action, and for the second round (1975-77) the choices were the Denver, Colorado area and the Portland, Oregon area. In all four, local panels were set up to work out proposals best suited for the particular area. One of the areas, Rochester, dealt with a single county while the other three were multicounty areas.

Rochester. The Greater Rochester Intergovernmental Panel (GRIP) worked hard to develop a two-tier model, and it spent a lot of energy deciding which level should handle what activities. A lower-tier task force developed two detailed models, one "ideal" and one "practical." The "ideal" model proposed dividing Rochester into several communities, each with its own local government, revising town boundaries in the suburbs to coincide with natural community boundaries, and creating neighborhood councils in the larger towns. However, the full panel rejected this scheme. The "practical" model, which the panel did adopt, wouldn't change boundaries but would set up community councils within the city and the large towns and neighborhood councils in the smaller towns and would also create more villages in the towns. (Along these lines, a new city charter proposed for Rochester contained provisions for community councils, but the charter lost in a 1973 vote; the loss was attributed to a proposed switch from the manager form to a strong mayor, whereas the idea of community councils had a generally favorable reception.) GRIP's upper-tier government would be Monroe County without major changes, continuing its manager form and the twenty-nine-member legislature elected from single-member districts; however, the county would take on additional functions, including a countywide police force, solid waste disposal, takeover of the water authority, fire protection in specialized areas, and countywide land use planning. (Greater Rochester Intergovernmental Panel, 1975). In the summer and fall of 1976 an effort was made to set up a joint city-county committee to work toward implementation of GRIP's recommendations, but nothing came of it.

Tampa Bay. The Suncoast Study Panel in the Tampa Bay area focused mainly upon the metropolitan level and produced no recommendations for reorganization of lower-tier government. The main recommendation was to create a regional council consisting of twenty-nine members elected from single-member districts of 50,000 population. Serving a three-county area, it would have authority to undertake comprehensive regional planning, establish regional policy, enforce regional standards, and provide for transportation, water resources, sewage treatment, solid waste disposal, and such other functions as may be added (Suncoast Study Panel, 1974). The Florida legislature must act to establish such a regional council, and this hasn't yet occurred.

Denver. The Denver Metropolitan Study Panel has concentrated much of its energies on working out the details of a proposal for some kind of an agency for the four-county area. Earlier action had occurred to try to establish a regional service authority with the successive passage of a state constitutional amendment in 1970, enactment of state legislation in 1972 to permit a choice of sixteen functions for such an authority, and then in 1973 defeat in a four-county referendum of a proposition to create a regional service authority with responsibility for solid waste disposal, land-soil preservation, and management services to local governments. A bloc of members of the new study panel advocated revival of the service authority idea, but they didn't gain a majority. Instead the panel in January 1977 voted to recommend a metropolitan council patterned after the Minnesota model (described later in this chapter). It would be an elected body in charge of metropolitan planning and management services but would perform no direct service operation. Thus, it would take over the planning and coordination functions of the Denver Regional Council of Governments and would handle such management services as purchasing and equipment pooling while already existing metropolitan agencies would continue to take care of such matters as water supply, sewage, urban drainage, and public transportation. The proposal passed one house of the state legislature in the spring of 1977 but not the other. The Denver panel also developed some ideas about how neighborhood advisory councils could relate to an areawide agency, but its main interest has been the region rather than small areas.

Portland. The Tri-County Local Government Commission for the Portland area likewise directed much of its attention to working out a better arrangement at the metropolitan level. It proposed an elected Metropolitan Service Council consisting of fifteen members chosen from single-member districts and a chief administrator elected at large. This would be done by legislation replacing the present appointed board of the Metropolitan Service District, which currently has authority to handle solid waste disposal, storm drainage, and the zoo and the option of taking over the public transit system, now handled by another metropolitan agency, if approved by a referendum. The reorganized agency would take over regional planning and coordination from the Columbia Regional Association of Governments, would be authorized (but not mandated) to deal with water supply, coordination of human services, regional parks and cultural facilities, and regional correctional facilities and programs, and would have the opportunity to submit to voter approval the possibility of taking over the functions of the Port of Portland and the Boundary Commission. In the fall of 1976 the Tri-County Local Government Commission submitted this proposal to the state legislature, and turned its attention to small-area government, that is, suburban municipalities, special districts, and neighborhood associations. The 1977 session of the legislature approved a measure calling for a local referendum on whether to convert the Metropolitan Service District into an elected metropolitan council. The vote will take place in May 1978.

Thus, all three of the NAPA-assisted study panels in multicounty areas recommended an elected metropolitan council with a limited set of functions, and if this comes about in any of them, it will be the first of its kind in the United States. In the fourth area the existing Monroe County legislature, which now has quite broad powers, would fulfill this role. All of them would keep in place existing county, municipal, and town units and special districts as a lower-tier government. Except for the rejected "ideal" plan in the Greater Rochester study, none of them proposed rearranging boundaries or consolidating units of local general government, but the Portland area panel did recommend consolidation or elimination of present special service districts and not to establish any new suburban cities. All but the Suncoast Study Panel came out in favor of neighborhood councils, but none of them advocated neighborhood government with substantive authority.

SUMMING UP

It has been over eighty years since the metropolitan study commission for the Boston area recommended a federated structure. Since then, federation has been repeatedly discussed and proposed, but not formally implemented. We are still awaiting acceptance of this idea by a state legislature and by metropolitan voters participating in a referendum, with the next test scheduled for Portland, Oregon in May 1978.

Experience in Other Nations

While Americans have toyed with the idea of metropolitan federation, other nations have brought this arrangement into existence. Great Britain and Canada in particular.

LONDON

When our nation achieved its independence from Great Britain, London was already a major metropolis of nearly one million people, consisting of the one square mile City of London and a number of surrounding parishes. As population spread outward during the nineteenth century, metropolitan bodies were created for police (1829), public works (1855), and schools (1870). Major restructuring occurred in 1888-89 with the establishment of two-tier government, composed of a new London County Council at the metropolitan level and twenty-eight boroughs and the City of London at the local level, achieved by withdrawing territory from three different counties. Functions were divided between the two levels, and the boroughs were quite strong. The next seventy years saw the enlargement of the London County Council's role but also the organization of sixteen separate special-service authorities. During the same period, population grew and grew, reaching a green belt perimeter created in the years following World War II (with new towns beyond). By the 1960s, governmental reform was overdue (Smallwood, 1965).

The response was the London Government Act of 1963, enacted by the British Parliament. The act created the Greater London Council and gave it jurisdiction over the territory of 620 square miles with a population of nearly 8 million people, taking in the London County Council area plus all of another county, parts of four others, 39 municipal boroughs and 15 urban districts within these counties, and three independent county boroughs. All local boundary lines were redrawn, except for one borough and the ancient City of London, producing a total of 32 boroughs having population ranging from 146,000 to 340,000 and averaging 250,000. The change reduced 92 governments to 34, each of them governed by a council elected by the people (Foley, 1972:32-38; also see Rhodes, 1970 and 1972).

The Greater London Council has responsibility for fire services, ambulance service, refuse disposal, trunk sewer lines and principal sewage disposal plants, main roads, traffic management, overall development planning, large scale developments, and some regulatory functions. The boroughs handled refuse collection, local sewer lines and some local disposal plants, street cleaning, off-street parking, planning within the context of the Greater London plan, most housing, health and welfare services, borough parks, and a variety of other activities. The Greater London Council is in charge of education in the twelve inner boroughs where the old London County Council previously functioned, but the twenty outer boroughs run their own schools. The Metropolitan Water Board provides the water supply. The metropolitan police are under the Home Office of the national government, transit is under the Ministry of Transport, and regional hospitals, electricity, and gas supply are also under the central government.

ELSEWHERE IN ENGLAND

During the 1960s local government in the remainder of England also underwent close examination by a royal commission under the chairmanship of Lord Redcliffe-Maud. At the time, England outside Greater London was covered by 45 counties and 79 independent county boroughs (really cities). The counties were divided into municipal boroughs, urban districts, and rural districts, categories of decreasing average population and density. This provided two tiers of government for the counties and one tier for county boroughs. In total there were 1,244 self-governing local units (counting Greater London), each with an elected council, for a country of 45 million people (Letwin, 1974:116-123).

This arrangement had several problems. The county boroughs couldn't expand their boundaries and gain land needed for public housing and other municipal facilities. It was difficult to plan for the interrelated needs of city, suburbs, and semirural fringe areas. And there was some confusion in the division of powers between counties and lower-tier units within them. This led the Redcliffe-Maud commission in 1967 to recommend drastic simplification. Three metropolitan areas would have two-tier government along the lines of the Greater London Council, and the remainder of the country would be divided into 58 unitary areas of 250,000 to 1,000,000 in population, each area with a single-tier government. After a lot of debate, the Labor government in 1970 added two more metropolitan areas which would have two tiers and accepted the rest of the proposal, but before it could pass the necessary legislation, the government left office. The new Conservative government, whose strength was greater in the counties than in the cities, rejected the scheme and opted for two-tier government throughout the land but with fewer units than previously. This was adopted in the Local Government Act of 1972 (Robson, 1974:517-520).

The result gives England a local governmental pattern consisting of Greater London with its 32 boroughs and one "city," six metropolitan counties containing 36 districts between them, and 39 other counties with a total of 296 lower-tier districts. This reduced 1,244 local governments to 395. Legislation also reduced local units in Wales from 181 to 45 and in Scotland from 430 to 65.

Under the new arrangement all county councils are in charge of overall development planning, main highways, traffic and transport, building regulations and air pollution control, refuse disposal and environmental health, police and fire protection, food and drug control. All district councils are responsible for local plans, most development controls, most public housing and rehabilitation, local road maintenance, and refuse collection. The two levels share responsibility for parks and open spaces, playing fields and swimming pools, museums and art galleries. In the metropolitan areas the local districts take care of education, welfare services, and libraries, and elsewhere the county councils handle these functions. In the nonmetropolitan counties, parish councils remain for advisory purposes, and they form a kind of third tier in rural areas.

TORONTO

Federated metropolitan government came to Toronto, Canada in 1953 when the provincial legislature of Ontario created the Municipality of Metropolitan Toronto, encompassing the combined area of the city of Toronto and twelve suburban municipalities, all of which remained in existence. In 1967 the province reduced the number of units at the local level to six by merging two small suburbs with the central city and by creating five suburban boroughs out of the remaining municipalities (Rose, 1974:33-48; also see Grumm, 1959; Kaplan, 1967; Mogulof, 1972; and Smallwood, 1963).

Different powers are assigned to Metropolitan Toronto, in many cases dividing functions into "wholesale" and "retail" activities, or large scale and small scale. Thus, water intake, treatment, and trunk lines are handled by Metro and local distribution by the municipalities; trunk sewer lines and sewage treatment are a metropolitan function while the municipalities install and maintain local sewage lines; Metro operates public transportation and metropolitan roads and the municipalities take care of the streets; there are metropolitan parks and municipal playgrounds, metropolitan hospitals and municipal health services; school operations are under six local school boards but financing is a metropolitan and provincial responsibility. Fire services are municipal, and so were the police at first but Metro took over this function in 1957. Since then Metro has also assumed responsibility for the central library, public welfare, and refuse disposal (leaving collection at the municipal level).

Albert Rose of the University of Toronto rates Metro a "huge success" in solving major problems of physical and quantitative nature: water supply, sewage disposal, public transportation, highways, school construction, community facilities. On social issues—the needs of the elderly, public housing, health and social services, quality of life—Metro is "somewhat of a failure." Moreover, social and fiscal disparities between the central city and the suburbs are far from resolved (Rose, 1974:41-45).

ELSEWHERE IN ONTARIO

The Province of Ontario has applied the federation idea elsewhere by creating ten new regional municipalities between 1964 and 1974. This makes this the predominant pattern for government in Ontario's urban areas. The reorganization process has been firmly under the control of the Ontario Municipal Board, which historically has had substantial powers over local government, including assessment appeals and approval of zoning laws, annexations, and incorporations. The board has successfully used commissions of inquiry to handle annexation cases, and it extended this device to review the structure of local government in specific areas. The process utilized hearings, fact finding, draft reports, and more hearings, culminating in reorganization acts passed by the provincial legislature (Fyfe, 1974:14-31).

The traditional governmental structure of Ontario has resembled that of the north central states in the United States, having counties, municipalities, townships, and a county council composed of township and municipal representatives, along the lines of the historic New York arrangement. Reorganization generally has followed county lines and has produced federations with the following principal elements (Fyfe, 1974:25):

(1) An upper-tier unit for the large urban center and its hinterland.

(2) A reduction in the number of local municipalities, mainly by consolidation, plus large annexations to give the urban center more control over its immediate hinterland.

(3) A regional council composed of members of local councils, chosen on an ex officio basis and roughly in accordance with population. (This follows the Toronto model.)

(4) The regional municipality is responsible for public health, police, regional planning, arterial roads, sewage disposal, bulk water supply, garbage disposal, capital borrowing, welfare, and regional parks. Education has previously been the exclusive responsibility of a county board and remains as a regional function.

(5) Local municipalities are responsible for local planning, roads, parks, local sewers, water distribution, garbage collection, fire protection, street lighting, and tax collection.

(6) The regional municipality is financed by a requisition on the local municipalities in proportion to their individual shares of the total assessment. The province bears some of the initial organizing costs, makes a special regional grant of $8 per capita to cover upgrading costs and the assumption of policing rural areas, previously handled by the province, and continues its regular grants.

COMPARISON WITH THE UNITED STATES

What strikes an American observer is the the ease with which the central government of Great Britain and the provincial government of Ontario have brought about significant reorganization of local government. In the United States the states have the legal authority to do the same, but except for a handful of special cases they haven't chosen to undertake this task. Partly this is a matter of our political tradition, which emphasizes a good deal of local autonomy even to the extent of writing municipal home rule into state constitutions. Partly it is a lack of administrative and legislative machinery and knowledgeable personnel with the capacity to design and carry out metropolitan reorganization. Whether state officials should muster their courage and develop needed capability is a subject for the last chapter of this book, but at this point that we can note that the states haven't followed the example of our neighbor to the north.

Federation-like Arrangements in the United States

Although no formal federated structure has been adopted for any metropolitan area in the United States, some federation-like arrangements exist in a number of areas. These are places where county government carries on a number of functions metropolitan in scope and municipal governments operate localized services within the same territory. The two levels aren't organically related, however, for each gets its power separately and directly from the state, and they may even be in competition. Moreover, in many instances the county may be providing municipal-type services to residents of unincorporated areas, and some municipalities may be contracting with the county for certain services. But in spite of the lack of purity in this style of federation, several approaches are worth noting.

PARTIAL FEDERATION IN DADE COUNTY, FLORIDA

When the Florida legislature in 1955 turned down the proposal for a federated government for Dade County, it offered as an alternative an opportunity for a home rule county charter. The state's electorate adopted a necessary constitutional amendment in 1956, and the county voters followed in 1957 with the approval of a new charter for Metropolitan Dade County. The twenty-six incorporated municipalities remained in existence to handle local services, but the county gained stronger powers, especially for services considered metropolitan in scope. In addition, a large portion of the county is unincorporated, and the county government has to provide municipal services to these residents, now numbering nearly half of the county's population, so that this part of the county has one-tier government. The other half of the population is served by two-tiers of government, though the division of municipal-county responsibility isn't uniform because some municipalities have transferred quite a few functions to the county and the others only a few. Thus, Dade County has a hybrid form (Lotz, 1973:6-10; also see Sofen, 1963).

The overall trend has been toward the county acquiring more functions. Welfare, assessment, and elections are traditionally assigned to counties in Florida, and in the 1940s Dade County took on responsibility for the public hospital, health services, the school system, and the airport. The new charter gave the county many more potential powers, but not all were used immediately. In the 1960s the county organized a transit authority, the metropolitan court took charge of traffic violations, and the seaport was transferred to the county. In 1971 the county library system took over the Miami libraries, which had previously been serving several suburban municipalities, but nine small cities still have their own libraries. In 1972 Miami's extensive water and sewer system became part of a larger Miami-Dade Water and Sewer Authority. All but two municipalities have their own police, but they all use the county's crime laboratory and more than half of them rely on the county for police communications and training. Thirteen municipalities have their own fire departments, the others having transferred this function to the county, but some of the city fire departments use the county's communication system. There are both metropolitan and municipal parks. Both levels engage in planning, the cities have zoning control within their jurisdiction, and the county handles public housing and federally aided community development. In other ways functional responsibilities are divided and intertwined.

In writing about Metropolitan Dade County in the ACIR substate regionalism study, Aileen Lotz (1973:10-12) concluded that reorganization eliminated considerable duplication and achieved a metropolitan approach to water, sewers, transportation, planning, and other areawide programs. There have been savings through the transfer of staffs from municipalities to the county, but the overall cost of government has gone up because services have expanded and previously low salaries have increased. In the unincorporated area, residents are receiving most essential municipal services, but some inadequacies in police services, public transit, and sewers are noted; however, general satisfaction is indicated by the lack of any successful attempt at annexation or incorporation. Economic and social disparities between the central city and suburban areas aren't overwhelming because enclaves of poor and rich are found in various parts of the county. However, there has been continuous friction between the municipalities and Metropolitan Dade County over the appropriate division of service responsibility. "In spite of this tension," observes John DeGrove (1973B:44), "the capacity to approach problems on a countywide basis has gradually increased as Metropolitan Dade County has taken over a growing list of services formerly performed by the cities." (Also see Mogulof, 1972.)

DE FACTO FEDERATION IN NASSAU COUNTY, NEW YORK

Elsewhere some metropolitan counties with no central city to rival county government have evolved into a federated-type arrangement. One such place is Nassau County, New York, formed in 1899 as three towns split off from Queens County when it became part of the New York City consolidation. With 1.4 million inhabitants in 1975, it is the most populous county in the United States without a central city. In this setting the county handles many areawide services even though it is part of the vaster Greater New York metropolitan region (Thomas, 1960:3).

The three towns cover all of Nassau County except for two small cities. Within the towns are sixty-four incorporated villages, all but one of them formed before 1933 when the state legislature expanded the powers of towns and allowed them to establish special districts. Thus, there are three levels of local general government in parts of Nassau County (town-village-county) and two levels in other parts (city-county or town-county for unincorporated areas). In addition, there are about one hundred sixty special districts run by the town boards for such functions as lighting, water supply, parks, and refuse collection, and also thirty-eight fire districts and fifty-seven school districts.

The Nassau County Board of Supervisors has six members consisting of supervisors elected from the three towns and the two cities (the largest town has two), and they cast weighted votes roughly equivalent of population represented. The county executive is elected at large, presides over board meetings, but may vote only in the event of a tie. Three of the supervisors serve as administrative heads of their towns and another supervisor has this role in his city, but in the other city the supervisor has only advisory authority. Through this dual role, the two levels of local government are formally interrelated. Beyond that, there are various interlocal agreements and service contracts.

The relative importance of the various units is indicated by employment patterns reported in the 1972 census of governments. Of 26,000 full-time employees, the county had 17,800, the towns 4,500 and the villages 3,600. This reflects repeated transfers of functional responsibility to the county from the other units. The school districts had 26,500 full-time employees and the independent special districts (fire services) only 117 because of their reliance upon volunteers.

In terms of functions, Nassau County administers its traditional functions of health, hospitals, welfare, courts, and corrections. Villages, towns, cities, and the county all are involved in police services, parks, sewerage, fire protection, highways, and libraries with the county spending the most on police, parks, sewerage, the towns most on highway maintenance, and the villages most on fire protection and libraries. The villages and towns, and not the county, handle water supply, urban renewal, and parking facilities.

This fairly complex pattern of local government in Nassau County has evolved over a long period and now functions as a kind of federation without the presence of a dominant central city and with a character of its own.

A MULTICOUNTY FEDERATION FOR
THE TWIN CITIES AREA, MINNESOTA

Another new kind of metropolitan federation is emerging in the multi-county area containing Minneapolis and St. Paul, Minnesota. In 1972 when the SMSA definition gave it five counties, this area had 113 municipalities (79 of them under 10,000), 34 townships, 26 special districts, and 40 school districts, for a total of 218 governmental units to serve a population of 1.8 million. Now the SMSA has been enlarged to seven counties with approximately 300 local taxing jurisdictions. This pattern isn't greatly different from some other multicounty areas, but the Twin Cities area is distinctive because of the establishment of a new areawide, general governmental unit known as the Metropolitan Council.

Background. Until 1945 Minneapolis and St. Paul contained nearly 90 percent of the metropolitan population, but in the post-World War II years suburban growth burgeoned, first residential and then commercial and industrial. Up until 1967 the Twin Cities area went through most of the same stages as other areas in responding to metropolitan growth: as early as 1888 a plan calling for growth of Minneapolis and St. Paul as one metropolitan area; steady expansion of the two cities by annexation; a voluntary metropolitan planning association (1927); the Minneapolis-St. Paul Sanitary District (1933); the Metropolitan Airports Commission (1943); the Metropolitan Planning Commission with its own property tax base (1957); gradual suburban incorporation; transformation of Hennepin County (one of the two core counties) into an urban service institution.

But all of this wasn't enough, for the institutional framework was insufficient to cope with increasing difficulties. The sewer problem was the worst, for growth was spreading far beyond the boundaries of the sanitary district and soil conditions were proving unsuitable for widespread use of septic tanks. Transit and open space were other problems. After several false starts, the 1967 session of the legislature established the Metropolitan Council as a planning and policy-making body, replacing the Metropolitan Planning Commission, and also set up the Metropolitan Transit Commission as a separate agency. Two years later the legislature created the Metropolitan Sewer Commission (Kolderie, 1973:114-138; also see Baldinger, 1971; and Mogulof, 1972).

Structure and finance. Local officials, civic leaders, and state legislators rejected the idea of a council of governments as unsuitable for the Twin Cities area and instead made the Metropolitan Council autonomous of other units of local government. At first there were fifteen members appointed by the governor: fourteen of them from districts formed by combining state legislative districts within the seven counties on a one person, one vote principle and the chairman chosen at large. The 1974 legislature enlarged the number of districts to sixteen, approximately equal in population but separate from the legislative districts. Earlier the chairman was part-time and there was a full-time executive director, but the latter position has been eliminated and the chairman is a full-time chief executive.

Initially the sewer board had eight members appointed by the Metropolitan Council, and the transit board was appointed by local government officials. The legislature changed this in 1974 to have eight members for each commission appointed by the Metropolitan Council from districts each combining two districts of the Council and the chairman appointed by the governor. The sewer board got the added responsibility of solid waste, and its name was changed to Waste Control Commission. A Parks and Open Space Board with similar composition was set up, and membership on the Airports Commission, previously made up of four representatives from each central city and one resident outside the cities appointed by the governor, was broadened to include more suburban representatives.

The Metropolitan Council draws up and adopts policy plans for each metropolitan commission and reviews and approves their development plans and capital budgets. The commissions in turn are the operating agencies. The Metropolitan Council is also authorized to review comprehensive plans of cities and counties within the metropolitan area and applications for state and federal aid, thus functioning as the A-95 review agency.

To finance its basic operations, the Metropolitan Council levies a property tax, which may not exceed seven-tenths of a mill. In 1976 its budget totaled $5.2 million, with $2 million from a property tax, $2.5 million from federal grants, and $700,000 from service charges to the metropolitan commissions and miscellaneous revenues.

Development guide and land use control. A major responsibility of the Metropolitan Council is the preparation of a guide for orderly and economical development, public and private, of the metropolitan area. As a major response to this responsibility the council in 1975 adopted a "development framework" chapter of the metropolitan development guide, following two years of staff work and consultation with local officials and citizens. This framework specifies areawide goals for urban development, social environment, natural environment, the regional economy, and citizen participation, and it has policies on metropolitan centers, fully developed areas, areas of planned urbanization, freestanding growth centers, and rural service areas.

The review powers mentioned earlier and the work of the metropolitan commissions will help implement this plan. In addition, the legislature in 1976 passed a land planning act to strengthen the Metropolitan Council's control over local plans. According to this statute, by July 1977 the council must prepare a metropolitan systems statement for each of the 245 local governmental units within the region to indicate existing and planned public facilities, population projections, and other information local governments will need as background for their own planning efforts. Local units then have three years to develop their comprehensive plans and submit them to the Metropolitan Council for review. The council will examine the local plans to determine compatibility with each other, and conformity with metropolitan systems plans and the development guide. If the council requires modification of a local plan, the locality may request a hearing by the State Office of Hearing Examiners or a special advisory committee, and the hearing report will go to the council for its consideration before making a final decision.

Thus, the Metropolitan Council gives the Twin Cities area a unique structure (so far), and its expanded powers have set the stage for fuller areawide controls over metropolitan development. As the council's authority has increased, there has been a rising demand that it should be directly responsible to the people through an electoral process. Therefore, every recent session of the legislature has seen a bill to bring this about, and although it always passes the House of Representatives, it is blocked in the Senate. If at some future time both houses agree upon such legislation, the Metropolitan Council will be a new kind of elected general-purpose government, not a metropolitan government modeled after an extended city or county government, but a new species shaped to its areawide responsibilities.

Analysis

Interest in metropolitan federation keeps recurring in the United States in spite of its poor record of formal acceptance. Partly this is a matter of intellectual and political preference. It is also partly because metropolitan unification has had only slightly more success, but not at all in multicounty areas; yet many feel that some type of metropolitan unit is necessary and federation offers a way. Furthermore, we have the examples from England and Canada to show the possibilities of federation.

FUNCTIONAL SUBDIVISION

Federation has the appeal of reason. It seems rational to think that some governmental activities require large scale operations while other activities can be best handled in smaller areas. Thus, most of the federation proposals give a lot of attention to which level should do what, and federations which come into being, both the formal and the de facto ones, demonstrate that functional subdivision is practicable.

I say "subdivision" because for particular functions—transportation, solid waste management, public safety, education, recreation, and others—specific activities are assigned to different levels. As we shall see in Chapter 13 when we get into this matter in depth, some activities are clearly metropolitan and others are predominantly local, but there are also some activities deemed metropolitan in one federation and assigned locally in another. But regardless, the principle of functional subdivision is inherent in all federations.

AREAWIDE GOVERNING BODY

A hallmark of metropolitan federation is the existence of an areawide, multipurpose unit governed by a council or commission with policy-making powers. This body can be chosen in several different ways.

It might be elected directly by the people, as happens in England and as has been recommended in most of the formal federation proposals in the United States. If election is the method, the issue arises of district or at large election, or a combination. The English areawide councils have a majority chosen from districts, and in the American proposals district election is the overwhelming choice, though one of the 1896 Boston alternatives had at large elections.

A second approach is for the areawide body to consist of persons who are elected to office at the local level and then become ex officio members of the metropolitan council. The Ontario federations are organized in this manner, consisting of city and borough councillors, mayors, and reeves (equivalent of a mayor). The Nassau County Board of Supervisors is composed of town and city officials.

The third possibility is appointment by a state or provincial official or perhaps by a number of local officials acting individually or jointly. Thus, the governor of Minnesota appoints the members of the Metropolitan Council: sixteen of them from districts (initially fourteen) and the chairman areawide;

in the beginning pairs of state senatorial districts were followed but now distinctive boundaries are observed. In Ontario the provisional government has appointed the first council chairmen of the new metropolitan and regional municipalities and thereafter the councils have elected their own chairmen.

LOCAL UNITS

For the local level of a metropolitan federation, Victor Jones and the 1970 CED report favor a rearrangement of governmental boundaries, as previously noted. The "ideal" plan of the lower-tier task force of the Greater Rochester study recommended this step, but the majority of the total panel rejected the idea. All the other specific American proposals have left the municipalities and townships in place.

At first no boundary change occurred in the Toronto federation, but in the second round thirteen municipalities were merged into six. Most of the smaller Ontario federations have reduced the number of municipal units at the beginning, and the number of local units in Great Britain have been sharply lowered. When the Greater London Council came into being, the number of lower-tier units in the territory covered fell from eighty-six to thirty-three, and in the rest of Great Britain the number of local units was cut to less than one-third of the previous total.

INTERMEDIATE LEVEL

Although the NAPA project was conceived to apply CED's two-tier proposal, as test sites it chose three multicounty areas which already have municipal units and counties so that a metropolitan body would be a third tier. None of the three local study groups gave serious consideration to consolidating the counties into a single metropolitan county at present, though the Portland group recorded this as a long-range possibility. This means that the counties would constitute an intermediate level or middle-tier unit, and in some respects the central cities would too because they might have neighborhood units as a lower tier. In the Twin Cities de facto federation, seven counties and the two central cities are intermediate levels of government.

The theory of federation, however, hasn't gone very far to define the role of middle-tier governments and their relationships to local and metropolitan tiers. In the Twin Cities example, Minneapolis and St. Paul each has a different mode of internal organization and a different approach to its neighborhoods. The two core counties, Hennepin and Ramsey, aren't alike, and the outlying counties offer other varieties. So the middle tier itself can't be defined with a single model.

PROBLEM-SOLVING POTENTIAL

Federation offers the same advantages as unification in achieving an areawide government to cope with metropolitan growth provided that the metropolitan unit has means for implementation of areawide plans. The Metropolitan Council of Minnesota has gained this ability through its policy control over the major operating commissions and its newly acquired authority to guide land use policy. The Canadian and English federations also are in a position to deal with metropolitan growth.

For its strategy to improve service delivery, federation promotes a division of responsibility scaled to the nature of particular services. Areawide services are financed by a metropolitan tax base, and there is a potential to use metropolitan taxes to fund local services, as Toronto does for education, and to redistribute a portion of local revenues, as the Twin Cities area does. This tackles the fiscal disparity issue.

As to social disparity, federation can have a positive, negative, or neutral effect. If local units control zoning and exclude low-income residents, the social separation produced by current multiplicity will remain. But an areawide body could work for a broader distribution of socio-economic groups by formulating a low- and moderate-income housing dispersal strategy, and its role in land use planning could lead to implementation measures in this direction. By having small units within the federation, different groups would have opportunity to control local governments serving their immediate communities and still be part of the larger body politic. This would probably increase citizen confidence and enhance public official accountability, though if the local tier were too highly fragmented with hundreds of small units, the uncertainty of who is accountable that now exists in the contemporary multitudinous arrangement, would still prevail.

Chapter 9

NEIGHBORHOOD DECENTRALIZATION

During this same period while advocates of a metropolitan approach have pressed for unification or federation and when councils of governments have emerged as a new kind of areawide body, a strong trend in the opposite direction has also occurred in metropolitan areas, producing considerable interest in neighborhood decentralization. This is partly a reaction to many years of increased centralization in governmental institutions, for as Herbert Kaufman has observed, there tend to be cycles of centralization and decentralization in American political life (1969:3-15). Interest in devolution of power is also associated with the human rights revolution which has swept the country during the last twenty years, resulting in a demand by minorities of various descriptions for a greater say in their own destiny. Both thrusts—the countercentralization and the human rights emphasis—have been given expression at the neighborhood level.

The Case for Decentralization

Two forms of decentralization might occur in neighborhoods: administrative and political. Administrative decentralization relates to management processes. It occurs when subordinates in an organization have discretionary authority to shape program details to the needs of the particular area or population served. Although physical decentralization usually takes place at the same time, mere physical dispersal of personnel doesn't constitute administrative decentralization unless they have discretionary authority. Political decentralization refers to policy-making by citizens and their elected representatives. It happens when decision-making authority is assigned to citizens or a representative body of a subarea within the territory of the central authority

It is possible for administrative and political decentralization to occur independently of one another: a district manager having discretionary authority without citizen involvement, or citizens having a policy voice without being in charge of operations. The two can also occur simultaneously, such as when a neighborhood board determines policy and hires staff to run programs.

DECENTRALIZATION MODELS

Neighborhood decentralization can take various institutional forms. To enhance our understanding of these varieties, Henry Schmandt provides five simplified models based on the degree of decentralization: exchange, bureaucratic, modified bureaucratic, development, and governmental (1973:18-26).

The exchange model emphasizes communication devices which facilitate a two-way flow of information between city officials and citizens. This can be taken to the neighborhood level through little city halls serving as information, complaint, and referral centers and through the use of neighborhood advisory committees.

The bureaucratic model involves delegation of greater authority to field staff. It can be accomplished in individual departments, and it can also come to focus in a district or neighborhood manager who has general authority over a number of decentralized services.

An advisory neighborhood council can be added to this arrangement to produce the modified bureaucratic model. This makes the neighborhood administrator responsible both to his superiors in the administrative system and, to a lesser extent, to neighborhood representatives.

What Schmandt calls the development model consists of community corporations which have responsibility for policy making and administration. They are organized as nonprofit corporations and are financed by grants and contracts.

When resident control of policy and operations is built into the structure of city government, it produces the governmental model. Under this approach, a representative body is in charge of specific public services for its territory.

The first three models constitute administrative decentralization, with citizen participation enhanced in the modified bureaucratic model. The last two are forms of political decentralization with administration also decentralized. The ultimate form combining both administrative and political decentralization is neighborhood government.

NEIGHBORHOOD GOVERNMENT

In his seminal work on neighborhood government, Milton Kotler identified the drive for local control with the political movement for liberty. He saw neighborhood organization as "the natural place for either founding new liberty or liberating local settlement from outside power" (1969:11).

Since then Kotler has been interested in developing a neighborhood-based ethics of politics with a heightened concern for justice. Both of these concerns were expressed in a "Neighborhood Bill of Responsibilities and Rights," adopted by the Alliance for Neighborhood Government in 1976. It starts in the following manner:

> The ideal of neighborhood government rests upon the belief that people can and should govern themselves democratically and justly. The essence of a democratic government is that people are responsible collectively to make choices which directly affect their lives together. The neighborhood is a political unit which makes this possible, since the smallness of the neighborhood enables all residents to deliberate, decide and act together for the common good (quoted by Kotler, 1976:581).

In my own book on neighborhood government, I summarized the case by stating that it "would contribute to improved urban governance by achieving a greater sense of community, redressing an imbalance of power, making public services more effective, promoting the public order, and opening new opportunities for personal development" (1974A:12).

In practice, neighborhood government hasn't been organized in any city, but a variety of approaches to neighborhood decentralization have been pursued during the last twelve years. Moreover, small suburban municipalities have many characteristics of neighborhood government.

A Dozen Years of Experiments

The right of self-government is an assertion which led to the American Revolution, and the desire for municipal home rule is a cause long pressed by local residents. Likewise the idea has an enduring place in urban life from the time that cities started growing big. The precinct was the foundation of the first urban political organizations. Settlement houses from their beginning in the 1880s had a neighborhood base, and after the turn of the century public schools began to be used as community centers. The 1920s had a vigorous community council movement, and the neighborhood unit emerged as a building block for city planning. In the thirties and forties neighborhood organizations were used to combat juvenile delinquency, and the neighborhood became the focus for urban redevelopment and conservation programs following World War II (Dillick, 1953; Hallman, 1973).

In the early 1960s the interest in neighborhoods picked up. This resurgence got a strong boost from the requirement of the Economic Opportunity Act of 1964 for maximum feasible participation of areas and persons served by the Community Action Program. The next ten years saw a dazzling array of experiments with widely varying forms of neighborhood decentralization.

COMMUNITY ACTION PROGRAM

In a 1967 study of the Community Action Program which I directed for a U.S. Senate subcommittee, we found that the dominant emphasis of community action agencies was upon services even though a few local programs had attracted a lot of attention in demanding power for the poor. However, not everywhere were they conducting services in the traditional sense, for institutional change was a strategy often utilized and residents were hired as staff in both professional and subprofessional capacities. The agencies themselves were different from previous ones because at least one-third of their boards were representatives of the poor, usually a majority, and these representatives were usually selected by neighborhood boards or area councils. Program operations in cities was focused in poor neighborhoods, so community action was very much a neighborhood program (Hallman, 1967:897-915).

Looking at five large community action agencies in the San Francisco Bay area, Ralph M. Kramer found four major modes of resident participation: policy making, program development, social action, and employment. The target area organizations took several forms; and some of them emphasized social action while others put more stress upon program development and services. On the whole, the experience showed that "people in low-income neighborhoods could certainly do more than protest. Residents of the target areas, including a very small proportion of low-income persons, demonstrated their ability to serve in policy-making, advisory, program planning, review, administrative, and budgeting roles" (Kramer, 1969:267).

COMMUNITY CORPORATIONS

In 1966 during the second full year of the Community Action Program, community corporations began forming in a number of localities as the neighborhood instrument for citizen participation. They took the form of a private nonprofit organization, governed by a board of directors selected by neighborhood residents. The boards set policy, controlled funds, and hired staff. Some of them dealt with community services, and others concentrated upon economic development.

When I visited a number of them in 1968, I concluded that they were producing feelings of self-pride and civic accomplishment and for the most part were adequately administered (1970:206-211). I took a second look in 1972 and discovered that some had faltered but some new ones had commenced operations and were flourishing (1974A:150-164). Both times I felt that good board and staff leadership was a key factor in achieving success.

In this same period Douglas Yates studied some community corporations and other decentralization experiments in New York and New Haven. He concluded that in these efforts citizens gained a forum for articulating their interests and grievances and achieved greater awareness of neighborhood needs. Their program results were modest, and none of them produced quick and dramatic solutions to major neighborhood problems. But they provided more jobs for neighborhood residents, and they revealed that decentralization doesn't greatly increase costs unless it is part of an innovative program intended to augment services. Fears of administrative chaos and abuse of power weren't born out by the experience of most of the decentralization experiments which he observed (Yates, 1973:64).

A distinct species of this form of organization is referred to as community development corporations (CDCs), and they emphasize economic development under resident control, especially in poor and minority neighborhoods. A task force set up by the Twentieth Century Fund studied the operation of a number of CDCs and concluded that they had demonstrated their value. "Community development corporations," the task force report indicated, "have a unique capacity for pooling a community's talents and resources; for ownership of businesses, homes and other property among the urban poor; for developing entrepreneurial and managerial talent; for linking together a variety of businesses and projects for mutual reinforcement and support; and for organizing the community to accept and effectively utilize resources and assistance from outside the poverty area" (1971:3-4; also see Ford Foundation, 1973).

COMMUNITY SCHOOL BOARDS

Community control of public schools was another demand voiced in the 1960s. School boards responded by expanding the advisory role of citizens, and New York and Detroit went even further by decentralizing control of the schools.

In New York this was first done on a trial basis in three experimental districts from 1967 to 1969, resulting in bitter disputes between some community leaders and the teachers' union over control of personnel. The state legislature ended this experiment with a new law setting up thirty-two school districts, each with an elected school board to oversee elementary and junior high schools. A reconstituted central board, appointed by the mayor and the five borough presidents, retained control over the high schools and basic personnel policies. The educational impact of decentralization was mixed, for there weren't many changes in educational methods, and attendance rates were unaffected. More blacks and Puerto Ricans got into supervisory positions, and there was a lowering of tensions between community organizations and school officials. One observer feels that the latter was one of the biggest accomplishments because the centralized system had been unable to cope with the demands of conflicting pressure groups (Ravitch, 1975:1-4).

School decentralization in Detroit came about in 1973 under a state law providing for eight regions of approximately equal population. Each region has an elected five-member board, and the top vote-getter is chairman and also the regional board's representative to the central board, which has five additional members elected citywide. Regional boards select their administrators and teachers from a central pool, but they have considerable discretion on school curriculum. Many more people are now involved in school affairs than before and sharp conflict between the community and educators has lessened. Student achievement has increased during the years of decentralization, but a trend in this direction had started before the regional boards were organized (Grant, 1975:5-8).

MODEL CITIES AND URBAN RENEWAL

The Demonstration Cities and Metropolitan Development Act of 1966 authorized what became known as the Model Cities Program. When it got rolling in 1967 and 1968 with two rounds of planning grants to a total of one hundred fifty cities, it was intended to be under the control of local government, and not private nonprofit organizations as was the case with about nine out of ten community action agencies. Nevertheless, there was a requirement for widespread citizen participation, and the insistence of leaders in the designated model neighborhoods led to considerable resident involvement. In a study of the Model Cities planning process in a number of cities, Marshall Kaplan, Gans, and Kahn found that all of them had some formal structure for citizen participation. The extent of the residents' role varied from city to city, ranging in a continuum of five basic patterns: staff dominance, staff influence, parity, resident influence, and resident dominance (1970:11-21).

In a study of the operations of eight local programs, George J. Washnis concluded that on the whole citizen participation efforts were worthwhile after city government worked out the proper relationships with the resident boards. He felt that the Model Cities Program showed that the following purposes could be achieved through a citizen participation process:

> (1) to develop an education and training process so that the average poor American can become honestly involved in the understanding and operation of local government and in making decisions that might affect his life, (2) to improve communication and trust between city hall and residents, (3) to develop new leaders from a class of people who otherwise might never have such an opportunity, (4) to get early agreement on the kinds of projects citizens want so that progress would not be held up, (5) to provide citizens with an effective process by which they can effectively criticize and evaluate services, and (6) to formalize participation structures so that they may become a genuine part of government (1974:20).

The U.S. Department of Housing and Urban Development (HUD) administered the Model Cities Program at the federal level, and it also handled the older Urban Renewal Program. In 1968 HUD issued new regulations requiring project area committees (PACs) for urban renewal projects and permitting federal funds to be used to pay their expenses. In 1971 the National Urban League undertook a demonstration project to provide technical assistance to PACs in five localities. To make its selection, the project surveyed 75 PACs around the country and found that "the great majority were weak, moribund or no longer exist. This overriding fact testifies to the failure of urban renewal agencies and HUD to take citizen participation seriously—either to encourage its development or to use it effectively" (1973:5). There were a few effective local project committees, however. They tended to be ones which had existed at least four or five years, had diverse membership and leadership, enjoyed wide community acceptance, had a good relationship with the urban renewal agency, and received technical assistance. The PAC's relationship with the renewal agency was the most crucial variable, but where they "work together despite differences, a better, more sensitive, more responsive urban renewal plan usually results" (1973:6).

LITTLE CITY HALLS AND MULTISERVICE CENTERS

While these various experiments with political decentralization were going on, ranging from modest advisory roles for project area committees to substantial control by community school boards, cities were also seeking ways to achieve administrative decentralization on the neighborhood level. Little city halls and multiservice centers were two devices designed for this purpose.

In 1971 the Advisory Commission on Intergovernmental Relations and the International City Management Association conducted a joint survey of cities over 25,000 to determine their experience with various forms of decentralization. Out of 460 cities reporting, 19 (4 percent) indicated they had one or more little city halls, defined as a neighborhood branch office for the chief executive, and 86 (19 percent) said they had multiservice centers, that is, a branch office providing two or more services from various public and private agencies. Resident advisory boards were used by about three out of ten cities with little city halls and by seven out of ten with multiservice centers (Stenberg, 1972).

Washnis visited a dozen of these cities and described several patterns: (1) traditional branch municipal facilities with regular city service personnel in field offices for efficiency and convenience (Los Angeles, San Antonio, and Kansas City); (2) multiservice centers providing many social services and some municipal services in one location (Chicago and Norfolk); (3) neighborhood city halls emphasizing communication, coordination, and a more personal involvement with individual citizens but with a minimal level of in-house services (New York, Atlanta, and Houston); (4) neighborhood city halls with all these functions plus a variety of services (Boston, Baltimore, Columbus); and (5) neighborhood outreach from the mayor's office (San Francisco). He concluded that these neighborhood units were functioning successfully. He favored combining a variety of services at one location in the neighborhood and having a representative of the chief executive in charge. He saw a commitment from both the chief executive and city council as a key factor in achieving success (1973).

DISTRICT CABINETS AND MANAGERS

After several years experience with various forms of neighborhood decentralization, New York City in 1971 embarked upon an experimental program of district management through the creation of district service cabinets in eight of the city's 62 planning districts. Each cabinet was chaired by a mayoral-appointed district manager, who had a staff of five persons and a budget in the range of $75,000 to $100,000. Field supervisors from twelve major operating agencies participated in the cabinets, and some of the agencies tried to make their own district boundaries coterminous with the planning districts in order to facilitate administrative coordination. The district service cabinets devised special projects, set up task forces to solve specific problems, and generally served as a place for information exchange. The mayor's office had a special unit to oversee this experiment and to work with headquarters of the various departments (Mudd, 1976:1-4).

An evaluation of this experiment by the Bureau of Applied Social Research at Columbia University found that there was strong public support for administrative decentralization and coordination at the district level from community leaders and local line officials of participating agencies. However, some resistance was noted at higher levels in the departments and among city council members, and this resulted in insufficient delegation of authority to field personnel. Problem-centered task forces were better able to handle most service problems rather than the whole cabinet. On the whole, more effective and more responsive services were produced at a relatively low cost (Barton, 1976:5-8; also see Barton, 1977).

OTHER EFFORTS

If space permitted, this summary of a dozen years of experience with neighborhood decentralization and citizen participation could be extended to include the use of program advisory committees for education, welfare, mental health, and many other federally aided programs; the opening of transportation planning to greater citizen participation at an early stage; a requirement for environmental impact statements and public hearings related to various programs. On the tenth anniversary of the enactment of the maximum feasible participation requirement of the Economic Opportunity Act of 1964, I concluded that "Year by year the citizen's role in local government has grown and organized neighborhood bodies have gained a larger voice in programs affecting their areas. Not a millennium, but steady progress" (1974B:14). Two more years have elapsed and the trend continues.

Neighborhood Councils of the Seventies

The newest development is the emergence of neighborhood councils with some kind of official or quasi-official relationship with local government. At the latest count approximately fifty cities and counties provide such recognition, and the number is growing. They go by various names, such as community councils, neighborhood boards, advisory neighborhood commissions, and other titles, but regardless of what they are called, it is their official role which separates them from the traditional civic association. Kansas City, Missouri has had such organizations since the 1940s and a few cities began to use this approach in the late sixties, but primarily the spread of neighborhood councils is a phenomenon of the 1970s, achieved through local initiative and not requirements of any federal program.

VARIETIES

In an analysis of thirty cities and counties where neighborhood councils function as a part of the local governmental process, I divided them into several clusters with similar features (1977). One group of five cities has specific charter authorization for neighborhood councils: Honolulu, Pittsburgh, District of Columbia, New York, and Newton, Massachusetts. All other places use an ordinance or policy resolution of city council or the county board, or have a less formal, de facto means of recognition. In New York community boards, as they are called, cover the whole city and all organize at the same time. In the District of Columbia and Pittsburgh there are fixed times for starting up but a neighborhood has the choice whether to organize or not, and in Newton and Honolulu neighborhoods can initiate the organizing process at any time.

Several cities using an ordinance or policy resolution provide for complete coverage of the entire city and all neighborhoods organize simultaneously. In Dayton, Birmingham, and Minneapolis neighborhood councils were set up with a close relationship to federally funded community development while ones in Simi Valley (California), Milwaukie (Oregon), and Wichita were started mainly to deal with local governmental activities.

The largest cluster of localities with neighborhood councils are those which phase them in over many months or several years. Usually the neighborhoods can decide whether to organize or not, and in most cases the city council or county board has procedures for granting official recognition to a neighborhood group after it is established. In this cluster are Anchorage, Salem, Eugene, East Palo Alto, San Diego, Fort Worth, St. Paul, Atlanta, and Jacksonville, and also Clackamas County (Oregon), Washington County (Oregon), San Diego County (California), and Guilford County (North Carolina).

In some cities the city council doesn't formally recognize neighborhood councils, but neighborhood associations have de facto recognition because of contacts with a city agency which renders them staff assistance and sometimes modest financial aid. Portland (Oregon), Kansas City (Missouri), Lincoln, and Fort Wayne are in this category.

And in the final cluster are privately organized neighborhood councils with a special relationship with local government. This occurs in Independence (Missouri) and Muskegon (Michigan).

ADMINISTRATIVE SUPPORT

Most cities and counties which recognize neighborhood councils assign some office or department to maintain contacts with them and perhaps provide technical assistance. Around the country several different types of administrative agencies handle this responsibility, and to some extent, the assignment relates to the program emphasis of the neighborhood councils.

Where neighborhood groups participate in developing a neighborhood plan, the planning department handles the liaison assignment but brings in other departments at appropriate times on their particular functions. Where community development is emphasized, the local agency in charge of the federal Community Development Program works with the neighborhood councils.

In a number of cities and counties, neighborhood councils deal with a number of programs, and a unit in the office of the chief executive (mayor, manager, county executive) works with them. In a few cities a special agency outside the chief executive's office is created for this purpose, and in some places a private nonprofit organization handles this task. And there are some cases where the charter authorizes recognition of neighborhood councils and leaves it up to the neighborhood residents to organize and gain acceptance without any city staff assistance.

FUNCTIONS

Neighborhood councils handle several kinds of functions, but all of them don't necessarily do the same things. For the most part their role is advisory, but here and there they are moving into program operations.

Communications. A major purpose of neighborhood councils is to facilitate communications between local officials and citizens. This is a two-way flow of information and viewpoints. City or county governments utilize legal notices, bulletins, letters, telephone calls, and public meetings to convey information to residents. Some localities use a central office and a common bulletin for this purpose while others let individual agencies handle their own communications to the neighborhoods. Likewise neighborhood councils utilize a variety of methods to convey their view to public agencies, including letters, phone calls, appearances at public hearings, interviews, and upon occasion protest tactics. Lastly neighborhood councils try to communicate with residents through public meetings, newsletters, and informal conversations.

Advisory and advocacy roles. For certain programs the advisory role of neighborhood councils is fulfilled through a structured process. This is particularly the case in developing a neighborhood plan. A planner will work with a neighborhood planning committee over a period of many months, a jointly prepared draft plan will be presented at neighborhood public meetings, and residents will testify at a formal hearing by the planning commission and the city council or county board. In helping develop the Community Development Program, neighborhood councils will participate on task forces and committees and will testify at public hearings prior to submission for federal funding. A similar sense of schedule will occur where the neighborhood is involved in preparation of the capital program and the operating budget. But many other matters, such as zoning proposals, program changes in local public services, and responses to specific problems will be handled as they arise. In these various efforts, citizens aren't merely technical advisers but also act as advocates of the neighborhood viewpoint.

Self-help activities. Quite a few neighborhood councils are getting into self-help activities which mobilize the volunteer efforts of residents. Examples of what they do are housing fix-up and paint-up, tool lending libraries, cleanup and beautification, recreation activities, neighborhood fairs, community crime prevention, services to the elderly, and community gardens.

Sometimes neighborhood councils do these things alone and sometimes in conjunction with public agencies.

Service delivery. Only a small number of neighborhood councils get into service delivery. When this occurs, they function like the community corporations mentioned earlier. The ones doing this tend to be descendants of the Community Action or Model Cities program. A special case is the East Palo Alto Municipal Council, consisting of five elected members, in an unincorporated community of 18,000 people in San Mateo County, California. It has a small staff and several subordinate advisory committees, and it oversees a variety of county and state programs conducted from offices within the community. Ultimately the county board of supervisors has final policy control on the county programs, but it has delegated a substantial role to the community.

RELATIONSHIP TO NEIGHBORHOOD GOVERNMENT

These neighborhood councils can't be considered neighborhood governments in the fullest sense because their policy voice is mostly advisory and their administrative responsibilities are light. Maybe some of then will move toward full-fledged neighborhood government, and others won't. In any case, they constitute a further development in the movement toward greater neighborhood decentralization of government in metropolitan areas.

Suburban Municipalities

Another form of decentralization on a neighborhood scale is the suburban municipality, though residents perceive their unit as an independent jurisdiction and not a "neighborhood government." But regardless of classification, the small municipality or township in the suburbs provides local services close at hand, and this can be considered a model for what neighborhood government might perform if the central city chose to delegate certain tasks to its neighborhoods. The suburban jurisdiction also represents its residents in dealing with the county, state agencies, special districts, and sometimes the central city, in this sense fulfilling advisory and advocacy roles similar to the neighborhood council in the city.

As we saw in Table 3.2 in Chapter 3, 80 percent of the suburban municipalities and townships in metropolitan areas contain less than 10,000 residents and are thus clearly a neighborhood size; another 13 percent are in the 10,000 to 25,000 range, a size similar to what a neighborhood council in a medium- to large-size city might serve. Altogether 29 percent of the total metropolitan population in 1970 lived in suburban municipalities and townships under 25,000 in population. Therefore, small-area government is now a reality for a considerable proportion of metropolitan residents.

When I examined the feasibility of neighborhood government several years ago, I looked at a number of small suburban municipalities and also at some small enclave cities, located in the midst of a larger city, in order to determine what they really do and how successful they are. I found that there are indeed small municipalities with 5,000 people or fewer which are able to conduct several kinds of public services, but a population of approximately 10,000 seemed a more desirable minimum in order to widen the range of services (1974:50).

Analysis

Looking at all phases of neighborhood decentralization, I find one of its greatest values is enhancing the sense of community. Where people have an organizational vehicle close at hand, they have a better opportunity to work together, and common action is a great booster of community spirit. Personal conflict between neighbors won't automatically disappear, but shared values are strengthened when people work together. Small-area government provides this opportunity.

It also gives some people their first taste of civic life, their first experience in political activities and in fulfilling the responsibility of elected office. Many will find this the place they prefer to work, some will learn that they don't care much for this role and will drop by the wayside, and others will build upon this experience and move into the broader arena, getting involved in city or county politics, state government, and, for a few, national politics. In this manner, the neighborhood can be an effective training ground for citizenship.

Many services can be improved by centralizing delivery to the neighborhood level, by giving field personnel greater discretionary authority, and by involving residents in advisory roles in program operations. This is especially true where personal service is a major factor, such as police, recreation, education, family counseling, and other social services. A neighborhood information and complaint office tied to a citywide or countywide management improvement program can make a contribution to better service delivery.

There are, of course, many kinds of services and facilities which can't be effectively decentralized because of genuine economies of scale (such as refuse disposal) or because of advantages of wide coverage (such as police communications). Not much can be done at the neighborhood level to overcome fiscal disparity; rather the opposite is true: neighborhoods are the victims of fiscal inequities.

Likewise, broad societal forces have produced segregated neighborhoods, thereby increasing racial and social separation in the metropolis. But also some people have used their control of small municipalities and neighborhood organizations to exclude other people, thus harming the wider good of the metropolitan community. Where this happens, the counterbalancing force of a broader jurisdiction is needed to overcome neighborhood exclusion.

It would be a mistake to claim too much for the potential of neighborhood decentralization because everything can't be done at a small scale. But it is also erroneous to dismiss it as impractical and a nuisance. Placed in the context of a federalist approach where responsibilities are shared among governments serving areas of different sizes, the neighborhood has an important role to play in the governance of metropolitan areas.

Chapter 10

STATE AND FEDERAL ROLES

The preceding seven chapters have reviewed the highly diverse ways local government is organized and functions in metropolitan areas. Frequently the discussion referred to actions taken by state government or by the national government. In this chapter we examine more fully the state and federal roles in metropolitan affairs.

Pattern of American Government

In an exploration of the metropolitan problem, Luther Gulick pointed out that in the United States we have three major "extensions" of government, each defined geographically. They are, he said (1962:30-31):

(1) A single government of *comprehensive extension*, covering the entire geographic hegemony of the nation, known as the "federal government";

(2) fifty governments, each of *intermediate extension*, known as the "states"; and

(3) over 100,000 governments, each of *limited, local extension*, known as "local governments."

He spoke of "extension" because the American scheme of government "is made up of partially autonomous governmental structures which differ primarily with respect to the *extent* of the constituencies and boundaries on which they rest." This terminology substituted for that of "levels" or

"layers" in order to avoid the implication of a hierarchy or order of prec-
edence. No, that's not the way a federal system operates, Gulick insisted.
"Our governmental services and controls are not exercised in hierarchical
layers. They are complete intertwined, *all at the same level*—the level where
you and I live and work" (1962:30).

Gulick's point is well taken. There is a state presence and a federal
presence in every metropolitan area, and metropolitan residents are constituents of their state and national government as well as one or more local
governments. All three "extensions" of government are present in the metropolis, each serving citizens and impacting on their lives: And what they do is
inextricably intertwined.

We will return to this notion in greater depth in the next chapter when we
take up the theory of local federalism. But here let us explore more precisely
what roles the states and the national government play in metropolitan affairs
and how these governmental extensions are interrelated.

Roles of State Government

State government is very much a factor in the governance of metropolitan
areas. It fulfills a variety of roles.

SOURCE OF LOCAL AUTHORITY

First and foremost, the state is the basic source of authority for local
government, and in a constitutional sense cities, counties, and townships are
creatures of the state. This assertion hasn't always been readily accepted by
local communities, which have sometimes claimed an inherent right of self-
government, reflecting a strong feeling for local independence. The issue was
settled legally by an 1868 Iowa supreme court ruling which the U.S. Supreme
Court subsequently upheld:

> Municipal corporations owe their origin to, and derive their powers and
> rights wholly from, the legislature. It breathes into them the breath of
> life, without which they cannot exist. As it creates, so may it destroy.
> If it may destroy, it may abridge and control (*City of Clinton v. Cedar
> Rapids and Missouri River Railroad Company*, 24 Iowa 475 (1868);
> quoted by Martin, 1965:29-30).

Indeed, what the state giveth, the state can take away. Reality, though, is
rarely this harsh, for local governments have considerable room for initiative
and they are a political force to be reckoned with. As Roscoe C. Martin
pointed out, "*de jure* the state is supreme, *de facto* the cities enjoy considerable autonomy" (1965:32).

But what is this "state" which determines the authority of local government? State government is an institution deriving its own powers from the people who adopt and amend the state constitution. The statutes are drawn up by the state legislature, a representative body with local people as its constituents. Thus, the state isn't a distant "them" in the state capitol but rather a collective "us," and we entrust certain persons to run it in our behalf. We are citizens of the state, and it is—or should be—responsive to our will.

Home rule. Because we are also citizens of a locality, we insist upon a fair degree of local independence. Therefore, the idea of home rule has entered into state law. But traditional legal doctrine looked askance at free exercise of powers by a locality. Thus, Judge J. F. Dillon, who wrote the Iowa decision quoted above, had this to say in his *Treatise on the Law of Municipal Corporations* (1872:101-102):

> It is a general and undisputed proposition of law that a municipal corporation possesses, and can exercise, the following powers, and no others: First, those powers granted in *express words*; second, those *necessarily or fairly implied* in, or *incident* to, the powers expressly granted; third, those *essential* to the declared objects and purposes of the corporation—not simply convenient, but indispensable. Any fair, reasonable doubt concerning the existence of power is resolved by the courts against the corporation and the power is denied.

Thereafter, Dillon's Rule was widely accepted by state courts throughout the nation.

Local citizens and their officials, however, haven't been content with such construction of their powers. Accordingly, they have pressed for home rule. The first legislative act permitting a local government to amend its charter came in Iowa in 1858. Missouri in 1875 was the first state to place a home rule provision in its constitution. A century later, according to William N. Cassella, Jr. (1975:448), "most states have recognized the importance of a degree of local autonomy and some form of home rule."

Even the Dillon Rule has been modified by what is sometimes known as the Fordham-AMA Rule, derived from a model constitutional provision which Jefferson B. Fordham prepared for the American Municipal Association in 1953. The National Municipal League worked out a similar proposal, and in 1962 the Advisory Commission on Intergovernmental Relations came up with the simplest expression of this idea: "Municipalities and Counties shall have all powers and functions not denied or limited by this constitution or by State law. This section shall be liberally construed in favor of municipalities and counties." Ten states now have home rule language of this sort in their constitutions, and court interpretation in another state has adopted this flexible approach to home rule (Cassella, 1975:446-448).

Local boundaries. Ordinarily home rule guarantees that local boundaries won't change without the consent of local voters. This idea developed for free-standing municipalities. Later when the suburbs began to incorporate on their own as municipalities, the home rule doctrine applied to them also, including the notion of inviolate boundaries. Local voters could agree to dissolve the municipal corporation, merge with another unit, or change the boundaries, but it was their decision.

During the last twenty years several states have modified somewhat this hands off approach by establishing boundary commissions to review and approve annexation proposals and boundaries of proposed new municipalities, as we saw in Chapter 3. Other states have set forth minimum standards for incorporation. But once a municipality is established, it has an expectation of remaining in perpetuity. Home rule to this extent applies to the smallest municipality.

Gone for the most part is any notion that the total settlement, the metropolis, has home rule to determine the governmental structure which best suits it, and its boundaries. Even where drastic metropolitan reorganization occurs, such as in city/county consolidation, small municipalities have the right to be excluded from merger (an exception was the Anchorage case where two small cities had no choice of remaining independent). In Indiana, which has no home rule, the legislature itself excluded four small cities.

However, no such reticence has prevailed in school reorganization where state mandated consolidation has occurred wholesale. But a different philosophy reigns. Education is generally perceived as a statewide responsibility delegated to local school systems, and not a locally initiated program which has the right of home rule. Historically counties, and to some extent rural townships, were also conceived as state subdivisions; a few states have abolished townships, but county boundaries remain scarcely unchanged and in some states are protected by the state constitution. Thus, boundaries of local general government are generally quite secure under prevailing practices.

FINANCES

Rarely is home rule absolute in the matter of taxation. The state may give local government a choice of a number of taxes, but even these are often hedged with maximum rates and other restrictions. In many states, localities are prohibited from tapping any tax source not expressly authorized by the state, and sometimes they are specifically banned from levying certain taxes. This keeps local government from utilizing such productive revenue sources as income and sales taxes, thus forcing them to rely primarily upon the property tax.

A local government may levy a property tax only on property within its jurisdiction, and in a metropolis divided into many local units, property values are distributed unevenly among local governments. So are retail sales and income if taxes on these sources are allowed, though a commuter income tax broadens a city's tax coverage. The product is fiscal disparity, a situation deplored by the commissions reviewed in Chapter 1 and a subject reserved for more detailed consideration in Chapter 14. The point to make here is that fiscal disparity is partly the result of a set of decisions made by state government on local governmental structure and tax arrangements.

Many states recognize this and take into account the unevenness of local tax resources in the distribution of state funds to local government. This redistributive capacity of state government has gone the furthest in education, as we saw in Chapter 5, but it has received modest application in state aid to local general government. To be sure, there are regional differences in wealth which only the national government can cope with, but it is within the authority of the states to eliminate a substantial portion of metropolitan fiscal disparity if the people and their representatives choose to do so.

PHYSICAL DEVELOPMENT AND SERVICES

Highways. Another way state government extends into metropolitan areas is in the construction of facilities. Chief among them are expressways and principal highways. Once perceived as a route to connect cities, the state highway, especially its expressway manifestation, has a major impact on the physical development of the metropolis. Extending as a radial outward, the expressway determines time-and-distance to work for commuters and the land most favorable for development. Interchange sites influence the location of commerce and industry and produce tremendous increases in land values. Plunging into the heart of the city, the expressway rips apart older neighborhoods and sets in motion numerous changes in land use and property values. Going around the city, the circumferential highway connects suburb to suburb and helps create an existence quite apart from the traditional central city.

By constitutional law, state government isn't beholden to cities and counties where it puts its highways, and for years the state highway engineers observed this law to the letter, yielding only to pressures exerted through state political processes. However, in recent years transportation planning in metropolitan areas has been a more cooperative venture, as told in Chapter 6, because metropolitan planning organizations involving both state and local officials have been delegated responsibilities for drawing up plans and determining priorities subject to state and federal review. In this manner, all three "extensions" of government are involved in local highway decisions.

Other facilities. State government also builds other kinds of facilities in metropolitan areas: universities, colleges, vocational schools, mental hospitals, and penal institutions. And it creates large parks and public beaches in or near the metropolis. Though not as universally present as highways, they have their impact upon the immediate environment, and they contribute to the local economic base.

Housing. Certain types of housing are built or financed by state agencies within metropolitan areas. Thirty-nine states have housing finance agencies to promote and assist in the construction of low- and moderate-income housing, and thirty-three of them have formed within the past ten years. New York has been doing this for several decades, and in 1968 it created a new body, the New York State Urban Development Corporation, to finance and also to sponsor new housing. It was authorized to override local zoning, a power it successfully used as a leverage to get suburban sites, but when it tried to invoke this authority in affluent Westchester County local resistance led to the state legislature revoking this power.

Services. State government furnishes many services directly to metropolitan residents—at state institutions and from other offices as well. State employment security agencies handle unemployment insurance and employment services, and another unit in the state labor department takes care of workmen's compensation. Thirty-six states directly administer the welfare program (the others delegate it to counties or share responsibility with counties). States license local occupations, regulate working conditions, inspect factories, enforce air and water pollution standards, license motor vehicles and drivers, enforce equal opportunity laws, inspect restaurants and nursing homes, and carry out many more activities. Clearly state employees are very much part of the governmental services picture in metropolitan areas.

PLANNING

As metropolitan areas spread across county lines and impacted on distant hinterland, the states have become more involved in developmental planning. They have done this by setting up substate planning districts, and a number of them have gotten into statewide planning.

Substate districts. Chapter 6 has told how forty-four states have delineated substate districts under the provisions of several federal acts. A few states actively promoted establishment of substate district organizations and some others offered technical assistance upon request, but for the most part it has been up to local leadership to take the organizational initiative. In looking at the process in 1973, ACIR discovered that the states were exerting relatively little influence over the continuing activities of the district organizations and furthermore state aid programs were not ordinarily put into the substate notification and review system which Circular A-95 established for federal programs (1973A:250).

Statewide planning. The states have instead directed their attention to statewide development planning, a process experiencing a resurgence in recent years. New York had a notable state planning process in the 1920s and other states took up the task in the New Deal period, but this activity waned in the years following World War II. A renewed interest in environmental concerns during the 1960s spurred states to pay more attention to statewide planning. Now all but Mississippi have some kind of state planning agency, twenty-seven of them part of the governor's office, eighteen assigned to some other agency, and four in a separate department. Some of these agencies get involved in land use matters, but others concentrate mainly on management planning (Council of State Governments, 1976:37).

Much of the state concern for land use is directed outside metropolitan areas, although obviously it responds to pressures resulting from urbanization. Thus, thirty states are engaged in coastal zone management supported by federal funds, twenty-six states are active in floodplain management, and twenty-two in wetlands management. Thirty-eight states deal with surface mining and thirty-four with power plant siting. Twenty-four states have some kind of a formal mechanism to coordinate land use related problems, nine states mandate local planning, and five have a permit system for certain types of developments, such as resort-area subdivisions (Council of State Governments, 1976:24-25).

As of the fall of 1975, seventeen states had completed growth plans or policy guidelines. Four of these states plus sixteen others have ongoing commissions and processes for state growth planning, and private commissions take on this task in five other states. After reviewing these activities, the Council of State Governments commented (1976:45-46): "Relatively few of these statements or studies have gone far beyond the recognition of need and the identification of some key components over which states may exercise initiative. In the handful of states that have developed sophisticated growth planning isn't very clear at the moment in most states, but the steadily increasing interest of state government in this field of concern will undoubtedly be felt in metropolitan areas in the years ahead.

The relationship between statewide land use planning and metropolitan planning isn't very clear at the moment in most states, but steadily increasing interest of state government in this field of concern will undoubtedly be felt in metropolitan areas in the years ahead.

STATE BODIES RELATED TO LOCAL GOVERNMENT

Community affairs agencies. About three-quarters of the states have established community affairs agencies (under various names) in order to improve their relations with local government and to help build local capacity. A good deal of their work involves provision of technical assistance and training to localities, particularly in land use planning under Section 701 but also in functional fields, such as housing and economic development. A number of community affairs agencies serve as conduits of federal funds, such as those under the Housing and Community Development Act of 1974, going primarily to smaller communities.

Some of the community affairs agencies get involved with major cities, but much of their work tends to be directed outside metropolitan areas to small places which have less capacity for planning and program management. Nevertheless, the state community affairs agency is a point of contact for the local governments of metropolitan areas, and particularly for regional councils.

Boundary commissions. Already mentioned are the state boundary commissions which exist in Alaska, Minnesota, Iowa, and Michigan. Mainly they deal with local proposals for annexation, incorporation, and formation of special districts. They haven't attempted to shepherd major local governmental reorganization in the manner of the Ontario Municipal Board (see Chapter 8, pp. 102, 103).

Special study commissions. From time to time, though, a state will set up a special study commission on local government. Thus, in 1969 the New Jersey legislature established the County and Municipal Government Commission, which proposed four alternative forms for county reorganization, and this set in motion forces leading to legislative adoption of county home rule in 1974. During this same period New York had a Temporary State Commission on the Power of Local Government. In Montana a new state constitution went into effect in 1973 with a mandate to modernize the local government system and to require voter review every ten years thereafter; as a follow up, the legislature set up a Commission on Local Government to assist localities and also allocated funds directly to local commissions. In this decade the Florida Commission on Local Government recommended a set of reforms which have gained legislative implementation, but similar study efforts in Ohio and California received no follow through.

STATE ROLES SUMMARIZED

When Roscoe Martin analyzed the role of the states in dealing with urban problems in the mid-1960s, he saw many shortcomings. For one thing he felt that "the states' concern for the vast new problems of metropolitan America, as measured by monetary contributions toward their alleviation, is quite casual" (1965:75). Part of the problem, he thought, was that states are suspended somewhere between total agrarianism and total urbanism, and this leaves them confused. They simply haven't given recognition to the complex problems of urban America as much as the national government has (1965:80-81).

In the intervening dozen years a lot has changed with state government. Reapportionment has given metropolitan residents fairer representation in the state legislature, in many cases with suburban representatives being the largest bloc. Governors have taken greater initiative in dealing with urban problems and have increased their staff capacity to do so. Creation of substate districts and regional councils has produced an instrument of local official communication and metropolitan cooperation. Some progress has occurred in making the state's monetary contribution more than just casual by increasing the amount of state aid to local government, though most states aren't seriously facing up to the problems of metropolitan fiscal disparity. And very few of them are displaying much interest in local government organization in metropolitan areas, an institutional framework which the states themselves created.

Roles of the National Government

Once upon a time American federalism was perceived as two-level arrangement consisting of the national government and the states. Local government was seen as subordinate to state government, and any dealings of the national government with localities were to be channeled through the states. No longer does this antique model describe the real world, for in actuality national, state, and local governments are all partners in the American federal system. Furthermore, multitudinous, direct national-local relationships occur, and during the last forty-five years the federal role in metropolitan areas has grown enormously, especially in the flow of federal aid to local government.

FINANCIAL ASSISTANCE

Grants-in-aid. This wasn't always the case. Federal aid started when the Morrill Act of 1862 authorized land grants to states to assist them in establishing colleges of agricultural and mechanical arts. The first money grant was for teaching material for the blind in 1879, and this was followed by other programs. All of them went to state governments, but in some instances the states could allocate part of the money to local governments.

The Great Depression of the 1930s forced a change in the practices of federalism because only the national government could mobilize the necessary resources to cope with economic disaster. The New Deal responses also changed the pattern of federal aid, bringing in local governments as direct recipients for the first time. Initially this came in the form of emergency assistance and then in the more permanent public housing program (1937). Airport assistance (1946) was the next major federal program directed to local government, though the states had the option of requiring the money to go through a state agency and about half of them did. Urban redevelopment grants (1949) came after World War II, and other programs followed until by 1960 local government could tap 25 different kinds of federal aid. By 1966, the number shot up to 68, and ten years later in 1976 local governments were direct beneficiaries of 85 federal assistance programs.

Most of these grants are for fairly limited purposes and are called categorical grants. During the last dozen years some efforts have been made toward consolidation into block grants encompassing a variety of activities in major functional fields. This has occurred for health (1966), law enforcement (1968), employment and training (1973), social services (1974), and housing and community development (1974). A new approach in the form of revenue sharing came in 1972. From all these sources, local government garnered $22 billion in federal funds in 1975, or 15 percent of local general revenue.

Taxes. The national government also takes money out of metropolitan areas in the form of taxes; naturally, for three-fourths of the taxpayers live there. Of total federal expenditures, 26 percent goes for national defense, 13 percent for other direct federal operations, 7 percent for interest payments, 16 percent for grants-in-aid, and 38 percent for direct benefit payments to individuals. These types of federal spending occur in precise locations so that money is returned to metropolitan areas, though in differing volume than when extracted and in different form.

Thus, through the combination of taxation and spending, the national government redistributes income. This occurs in three ways: between generations (the working population supporting the elderly retired); between income groups (the rich paying taxes to support job creation and income-support programs); and between geographic areas (transfers from one region to another and from one part of the metropolis to another). All three methods have an effect upon metropolitan fiscal disparity, and on the whole they lessen the disparity to the advantage of poor communities but the process is very uneven.

THE A-95 PROCESS

The federal regulation having the greatest effect upon metropolitan structure is Circular A-95 of the Office of Management and Budget (OMB), which we have come across several times. Chapter 6 related how it was set up by OMB's predecessor, the Bureau of the Budget, to carry out provisions of the Demonstration Cities and Metropolitan Development Act of 1966 and the Intergovernmental Cooperation Act of 1968.

When ACIR reviewed this system in 1973 after four years of operation, it found that the A-95 clearinghouses had brought about improved communications among local officials, leading to better local project coordination and thus indirectly saving public funds. Applications were reviewed without undue delay and without building up a large bureaucracy. On the negative side, ACIR reported that many local officials considered the A-95 process to be added red tape, that comments by the clearinghouse were almost never negative, and that anyway they were only advisory to the federal agencies. Furthermore, state-funded projects weren't part of the system, and the whole

A-95 process lacked cohesion (ACIR, 1973A:163-164). However, on one of these points, areawide clearinghouses rebutted that few negative comments came in because they had already resolved local disagreements.

A 1976 OMB Handbook, *A-95 What It is—How It Works*, acknowledges the limited purpose of the system (1976:4): "A-95 is an instrument for facilitating the needed coordination without encroaching on the constitutional domain of the States or the statutory responsibilities of Federal program administrators." Continuing, OMB explains that it is based upon the premise that communication is fundamental to coordination and that A-95 creates a climate for intergovernmental cooperation. The handbook admits that the recommendations, positive or negative, are not binding on federal officials.

ACIR looked at the A-95 process again in 1976 and reviewed a variety of evaluative studies (1977B:216-234). The commission concluded that some improvements had been made in the process, but governors, mayors, county executives, and managers weren't taking advantage of the opportunity to assert general policy concerns over functional interests. This stems in considerable measure from the lack of consideration given by federal agencies to A-95 comments in program implementation and the very limited staff OMB assigns to managing the system (1977B:250-251).

In its latest revision (January 1976), Circular A-95 covers 199 federal programs. Approximately 54 state and territorial and 550 areawide clearinghouses are in operation, including some 220 in metropolitan areas. Because Section 204 of the 1966 act gives preference to areawide agencies composed of or responsible to local elected officials, the A-95 process has been the strongest force behind the promotion of regional confederalism. This is why confederation, weak though it may be, is today the most common pattern of government in metropolitan areas.

FUNCTIONAL PLANNING AND COORDINATION

The national government, however, is a pluralistic institution, and not even OMB, situated in the Executive Office of the President, seems able to prevent the federal departments and Congress from pursuing other means of regional coordination. Thus, in recent years several functional programs have created opportunities for other areawide planning agencies to develop separately from the A-95 clearinghouses—though most of them can be assigned to a common areawide agency at state and local option. Chapter 6 (p. 75) mentioned metropolitan planning organizations for transportation and Section 208 water quality planning agencies, both frequently but not always a part of the A-95 clearinghouse agency. Here let's look at a couple of examples which are not.

Employment and training. From early 1969 until December 1973 Congress gave consideration to consolidating a number of diffuse federal-aid programs related to employment and training. An early proposal called for federal funds to be allocated and local programs conducted on a metropolitan basis, but pressures from city and county interests prevented this from happening. Thus, the Comprehensive Employment and Training Act of 1973 (CETA) allocates money to prime sponsors, which can be cities of 100,000 or more in population, counties with 100,000 outside eligible cities, and state government for the balance of the state. However, if local units combine into a consortium, they can get a little more money, thus providing a financial incentive to function on an areawide basis. Out of 445 state and local prime sponsors in the spring of 1977, 139 were consortia, almost all of them in metropolitan areas. (In addition, many states were using substate town-and-country districts for balance-of-state allocations.) Rarely was the areawide A-95 clearinghouse used as the CETA prime sponsor, though CETA applications do go through A-95 review. A major reason is that most clearinghouse agencies originally concentrated on physical development planning, and they aren't as heavily into human resource programs.

Health systems. One of the newest in the panorama of federally encouraged and mandated areawide planning enterprises is the network of health systems agencies. Functioning in a health service area designated by the secretary of health, education and welfare after consultation with the governor, a health systems agency sets goals, reviews health services, and develops an annual implementation plan for health services, personnel, and facilities. It also has the authority to review and approve or disapprove applications for federal programs funds for its area. The federal law, the National Health Planning and Resources Development Act of 1974, requires a minimum population of 500,000 for a health systems planning area, except where an entire state has less and in a few unusual circumstances. And the act gives preference to private nonprofit corporations, except that a regional body of elected officials or even a single unit of local general government may serve if its territory is identical to the health service area. As a result most of the health service areas are much larger than SMSAs and the substate planning districts previously created by the states, and almost nine out of ten are nonprofit corporations. Of the A-95 metropolitan clearinghouses, only the Metropolitan Council of Minnesota and four in Texas have taken on health systems planning, but even these have to have separate governing boards. There are also several separate regional health agencies under public official control and three counties and one city (Chicago) have gained this authority.

Observations. Other functional federal programs also have areawide planning mechanisms, such as law enforcement, economic development, resource conservation, air quality, and social services. As of 1976, 20 federal aid programs operate at the substate regional level and altogether have approximately 4,000 geographic program areas (ACIR, 1976A:106). In any particular metropolitan area, some of these will come under the jurisdiction of the regional council which is the A-95 clearinghouse agency, but others will go their separate ways.

The General Accounting Office delved into the situation in three substate areas and found widespread deviation from the idea of a single areawide organization to plan or to coordinate planning (Comptroller General, 1977:ii). This occurred because programs were initiated haphazardly over the years to satisfy particular needs and each program built its own constituency. Federal agencies often ignored the designated comprehensive planning agency and instead set up their own separate planning groups, sometimes of their own volition and sometimes because of legislative requirements. This despite encouragement from OMB to achieve coordinated planning.

OTHER RELATIONSHIPS

Services and law enforcement. Metropolitan residents are citizens of the United States, send representatives and senators to Congress, and vote in presidential elections. Conversely the national government has direct relationships with the people of metropolitan areas through the delivery of specific services and the enforcement of federal laws. Among these are social security, home mortgage insurance, environmental standards, equal opportunity laws, occupational health and safety standards, and many more. In such efforts, the national government extends its operations throughout the land and isn't merely a distant institution residing in Washington, D.C. It interrelates with other "extensions" of government within metropolitan areas, and all of these governments provide services to the people.

Information. The national government is also a gigantic dispenser of information. A lot of this is part of federal grant-in-aid administration, and federal preferences often shape the structure of local government. For example, special districts for soil conservation, public housing authorities, and regional councils as confederations of local officials all came about by federal encouragement. In the 1920s the Department of Commerce widely circulated a model zoning ordinance which set the standard for this method of land use control. Technical assistance guides continue to flow out of Washington.

FEDERAL ORGANIZATION

Three-fourths of the U.S. population reside in metropolitan areas, and their lives encompass the broad range of human existence. As numerous local agencies serve them so virtually every federal department has some impact upon metropolitan life. Yet, in a mostly urbanized nation, there is no national policy on metropolitanization.

Executive branch. In a way the Department of Housing and Urban Development has the broadest mandate for dealing with metropolitan problems, but it is only slowly emerging from its derivation in the Housing and Home Finance Agency. For HUD, planning still relates mainly to the physical, and community development barely gets into the social aspects of urban life. Local finance gets some attention from HUD, but when New York City got into fiscal difficulty, the Treasury Department got the assignment to work with it and has since created an urban finance unit. A department of cities or metropolitan areas HUD is not.

Other departments are even more strongly functionally oriented. The Department of Health, Education and Welfare administers a raft of programs bearing the departmental titles. Most of its grant-in-aid programs go to the states, and it displays very little understanding that many of the local service systems it helps finance are metropolitan in scope. The Labor Department keeps track of labor market areas roughly corresponding to metropolitan areas, but the local employment and training programs it funds aren't aligned to plan for the whole metropolis unless coincidentally a local consortium of metropolitan scope happens to emerge. As we saw, areawide transportation and water quality management are somewhat more attuned to the whole metropolis, but the Department of Transportation and the Environmental Protection Agency tend to go their separate ways.

Supposedly the Executive Office of the President pulls together the diverse forces of the federal departments, but the Office of Management and Budget, which has this task, assigns only one person to handle the A-95 process and has no staff delving deeper into how the national government might be better harnessed to contribute to long-lasting metropolitan solutions.

Congress. Even more functionally specialized, Congress is not well equipped to understand and deal with metropolitan problems. The legislative committees focus on specific programs or problems in particular functional fields, but a general subject like metropolitan organization doesn't fit into any niche. To be sure, intergovernmental relations subcommittees hold hearings on metropolitan issues from time to time, but there is no across-the-board, sustaining interest comparable to what Congress gives the national economy and the federal budget through the Joint Economic Committee and the Budget Committees. Congress simply hasn't a good focus on the metropolis as the dominant mode of settlement in the United States.

ACIR. The only agency in Washington with a continuous concern for metropolitan problems and governmental organization is the Advisory Commission on Intergovernmental Relations. Created by Congress in 1959, ACIR is a bipartisan body composed of twenty-six members, nine from the national government, fourteen representing state and local governments, and three citizens at large; both legislative and executive branches of the federal, state, and local government are represented. Its task is to monitor the operation of the American federal system and to recommend improvements. The numerous ACIR reports quoted in this book are evidence of the deep and sustaining interest which the commission has displayed in metropolitan issues. ACIR recommends and tries to persuade, but implementation depends upon others. Many different states and local governments have utilized model legislation which the commission has drafted, and Congress and federal executive departments often take its advice. ACIR is a worthy servant of American federalism.

The spirit which ACIR conveys is sometimes called "cooperative federalism," emphasizing the importance of shared responsibility and joint endeavors. As Luther Gulick has affirmed (1962:129), "all 'extensions' of American government must take a hand in dealing with our rising metropolitan problems. No one of the partners can do it alone." The entire federal system must be mobilized, and the whole citizenry, functioning as individuals and in various associations. This is the way a pluralistic, democratic society seeks solutions to its problems.

PART III

BASIS FOR FUTURE REFORM

Chapter 11

THEORY OF LOCAL FEDERALISM

Practical adaptation has been the dominant approach utilized in the United States as we have adjusted our local government institutions to the service needs of the expanding metropolis. More drastic structural change has occurred now and then but this has been the exception. This evolutionary course has been based primarily upon year by year responses to specific challenges, and it hasn't derived from any clearly expressed theory. Nevertheless, certain philosophical ideas and assumed values underlie the adaptive means utilized, and during the past twenty years the pattern of multiple local governments has gained a rationale in the development of public choice theory. Furthermore, advocates of structural reform have articulated some basic theories for the changes they recommend.

Theories matter, whether stated or left unsaid, for what we think affects how we act. It is important, therefore, to have a firm theoretical foundation for any future reforms we undertake. Thus, I want to lay out my own ideas. But before doing so, let me review the main contemporary theories, presented in previous chapters, and describe their practical effects and extent of acceptance.

Four Theories of Metropolitan Organization

THE THEORIES

Four principal theories are used to justify the existing pattern of local governmental organization in metropolitan areas or to advocate reorganization. The patterns they favor are these: unification, federation, confederation, and multiplicity.

Unification is the course recommended by those who believe that the metropolis is one large community with a common local economy, a complex nexus of social interaction, an interdependency of institutions, a broad array of mutual interests. Many of the service needs of the metropolis, such as water supply, transportation, and others, require areawide action, and a proliferation of numerous local governments confuses administration and fails to provide adequate services. Therefore, a single government is needed for the whole metropolitan area so that citizens may express their common purposes and achieve joint solution to the problems they all face.

Federation is proposed by persons who agree that areawide government is needed but who also insist that there are local communities within the metropolis with their individual characteristics and special needs. Just as there is a need to centralize some functions so also there is a need to decentralize others. Thus, the formal structure of local government within a metropolitan area should have both an areawide unit responsible directly to the people of the whole metropolis and also local community units responsive to the will of persons living in various subareas. Between the two can be a rational division of functions.

Confederation is the arrangement favored by people who recognize the necessity of dealing with the entire metropolis as well as its local communities, but they propose that the areawide organization be under the control of local governments, which would join together for this purpose, rather than have elected areawide officials. They come to this approach because of doubts that structured federation can ever be achieved and also because of a preference for voluntary, interlocal cooperation.

Multiplicity of local governments, all basically co-equal, is, however, the dominant pattern in metropolitan areas, having come about through evolutionary change. Advocates of *public choice theory* say this is a good arrangement because intergovernmental competition enhances performance. Where some of the overlapping jurisdictions are larger than others, there can be a sorting out of functional assignments based upon economy of scale and each function can be performed at the level achieving the greatest efficiency and responsiveness.

PRACTICAL EFFECTS AND PUBLIC ACCEPTANCE

Unification has been proposed many more times than it has been adopted. This is because voters, when they have an opportunity to express their will, have indicated that they favor continuation of a more pluralistic governmental structure for the metropolitan area. They feel there is more to gain in keeping present arrangements than in centralizing authority in a single, areawide government.

It seems to me that to the extent the voters oppose centralization of *all* services, they make a sound judgment that not everything can be best performed on an areawide basis. We will get into this subject in depth in the chapter after next, but here we can note that many activities of local government can be handled better on a small scale. In its place decentralization is as valid as centralization, depending upon the nature of the service. Moreover, centralization of all services runs the risk of producing excessive concentration of power in a jurisdiction so large that the average citizen is far removed from the elected officials.

Where federation has been proposed and put to a vote, it has most often been perceived and opposed as centralization, or metropolitanism as opponents derisively call it. And it is, in the sense that it creates a metropolitan institution where none previously existed. Moreover, many of the proposals have been quite ambitious in the tasks they would assign the metropolitan government, often going well beyond the bare minimum produced by a more cautious definition of what must be performed areawide. As proposed by the Committee for Economic Development (1970), federation would take the form of a strict two-tier structure and would break up the central city by dividing its functions between an areawide government and a number of community governments. This prospective abolition of a known institution, supported by many vested interests, by an unknown arrangement generates a lot of opposition and little support. A more asymmetrical approach, such as three tiers for the suburbs (municipal, county, areawide), two tiers for the central city (city and areawide), might gain more support, but this arrangement has rarely been articulated by local studies and reform proposals.

Public choice theory as it has developed in recent years recognizes the need for some areawide action as well as local activities but would have this come about through cooperative agreements and specialized areawide agencies rather than by creating a strong multipurpose unit for the entire metropolis. Moreover, at the local level this theory sees positive values in numerous special districts. What this leads to is dominance by functional specialists and ineffective means for achieving the interconnection between closely related services. The view of the whole is lost for the total metropolis and for smaller communities as well. Furthermore, public choice theory ducks the issue of gross social and economic inequities in the existing arrangements within metropolitan areas by deferring redistributive measures to national action rather than designing areawide means for achieving greater equity.

Confederation tries to produce wholeness through a council of governments while retaining the integrity of the multiplicity of local governmental units, but this voluntary approach creates a powerless vehicle for dealing with crucial areawide problems. But if a confederation could somehow gain greater authority, it would run the risk of being unaccountable power because officials elected at one level would be making decisions at another level, oftentimes with their own vested interests at stake. Confederation produces no metropolitan-wide political process, no leadership chosen to deal with areawide issues, and this absence makes it harder to develop the sense of metropolitan community to go along with the feelings for local communities.

None of these theories is wholly erroneous. All of them contain measures of the truth, but they suffer from the indicated shortcomings. What is needed theoretical foundation which extracts the best elements and synthesizes them creatively into a more serviceable approach. I believe that this can be achieved through a theory of local federalism.

Local Federalism

Federalism is a mode of governmental organization usually conceived as defining a particular relationship between a national government and the governments of distinct territories, such as states, provinces, or regions into which the nation is divided. Because this arrangement describes a number of nations, existing and past, scholars have developed general theories of federalism—always influenced by the American federal union, which is the longest enduring federal system in the world. Therefore, it is useful to review the theory of federalism in general and American federalism in particular before applying these ideas to metropolitan areas.

FEDERALISM IN GENERAL

In a study of what federal government is, K.C. Wheare set forth the essence of the federal principle as "the method of dividing powers so that general and regional governments are each, within a sphere, co-ordinate and independent" (1964:10). Each citizen is subject to two governments, but that alone doesn't make the system federal because this can occur when the regional governments are subordinate to the general government. It is their coordinate status, each having independence within its own sphere, that makes it a federal system. If this principle is to apply in practice, says Wheare, it is necessary that "both general and regional governments must each have under its own independent control financial resources sufficient to perform its exclusive functions. Each must be financially co-ordinate with the other" (1964:93).

Rufus Davis reinforces these ideas by emphasizing three features of relative power and authority possessed by a member of a federal union: (1) independence within its ambit of power, (2) financial means to be master, and (3) political ability to be master. He realizes that in exercising its powers, each level impacts upon the other so that total independence doesn't exist. "In one sense, and one sense only is the 'independence' of all units within all federal systems indistinguishable in degree or kind—the mutually irrevocable freedom of each unit to initiate those measures and pursue those ends it believes to be within its ambit of power" (1967:15). Control over its own financial resources is an essential part of this freedom to act. As to political power, Davis emphasizes the role of political parties as instruments through which politicians of each level influence each other. That is to say, federalism has relationships between political actors as well as governments.

Another perspective is added by William S. Livingston who emphasizes federalism as a sociological phenomenon. "The essence of federalism lies not in the institutional or constitutional structure but in the society itself. Federal government is a device by which the federal qualities of society are articulated and protected" (1967:37). Society is diverse and where these diversities are grouped geographically rather than along functional lines, that society is federal.

Looking at nation-states, William H. Riker sees federalism as "the main alternative to empire as a technique for aggregating larger areas under one government" (1967:53). The federal constitution is produced through a political bargain. The politicians who want to expand their territorial control offer concessions to the rulers of constituent units. The politicians who accept the bargain give up some independence for the sake of union, which they perceive as offering benefits to them. Both sides gain something and therefore the participants are willing to make the federal bargain.

For Daniel J. Elazar, federalism deals with the concentration, diffusion, and sharing of power in political and social systems.

> Federal principles grow out of the idea that free men can freely enter into lasting yet limited political arrangements to achieve common ends and protect certain rights while preserving their respective integrities. As the very ambiguity of the term "federal" reveals, federalism is concerned simultaneously with the diffusion of political power in the name of freedom and its concentration on behalf of energetic government (1971:3).

Although federal union might be expressed in a constitution, it is more than a legal document or a set of fixed relationships. As Richard H. Leach indicates (1970:1-2), "Federalism is concerned with process and by its very nature is a dynamic, not a static concept. In operation, it requires a willingness to cooperate across governmental lines and to exercise restraint and forebearance in the interest of the entire nation."

AMERICAN FEDERALISM

After the framers of the U.S. Constitution completed their work and produced a federal union to replace the failing confederation of states, they had to explain and sell it to the people. This they did in the serial publication of essays later collected as *The Federalist.* In the forty-sixth of these James Madison gave a succinct definition of American federalism: "The federal and State governments are in fact but different agents and trustees of the people, constituted with different powers, and designed for different purposes" (n.d.:304-5). Forty years later Alexis de Tocqueville made a similar observation when he indicated that the American citizen is a member of "two distinct social structures, connected, and, as it were, encased one within the other" (n.d.:66). He also pointed out that in contrast to all previous confederations, the American federal union permitted the national government to enact and enforce its own laws and levy taxes directly upon the citizens and not be dependent upon the states for law enforcement and tax collection. Yet, the states could enact and enforce their own laws and collect taxes for themselves.

Althouth in a constitutional sense local government is subordinate to state government, operationally it has considerable independence within its ambit of power and the financial means and political ability to be its own master. So we really have a de facto kind of three-level federalism in the United States. This was understood by Thomas Jefferson, who wanted to extend the concept to a fourth level—wards or townships:

> We should thus marshal our government into, 1, the general federal republic, for all concerns foreign and federal; 2, that of the State, for what relates to our citizens exclusively; 3, the county republics for the duties and concerns of the county; and 4, the ward republics, for the small, and yet numerous and interesting concerns of the neighborhood; and in government, as well as in every other business of life, it is by division and subdivision of duties alone, that all matters, great and small, can be managed to perfection. And the whole is cemented by giving to every citizen, personally, a part in the administration of the public affairs (Padover, 1943:290).

A division of concerns was also highlighted in *The Federalist.* Part political philosophy and part pragmatic justification for the new constitution, this document stressed the many powers residing in the states even though the national government was gaining more power. Madison (n.d.:304-305) speculated that "the first and most natural attachment of the people will be to the governments of their respective states." However, if "the people should in the future become more partial to the federal than to the State governments, the change can only result from such manifest and irresistible proofs of a better administration." In other words, the assignment of functions is changeable, not locked into the system forever.

As the nation grew, as more states joined the union and numerous local governments formed, and as the powers of government expanded at all levels, a notion developed that we have three distinct governmental layers in our federal system. In the 1950s there was quite a bit of talk about sorting out which function could be best handled at each level and reassigning functions to the appropriate level. Morton Grodzins (1966:8) attacked this view of a three-layer cake of government where the institutions and functions of each level were considered separately.

> In fact, the American system of government as it operates is not a layer cake at all. It is not three layers of government, separated by a sticky substance or anything else. Operationally, it is a marble cake, or what the British call a rainbow cake. No important activity of government in the United States is the exclusive province of one of the levels, not even what may be regarded as the most national of national functions, such as foreign relations; not even the most local of local functions, such as police protection and park maintenance.

His studies developed detailed descriptions of how activities within various functional fields are handled by different levels, sometimes alone and sometimes in connection with another level, but for the function as a whole all levels are involved in some way or other.

> If you ask the question, "Who does what?" the answer is in two parts. One is that officials of all "levels" do everything together. The second is that where one level is preponderant in a given activity, the other makes its influence felt *politically* (here the voice of the peripheral power units are heard most strongly) or through *money* (here the central view is most influential) or through *professional associations*.

Money is the sugar which sweetens the marble cake, and the last forty years have seen a substantial increase in intergovernmental financial transfers, as documented in Chapter 5. Mainly this has been the broader geographic areas (national and state) channeling funds to the smaller areas (the states and localities). With money go conditions, and, while not the same as hierarchical commands, these at best complicate the relationships between the three levels and at worst threaten local governments with a subordinate status. Although ultimately their political power enables local jurisdictions to preserve their independence, fiscal interdependency is now very much a part of American federalism.

Along these lines Elazar calls upon us to resist the idea of American federalism as a form of decentralized power. "Decentralization," he points out, "implies the existence of central authority, a central government that can decentralize or recentralize as it desires." Instead he insists we should think of our arrangement as a noncentralized political system where "power is so diffused that it cannot be legitimately centralized or concentrated without breaking the structure and spirit of the constitution." In this arrange-

ment "there are no higher or lower power centers, only larger or smaller
arenas of political decision-making and action." So he urges us to discard the
imagery of higher and lower levels and instead to think of different arenas of
decision-making and the lines of communication between them
(1975B:23-25). This is similar to Luther Gulick's comment, quoted in the
previous chapter, that we have three "extensions" of government—federal,
state, and local—and that all three function and are intertwined at the same
level, where people live and work.

METROPOLITAN APPLICATION

Many of the attributes of federalism could be applied to the governmental
structure of metropolitan areas, not with precise duplication of the patterns
of national, state, and local governments, but with many similarities in
principle.

Under the concept of local federalism a metropolitan area would have two
or more coordinate arenas for government—areawide, central city and suburban county, city neighborhood units and suburban municipalities; and each
would be independent within its ambit of power. Each arena would have a
direct relationship with citizens in two ways: serving them and being accountable to them through an electoral process. Citizens would be subject to and
served by two or three local general-purpose governments. These governments
would be different agents, designed for different purposes, constituted with
different powers but all of them trustees of the same people.

Independence is the crucial issue, and to be realistic it will be relative
independence, not absolute. All local units derive their legal authority from
the state, so they are all subordinate jurisdictions in a constitutional sense.
But with enactment of broad, general enabling legislation and provisions for
local home rule, counties, municipalities, New England towns, and the strong
variety of townships all have substantial powers. While these powers can be
revoked, historical experience and a projection of future political realities
suggest that they won't be terminated capriciously. By state law the same
degree of permanence could be given to an areawide government and also to
neighborhood governments, though possibly with a more limited range of
substantive authority for both of them, the largest and smallest areas of the
metropolis.

Since each local governmental unit derives its authority from an outside
source, the state, none is subordinate to any other local unit. If neighborhood government were set up by state law, it would fit into a system of local
federalism. If it were established through delegation of power from a city or
county to its neighborhoods, the resulting units would be legally subordinate
to the broader jurisdiction, thereby having less independence, but politically
they still might function within the spirit of federalism. Where an areawide

government is set up through joint action of counties and municipalities, it would be a confederation, not an expression of local federalism. So any areawide government must have an independent source of authority, either from the state or from the people through a referendum, if there is to be true federalism in the metropolitan area.

Adequate financial resources must be available if independence is to be meaningful. This requires that at least part of a unit's funds must derive from one or more revenue sources which the unit is authorized to tap for itself. This might consist of direct taxes, it might be shared revenues as long as the local unit is assured of receiving and can spend as it chooses, or it might be a combination. Grants-in-aid and contributions could be other sources of funds, but if these are the sole means of support, the unit has very little independence. Thus, an areawide government under local federalism must have taxing authority, either directly or through a guaranteed, shared-revenue arrangement. The same holds true for neighborhood government, but for neighborhoods the primary source might be a revenue-sharing arrangement which draws on a geographically broader tax base (citywide, county, metropolitan) and redistributes funds to neighborhoods on a needs basis. So fiscal interdependence would be very much present in local federalism.

The division of responsibility within local federalism would look like Grodzins' marble cake. Each arena of action would be performing specific activities in various functional fields (such as health, law enforcement, parks and recreation), and all arenas would be involved in virtually every function. Generally there would be a sorting out of activities in accordance with which area can best handle them, but this would be constantly shifting and the pattern wouldn't necessarily look the same from one metropolis to another. Since activities for a particular function would be operating in different sizes of geographic areas, articulation of a total service system would be necessary for each functional field, and this would be expressed through interlocal cooperation, not hierarchical authority. However, it's conceivable that the metropolitan unit would have sufficient control of federal, state, and areawide funds for a particular function to have some leverage over other local units and in that manner achieve effective service systems. Just this kind of leverage is what federal and state agencies apply as they administer grants-in-aid.

And as in the broader federal system, a lot of political bargaining would also occur in local federalism. Much of this would take place in decision-making processes where approval by two or more jurisdiction is required. The bargainers would be elected and appointed officials, political parties, civic associations, interest groups, private individuals, that is, the same types of persons who enter into bargaining between national, state, and local governments. One difference, though, is the possibility that local bargainers in metropolitan federalism can appeal to the outside authority of state and national governments to side with them, for both these broader extensions enter the scene when they supply money and in addition the state is the source of power of all the local units.

The bargaining process could also be present in establishing a system of local federalism in the first place as local political and civic leaders endeavor to fashion two or three sizes of arenas for local government and work out an initial division of responsibility and financing arrangements. This echoes Riker's observation that a federal system is almost always produced as a result of a political bargain.

Looking at these dynamics underscores Livingston's emphasis upon federalism as a sociological phenomenon. Thus, local federalism would express the diversity which exists within the metropolitan area. The people would accept their differences and honor them but would also acknowledge their common values. Social pluralism would have political manifestations in governmental units organized in several sizes of geographic subareas. Communities within communities and governments within governments would be the pattern. Local federalism of this sort would champion wholeness within each arena, given expression in general-purpose units rather than a lot of functional special districts.

Local federalism in metropolitan areas would therefore be more than a particular kind of governmental structure. It would express the relationship of interdependence, the process of working toward mutual solutions of common problems. It would have intermingled governments to articulate the needs of the areawide community, the neighborhood communities, and intermediate-sized communities. Local federalism would bring small and large together into an interrelated whole.

RELATIONSHIP TO OTHER THEORIES

In relation to other theories of metropolitan organization, local federalism agrees with the contention of the unifiers that an areawide perspective is needed for solving metropolitan problems, but it disagrees that a single, consolidated government is the answer. Yes, an areawide government is required for certain tasks, but not to do everything. Other arenas for governmental action are also necessary.

Thus, local federalism joins public choice theorists in their appreciation of decentralization and a pluralistic mode of organization, but it parts company with them in their aversion to areawide general government and their admiration for special districts. Local federalism rejects the functional approach and throws its weight to two or three sizes of elected, general-purpose governments in the metropolitan area. (Reasons for this preference for general-purpose government are spelled out in the next chapter, pp. 162-164.)

The proponents of confederation also favor general government instead of special districts and thus advocate an "umbrella multijurisdictional organization" to deal with areawide issues. This would be under the control of local governments' representatives, but local federalism wants the areawide government to be elected directly by the people. It is precisely this point that distinguishes federalism from confederalism.

As the semantic similarity suggests, federation is a structural expression of federalism. The reason I risk confusion by using two separate though similar terms is that metropolitan federation has been associated with a fairly rigid structural approach, especially the CED proposal for two-tier government which would break up the existing central city. In contrast, local federalism emphasizes the relationships and processes of intermingled governments and indicates that this can take varied configurations: two sizes of governmental arenas; three sizes; perhaps two sizes in part of the metropolis, three in other parts; even a fourth arena for the largest metropolitan regions. It can build on and adapt existing units without designing a completely new structure, thus being as pragmatic as the broader American federalism which has continuously changed since 1789. Local federalism stresses the spirit of having several arenas of government serving as different agents for the same people and allows this to take whatever form is most suitable for a particular metropolitan area.

Self-Interest and Social Justice

I can talk about local federalism, but the people of the metropolis have been mostly disinterested in or opposed to any kind of major change in the local governmental structure. Compared to the reforms proposed, a majority seems to favor the present pattern of multiplicity.

In a book entitled *Political Change in the Metropolis* (1976), John H. Harrigan argues that the whole course of urban politics is determined by sets of biases held by various participants. He maintains that the "multicentered metropolis" developed and is retained because it is biased in favor of three main, dominating groups: suburbanites who want to keep out the poor and racial minorities; land speculators, real estate developers, and large retailing enterprises who profit from uncontrolled sprawl; and functional fiefdoms, particularly special districts operating quite independently of the electorate (1976:191-192). In sum, special interests preserve the status quo.

The role of self-interest in politics has long been apparent. As George Washington told a committee of Congress in 1778, "A small knowledge of human nature will convince us, that, with far the greatest part of mankind, interest is the governing principle; and that, almost every man, is more or less under its influence" (Padover, 1963:41). *The Federalist* dwelt upon self-interest extensively and claimed that the federal system helped contain it by preventing excessive concentration of power. But what these renowned authors didn't acknowledge was that the division of authority can also work to the advantage of special interests. This is Harrigan's point.

Are we then in a Catch 22, no-win situation? No, I think not, unless we seek perfectionistic solutions. For along with self-seeking, people are also self-giving, and the two attributes are intertwined in human nature. Self-giving is expressed in family relationships, in friendships, and in private charity, and it enters public life in a quest for social justice.

In our society a commitment to social justice has religious and philosophical roots. Both roots affirm that each human being has intrinsic value and that persons have a moral obligation to treat one another with respect and concern. So too, society as a whole should function justly.

Because suburbanites and city dwellers have a concern for social justice, they are oftentimes willing to support measures which go beyond narrowly construed self-interest. Thus, progressive taxation levies a higher rate on the rich than on the poor, and numerous public programs benefit the needy, paid for by those better-off. But because metropolitan inhabitants are also motivated by self-interest, most of them place limits on how far they will sacrifice to benefit others. I am firmly convinced that a commitment to social and fiscal equity is within those limits and that a governmental system can be designed within a metropolis to produce greater equity. Not absolute equality, not complete population heterogeneity, mixing together all social classes and races in every neighborhood, but certainly a fuller measure of equity than now prevails.

The federal principle provides a governmental structure for handling the competing demands of self-interest and social justice. Both factors will be present in all arenas of dicision-making and action—metropolitan, city and county, neighborhood and small municipality. Just as self-interest has used local control of zoning for its own advantage, it will try to benefit from areawide government, but if this unit is under democratic control, the broad electorate can prevent special interest domination. The redistributive potential of a metropolitan tax base can be mobilized to promote greater equity, and the intimate scale of neighborhood government can make services more humane. Minority groups, which have opposed metropolitan unification because it would reduce their political gains within the central city, will find that under local federalism they can retain control or influence over many important local activities, including the police, while benefitting from the equalizing attributes of areawide taxes and areawide financing of capital intensive facilities.

Division of governmental power prevents excessive concentration of authority in a central government, and the dynamics of a federal system provide a check on abuses occurring because of factional control of one of the smaller units. The ongoing relationships between the several arenas, sometimes expressed in open conflict and sometimes in cooperative endeavors, helps the broader public interest to emerge. Although local federalism offers no surefire guarantee of success, on the whole it holds a stronger possibility for balancing self-interest and social justice than either a single consolidated government or multitudinous local governments without an areawide unit.

Chapter 12

COMMUNITIES AND LOCAL GENERAL GOVERNMENTS

Local federalism sees a metropolis consisting of communities within communities. It favors units of local general government for such communities of different scale. These and related concepts need more elaboration.

Basic Concepts

COMMUNITY

Community is an elusive concept, and there are almost as many definitions as there are social scientists and philosophers who have tried to define community.

Along these lines a recent social science panel of the National Research Council, seeking to determine the significance of community in the metropolitan environment, defined the term in this manner (1974:2): "A community consists of a population carrying on a collective life through a set of institutional arrangements. Common interests and norms of conduct are implied in this definition." Acknowledging different usages, the National Research Council panel indicated: "One use of the word community then is to refer to a grouping of people who live close to one another and are united by common interests and mutual aid. . . . On the other hand, the term may be used in the broader sense to refer to any population that carries on its daily life through a common set of institutions." The first usage suggests a fairly small population possessing considerable solidarity; the second could be much larger in size and would feature division of labor and interdependence. But the panel also noted (1974:3) that "community is used increasingly to refer to interest groups whose common activities are relatively independent of location factors." Thus, the National Research Council panel concentrated upon institutional arrangements and offered two spatial concepts at different scales and one concept not tied to particular space.

Philosopher Lawrence Haworth has taken a different tack and has emphasized another aspect of community (1963:86): "In any genuine community there are shared values: the members are united through the fact that they fix on some object as preeminently valuable. And there is a joint effort, involving all members of the community, by which they give overt expression to their mutual regard for that objective." The value they share may be a goal they consider worth achieving, a memory of mutual heritage, a common religious faith (1963:20). Whatever they are, the common values give a characteristic quality to the people's view of the world and their place in it. But this isn't a passive existence, for members of a community undertake joint endeavors to express the values uniting them.

Sociologist Robert Nisbet adds yet another attribute of the concept of community (1966:47): "Community is founded on man conceived in his wholeness rather than in one or another of the roles, taken separately, that he may hold in the social order." This distinguishes a community from an association dealing with special concerns or interests, such as economic, recreational, political, or social service matters.

Drawing upon all of these definitions, I would emphasize shared values, interdependence, and wholeness. These attributes might be manifested by people living within a particular locale, such as a housing project, a neighborhood, a suburban municipality, a city, but they might also be expressed by people bound together by common traits, such as race, ethnicity, or religion. Under most circumstances a particular interest group—business, trade, professional, labor, environmentalist, government reformist—wouldn't constitute a community, but where that interest dominates its members lives, as occurs from time to time in social movements, a kind of community emerges.

In this book I am primarily interested in spatially located communities. Each resident of a metropolis occupies space, but not everybody feels a sense of community contained within a neighborhood, the city, or even the whole metropolis. Yet many do. Perhaps for a few, the neighborhood is the preeminent experience in their lives and they can be considered urban villagers, but most metropolitan residents are part of more than one community in the spatial sense and may also be part of one or more communities without a precise geographical base, such as a racial, ethnic, or religious community. Therefore, rarely would a person live in a single community of absolute wholeness, encompassing all values and activities of life, but the several communities a person belongs to can provide a considerable measure of wholeness.

For me, the sense of community is a necessary ingredient for satisfactory living in the metropolis. Therefore, the institutional arrangements of local government should build upon and reinforce the spatially located communities, should enhance common values, and should contribute to wholeness of life.

POLITY

In pluralistic urban society people have diverse values and usually are members of more than one community. In a particular spatially located community, the residents will reflect this diversity but will also have common values, not the least of which is a concern for the social and physical environment they share and the personal relationships occurring in that locale. They will be conscious of their mutual interests and will seek an organized means to work toward common objectives, such as preservation of order, maintenance and improvement of environmental conditions, provision of public services, and cooperative problem solving. They may enter into a process of decision-making and institute some kind of organization to carry out these decisions. Officials of the organization may be authorized to take actions in behalf of the community, maybe even to enforce standards of conduct upon community members. In this manner, the people are associated in a political community, sometimes referred to as a polity.

The term "polity" is gaining increased usage but with varied emphases, just as the concept of community has several meanings. In personal conversation, Norton Long recalls the Greek idea of the city and the key role of citizens, and he stresses common purposes and citizen identification with the city as a polity, or with the neighborhood as a polity. York Willbern speaks of polity as a state of consciousness of people who perceive themselves as a political community. Daniel J. Elazar describes polity as a system of governance which may involve a territory (such as a city polity) or may not (such as an ethnic group polity). Milton Kotler thinks of polity as a community whose purpose is self-government.

Combining elements of all these perceptions, we can look upon polity, or political community, as a people sharing common identity and a governing system to which they relate as citizens. This usually gains expression in some form of government.

Which comes first, a political community as self-identity and a set of relationships or government as an organization? It can happen either way.

Historian Daniel J. Boorstin has noted (1965:65) that often in the course of settlement of this land, "communities existed here before there were governments to care for public needs or to enforce public duties." He cites the Pilgrims aboard the Mayflower about to land unexpectedly in Plymouth outside the jurisdiction of any government. Before disembarking the leaders adopted the Mayflower Compact to set up a government for the already existing community. So also in westward expansion, settlement frequently preceded the establishment of formal government. The people so associated adopted their own set of rules and processes for dealing with offenders. They functioned by majority rule and officers usually had brief tenure. This occurred as settlers burst beyond the Appalachian Mountains into Kentucky and the Northwest Territory, and then across the prairie into the Great Plains. It happened in the gold rush communities which sprang up almost overnight. Even persons journeying in wagon trains along the Santa Fe, Oregon, and California trails formed rudimentary governments to manage their temporary communities and to provide rules of conduct.

Yet the opposite can also occur. Government can form first, and then as people associate around the governmental process, their sense of a political community emerges. Again looking back to early settlement, some cities were chartered and the first officials appointed before streets were laid out and houses built, and the preexistence of government provided a social foundation for settlers coming from varied backgrounds. A township or county, plotted on a map when it was rural territory but now has become urbanized, forms a political community because people relate together around a long-established governmental institution even though the boundaries might not coincide precisely with what a sociologist would describe as a "natural social community." Similarly a central city long ago surpassed by metropolitan growth remains as a political community because of the processes, services, laws, and institutional arrangements that revolve around city government.

In a metropolitan area, a person is usually part of more than one spatially located, social community: the neighborhood community, the city or suburban county community, the metropolitan community. Likewise, people are also part of two or more polities, or political communities, whether or not they are formally organized as governments.

GENERAL GOVERNMENT AND CITIZENSHIP

In my view it is desirable for these political communities of different scale to take form in units of general government. In this regard, Luther Gulick has given us an excellent definition of what general government is (1962:84):

The essential character of "general government" is the bringing together under a single decision-making structure of a considerable number of activities which are directed toward separate and identifiable special goals, generally using separate professional skills and requiring an allocation to each of money and other limited community resources. In addition, there must be a democratically responsible policy-making organ and a feeling on the part of the local community that the agency is "general" rather than "special" and there is no other general agency with the same jurisdiction.

Paul Ylvisaker also believes that each geographic area should have a general government "covering the whole range of governmental functions rather than a partial one related to only particular functions." Meaningful choices of priorities can come only when a full range of alternatives is presented in one setting, and the countervailing power of competitive interests can occur as a check on the desire of each functional speciality to gain supremacy. The citizen as a whole person needs to be drawn into a government which is comprehensive. Furthermore, concludes Ylvisaker, a governmental unit for a particular area is more likely to be viable and survive if it has a variety of responsibilities (1959:34-36).

There is no absolute list of functions which a governmental unit must handle in order to be considered a "general government," though it does need basic authority to adopt and carry out policies and to appropriate and spend money. The precise tasks will vary with the size of the area, for a neighborhood general government would undertake quite a different set of activities than an areawide general government. Regardless, there is a "critical mass," subjective in nature, which gives people an idea that the government is general rather than special purpose.

Where governmental units specialize, people tend to relate to them as consumers seeking a particular service—water from the water authority, fire protection from the fire district, books on loan from the library district. Missing is the role of people as citizens who are not merely subjects of laws but who through their participation can influence governmental decisions and can choose who the officials will be. As Elazar has emphasized (1976:3):

> Particularly in a republic and particularly in a democratic republic, those who share in the polity cannot be less than citizens if the polity itself is to survive in its chosen form. Consumers, at most, pick and choose among goods offered them by others, in whose offering they have no real share. How different such a course is from that of citizens who must share in determining the activities of government as well as utilizing its products.

Looking at the broader American republic, Long indicates (1976:13): "We are at once citizens of the nation, the states and their local governments. To the extent this citizenship is more than a legal formality, it implies a loyalty, a loyalty of varying degrees to three distinct though by no means separate political communities." This idea can be translated to the metropolitan scene by saying we are at once citizens of our neighborhood, our city or county, and the whole metropolis. As members of political communities of these different scales, we need a general government in each through which we can perform our citizenship responsibilities.

LIBERTY AND DEMOCRACY

Community emphasizes the collective life of the people, and general government gives the political community an institutional form. This is good and proper but has dangers if carried to an extreme. Persons in power, or seeking power, can make community into an absolute value and, claiming to speak for the "good of the community" or purporting to express the "general will," they might repress dissent and inhibit individual freedom.

In this century we have seen just such occurrences in totalitarian regimes where dictators have used a distorted idea of community as a justification for their despotic practices. On a less repressive scale, local leaders sometimes use coercive tactics to press for unanimity in order to "benefit the community" without reckoning the cost to some individuals. Planners and administrators from time to time push projects they maintain are in the total community's best interest without taking into account how specific persons might be harmed.

The antidotes to these distortions of the community idea are liberty and democracy. "The individual is indisputably the original, the first fact of liberty," wrote Woodrow Wilson (Padover, 1963:119). "There is no such thing as corporate liberty. Liberty belongs to the individual, or it does not exist." The founders of the American nation believed this, too. Liberty for them was an inalienable right, a blessing to secure for themselves and all posterity. Their belief gained concrete expression in the Bill of Rights, adopted to preserve essential freedoms for individuals and to offer protection against arbitrary power of government.

Especially crucial is the First Amendment which provides freedom of speech and the press, free exercise of region, the right of assembly (and by implication the right of association), and the right to petition government for redress of grievances. This amendment, the rest of the Bill of Rights, the Fourteenth Amendment's equal protection clause, and all the other rights enumerated in the U.S. Constitution place strict limits on the powers of government and should apply to neighborhood government, metropolitan government, and the governments for areas of intermediate size. We should never forget this.

If these and any other governments are to be just, their powers must be derived from the consent of the governed, so the Declaration of Independence has instructed us. This might occur through direct democracy in the form of neighborhood assemblies and referendums on public issues. More likely it will be achieved through representative democracy in which people elect legislative and executive officials to make governmental decisions. It might even be done by indirect democracy in the form of a metropolitan confederation, with officials elected at one level serving also at the metropolitan level, though I have doubts about the adequacy of this approach because it removes the decision makers too far from popular control. Whatever the form, the broad band of American experience on how to make democracy work needs to focus on all the governmental institutions of metropolitan areas.

De Tocqueville perceived the importance of democratic control at the grass roots. He observed (n.d.:Book I, 62) that

> local assemblies of citizens constitute the strength of free nations. Municipal institutions are to liberty what primary schools are to science; they bring it within the people's reach, they teach men how to use and how to enjoy it. A nation may establish a system of free government, but without the spirit of municipal institutions it cannot have the spirit of liberty.

As it was then when the United States had 13 million inhabitants so it remains true today when the population exceeds 216 million, three-fourths of them living in metropolitan areas.

Finally, having several geographic arenas for governmental action under local federalism offers a protection against the coercive use of the community concept. People won't be members of a single community but rather will partake in several communities, so no one community can dominate their lives. Pluralistic government builds some checks into the system, and non-centralization of various governmental tasks avoids the dangers inherent in concentration of too much power in a big, centralized, unitary metropolitan government.

Units of Local Federalism

Under local federalism, different kinds of general governmental units would give form to the several polities of the metropolis and would function in communities of different sizes. Activities of these units would intermingle, but for ease of discussion let us consider each geographic area by itself.

SMALL UNITS: NEIGHBORHOOD AND SUBURBAN

Let us start with the smallest areas: neighborhoods. They might be part of a city, sometimes with clearly defined boundaries but sometimes not sharply delineated. In some instances a small suburban municipality will encompass a single neighborhood when viewed from a metropolitan perspective, but a larger suburb might have several neighborhoods. Unincorporated sections of urban counties also have neighborhoods, but the lower the density and the more scattered the houses, the less identifiable they are.

Are there really neighborhoods? Some people, though, doubt that there actually are neighborhoods in today's metropolis. A continual debate occurs among intellectuals about the validity of the neighborhood idea.

Part of the difficulty of this debate is the ambiguity of the meaning of neighborhood. Sociologist Suzzanne Keller explored these differences and came up with her own definition of neighborhoods (1968:87): "Essentially, it refers to distinctive areas into which larger spatial units may be subdivided, such as gold coasts and slums, central and outlying districts, residential and industrial areas, middle class and working class areas." The distinctiveness of an area, she continued, comes from one or more of four characteristics:

(1) geographical boundaries, (2) ethnic or cultural characteristics of the inhabitants, (3) psychological unity among people who feel that they belong together, or (4) concentrated use of an area's facilities for shopping, leisure, and learning. Neighborhoods combining all four elements are very rare in modern cities. In particular ... the geographical and the personal boundaries do not always coincide (numerals added).

The National Research Council's social science panel on the significance of community in the metropolitan environment looked at the neighborhood, which it classified as a "microcommunity," and concluded that it had lost its significance as a locus of interaction because people's interests and personal relationships are now widely dispersed due to heavy reliance on the automobile, lower residential densities, increasing specialization, and rising household incomes. The neighborhood is also less of a force in personality formation, the panel claimed. What is left for the neighborhood?

It survives principally as a means of control over the immediate physical environment and in that respect tends to operate as a unit only when it is threatened. Poor and minority neighborhoods are somewhat of an exception. In these neighborhoods, social interaction is more intense and community efforts are more concerned with obtaining responsive public services than with the exclusion of threats to the community (1974:74-75).

I think these social scientists exaggerate the decline of the neighborhood. Although not everybody in the metropolis feels a sense of neighborhood identity, many people do. The evidence of Chapter 9 indicates that the neighborhood as an organizational unit and as a kind of small community has had a resurgence during the past dozen years. Officially recognized neighborhood councils in cities and urban counties are functioning in middle and upper income areas as well as in poor and minority neighborhoods. Although defense is one of their purposes, they are going well beyond the narrow concerns of the old-style property owners' association and are approaching neighborhood planning and problem solving in a positive manner. Where coalitions of neighborhoods function, they produce interchange among different social classes and racial and ethnic groups.

Today's neighborhood isn't an urban village, so it doesn't serve as the exclusive focus for social interaction, and people's perception of neighborhood boundaries overlap. Nevertheless, neighborhoods in hundreds of cities and urban counties continue to play a significant role in community life. This role could be enhanced, in my opinion, if it had a clearer place in the governmental structure of the metropolis.

Small-area governments. Looking at the neighborhoods of the metropolis we can identify four main situations in their relationship to governments of larger scale. They are the central city neighborhood, the incorporated suburb, the developed but unincorporated suburb, and the unincorporated fringe area with scattered development. Each of these requires a different organizational response.

How to best organize central city neighborhoods depends upon the size of the city. At a minimum, every neighborhood should have a neighborhood council, that is, a body controlled by residents through democratic processes and granted some kind of official recognition by city government. The city would seek the advice of the neighborhood council for all proposed actions affecting the neighborhood. The neighborhood council would serve as an advocate of the residents. It could sponsor self-help activities, and it might take responsibility for the delivery of specific services. (For more about neighborhood councils see Chapter 9 and Hallman, 1977.)

For small central cities, neighborhood councils would be sufficient, but as city size increases, stronger neighborhood vehicles are needed. A city beyond 100,000 and certainly those over 250,000 ought to consider full-fledged neighborhood government. By this I mean a unit governed by a representative body which is elected by the residents, exercises power delegated to it by the city, hires its own staff, runs programs and provides services, and acts as an advocate of neighborhood needs. In the largest cities where districts for community government might have 100,000 or more residents, these units themselves should have neighborhood councils for smaller subareas. A neighborhood government should have enough program initiative, fiscal capacity, and political freedom to resemble an independent general government in a federalist system even if legally the neighborhood unit is subordinate to the city. (For more on how to organize, operate, and finance neighborhood government, see Hallman, 1974A:166-277.)

Incorporated municipalities in the suburbs already have such independence, so they now constitute small area government as part of local federalism. Some of them, however, serve too few people and have insufficient resources to be able to perform enough functions adequately, and this weakens their administrative viability. (What is too small will be taken up in the next chapter.) It would be desirable, therefore, for clusters of the smallest suburban units to merge into somewhat larger municipalities. At the other extreme, some suburban municipalities are already quite large, and they need neighborhood councils, just as small- and moderate-size cities do.

Fully built-up, unincorporated suburbs in states without strong towns or townships have no effective general government smaller than the county. Three main courses are available to give governmental form to neighborhoods so situated. The urban county could organize neighborhood councils or set up neighborhood governments with delegated powers, following the model suggested for the central city. Or, the central city could annex them and establish neighborhood councils or neighborhood governments for such areas. Or, new municipalities could be incorporated. If the latter, existing special service districts should be folded into the new units so that general government would replace the functional fiefdoms. Likewise, other special districts serving small areas should be merged into the existing incorporated suburbs.

For the developing fringe not part of any municipality, suburban and rural community councils should be set up. They might cover fairly wide territories, and as urbanization occurs, the denser areas can be split off as neighborhood councils or incorporated municipalities.

For a particular metropolis, this arrangement might produce a combination of neighborhood councils, neighborhood governments, incorporated suburbs, and suburban/rural community councils as the small area units of local federalism. Although those preferring symmetry of governmental form might object, this pattern would meet the diverse needs of subareas of the metropolis while giving neighborhood communities the forms of general government best suited to their needs.

CITIES: CENTRAL AND SATELLITE

The next size of area to consider is the city. Mainly this is the traditional central city, the place settlement commenced, the dominant municipality of the metropolis. There also might be a pair or trio of small- to moderate-size central cities, located near one another, whose overlapping growth patterns produce a metropolitan area. Or there might be a satellite city, once free-standing but now swallowed up by metropolitan expansion from a nearby larger central city. The satellite isn't a big city, but compared to the usual suburban municipality, it is more complete in its land use and economic functions.

Berlin's experience. The 1970 CED proposal for two-tier metropolitan federation called for breaking up the central city with some of its functions going to a new areawide government and others going to community districts into which the old city would be divided. Such a drastic reorganization has never occurred in the United States, but something along these lines came about in Berlin, Germany in 1920. Federated government was created by consolidating 95 units to produce an areawide government serving nearly four million people, almost twice the size of the old city. At the same time 20 districts were formed, each with a district council, a district executive committee, and district administrative functions; all the district council members combined to make up a 225-member assembly for the whole metropolis. Rowland Egger has explained the reasons (1933:102-103):

> The division of the former city of Berlin into six administrative districts proceeded from the belief that the pre-consolidation metropolis was too large economically to administer the developed administrative functions with the administrative apparatus best suited to the needs of the outlying districts. It proceeded further from the conviction that the old city was not, within itself, a unified municipality from a social and economic point of view in the sense which the outlying districts were expected to constitute such. Finally, the outlying districts themselves felt that if the old city were continued as a single administrative district it would completely dominate the new city, and that whatever local independence which might otherwise accrue to them by virtue of the federated administrative structure would be abrogated.

The Nazis ended this arrangement by centralizing all authority and eliminating the district units, but after World War II federation was restored to West Berlin and 12 district councils are now responsible for various activities absorbing about one-third of the city budget (Weiler, 1971:13-22).

American central cities. The point of whether the central city is really a community from "a social and economic point of view" can be raised about American cities. Diversity not homogeneity characterizes the city's people, and various racial, ethnic, and social-class groups may feel more competitive than united by mutual bonds. Yet the historical existence of the city has drawn this heterogeneous population together and has provided a forum for interaction. This fulfills the second of the National Research Council's definition of community: a population carrying out its daily life through a common set of institutions. The city is this kind of community. Furthermore, it has an established system of governance which makes it a polity, or political community.

This doesn't mean that subdivision of the central city can't or shouldn't happen in the United States as part of local federalism, but it would be one of the most difficult structural changes to achieve. Numerous vested interests in existing arrangements would mount tremendous political opposition, and such practical matters as reassignment of personnel, sanctity of labor contracts and pension rights, bonded indebtedness, and continuation of existing laws would all have to be dealt with. None of these are insurmountable barriers, but prevailing over them would take strong determination to achieve locally and marvelous skill if handled in the state legislature.

Most likely the central city in a larger metropolitan area will remain intact as an intermediate area of local federalism. It will need neighborhood units of some variety to provide more intimate government in small areas, and it will relate to an areawide government which handles some specific metropolitan functions. Thus, questions of the proper functional division, the possibility of revenue sharing, and the political relationships among the several governments become the principal concerns. The role of the central city might change, but it will continue to stand as an important local government, not dominant but nevertheless exercising considerable responsibility for a broad array of services for its residents and for contributing to solutions to metropolitan problems.

In a smaller metropolitan area the central city's role might be even broader. In states where annexation is easy and suburban incorporation difficult, the city can expand to keep pace with metropolitan development and through exercise of extraterritorial powers can guide growth beyond its boundaries. In this situation the city is the dominant government, and the county handles mostly its traditional, nonmunicipal functions and some rudimentary services for rural areas. This comes closer to unified government than to local federalism, and neighborhood councils would be especially appropriate as a counterbalance to centralized authority of the city. Where the small central city doesn't contain so large a portion of the metropolitan population, it will need to work out its relationships with surrounding municipalities, towns, and townships, with the county, and with its own neighborhoods. And the same is true for twin cities and triplets, adding their own interrelationships to the equation. As stated before, political bargaining is a necessary part of local federalism.

Satellite cities. The satellite city has a special position, for it possesses many attributes of the central city, including in many instances old buildings and poor people, but it isn't as influential in metropolitan affairs. Yet it is more than a large suburb. In some metropolitan areas the satellite city is in another state across the river from the central city, and there it is the heart of a submetropolitan area. These several factors should be recognized in defining the place of the satellite city in local federalism.

COUNTIES AS INTERMEDIATE-AREA GOVERNMENTS

In the multicounty metropolis, counties can function as intermediate-area governments of local federalism, but their role might vary depending upon their location within the metropolitan area. Four types can be identified: a core county containing the central city and some suburbs, a suburban county without a central city but with substantial urbanization, a satellite county holding a satellite city usually geographically removed from the central city, and a fringe county with scattered development and older towns being pulled into the metropolitan orbit.

The *core county's role* is closely intertwined with the role of the central city, and to a considerable extent they are counterbalanced: the heavier the one, the lighter the other. Perhaps through functional consolidation the core county has taken over services once performed by the central city, such as public health, solid waste disposal, the airport, and it has more employees than the city. At the other extreme, the central city and incorporated suburbs might handle most basic services, leaving the county with its more traditional functions plus a few services for unincorporated areas. Or the county might render some services in the suburbs it doesn't provide in the city, with or without tax districts reflecting these differences. Whatever, county/central city political relationships are likely to have a different quality than the county's relationship with suburban municipalities because of the size and historic centrality of the city.

The *suburban county* without a large city is another matter. The county's role is usually much larger in states where county modernization has proceeded than in states where county government is still relatively weak. In states without strong townships the county will probably be drawn into more urban services for unincorporated areas than in states where townships function like municipalities. In both kind of states there will be a two-layer pattern of the county plus small area governments consisting of municipalities and possibly townships. In Virginia, though, the suburban county is largely a unitary government except for a handful of small "towns" with minimal functions.

The *satellite county* has some urban characteristics because of one or more small cities and their suburbs, but its developed area isn't part of a continuous band of urbanization extending outward from the metropolitan center. The satellite city may be a stronger governmental institution than the county, but as metropolitan growth continues and scatters here and there, county government will have to play a larger role.

The *fringe county* is beginning to feel the impact of metropolitanization and is confronting the need for subdivision control, sewerage systems, water supply, and increased services of various kinds. The long-established towns have some of these services and facilities, but growth may be dispersed into local jurisdictions unequipped to deal with it. This challenges the fringe county to undertake tasks it never before performed.

One might ask whether any of these counties in the multicounty metropolitan area can be considered a true community. Yes, they are in the same sense that the central city is, that is, a population with a political system and a common set of institutions. The strength of community bonds will be affected by how dependent people are on county services, how visible the county political process is, and also by geography, which determines how much physical interaction occurs.

METROPOLITAN AND REGIONAL

City government is a major service institution, and so is the urban county. Both are also political institutions functioning with conscribed boundaries, and their residents are citizens as well as service consumers. In short, the city and the urban county are polities, that is, politically organized communities. To a considerable extent their existence as units of local general government is the primary basis for their status as communities, for other bases tend to occur more in smaller and larger areas—social interaction and mutual aid in neighborhoods and economic interdependence at the metropolitan level.

Metropolitan community. The opposite is the case with the metropolis as a whole. It is a community because the population is bound together by complex networks of social and economic interrelationships, reaching out to the hazy fringe of the commuting range and readership area of the metropolitan daily newspapers. Among others, advocates of consolidation in Philadelphia in the 1850s recognized this, and so did Paul Studenski in his 1930 study of government in metropolitan areas. The latter's contemporary, R.D. McKensie, affirmed this idea when he wrote about the rise of the metropolitan community (1933:70):

> The coming of the motor vehicle and the paved highway, the expansion of the press and other agencies of communication have brought the city and its hinterland into a closer functional relationship. The institutional division of labor which formerly characterized the inner life of the city has been extended to include a wide range of surrounding settlement, effecting what almost amounts to a revolution of the pattern of local relations. This new type of multi-center community is what is meant by the term metropolitan, or city, region.

> The metropolitan region is thus considered primarily a functional entity.

In our own era Kent Mathewson has devoted a lot of attention to metropolitan regions containing a major city (sometimes two or three) and two or more counties. He conceives of a metropolitan region in this manner (1974:51): "Geographically, it is a central city and its surrounding suburban ring. Psychologically and sociologically, it is that collection of local communities in which the citizens are interdependent in terms of their employment, residence, health and medical care, education, recreation and culture, shopping and religious experience." Politically, though, observes Mathewson, the metropolitan region lacks a governmental arrangement to provide a problem-solving capacity to match the scale of the problems. In this sense, the metropolis is a community in search of a government.

Is this really true? Do communities of interdependent people instinctively form a kind of natural polity and then seek a government to give it an institutional expression? Something like this has indeed occurred in metropolitan areas, as we reviewed in early chapters. At first it was the city expanding outward, then metropolitan special districts to handle functions where interdependency is greatest, next metropolitan planning bodies without much power but with an ambition to provide guidance for orderly growth for the whole area, and in the last twenty years councils of governments as weak confederations, bringing together elected officials of submetropolitan, general-purpose governments.

Areawide government. The time is ripe for the next step: general-purpose, areawide government. Except for some smaller metropolises and a handful of moderate-size, single-county areas, areawide government isn't likely to be a unitary jurisdiction but rather a government for the widest arena of decision making and action in a system of local federalism. Accordingly, its functions should encompass those activities which clearly demand areawide administration because of the nature of the facility (such as an airport), the service (such as mass transportation), or the process (such as planning guidance for metropolitan growth). There should be enough of these activities under one umbrella to constitute a general-purpose government, but the areawide unit need not get into everything that municipalities and urban counties deal with.

For single-county metropolitan areas, the county can become the areawide government, perhaps in the process shucking off some of its service delivery functions to more localized governments. For multicounty areas, the multi-town-and-city areas of New England, and the multi-city-and-county areas of Virginia, American ingenuity can figure out various ways to organize areawide governments. For starters, we have two models extant. One is the Metropolitan Council of Minnesota, which conducts metropolitan planning, facilitates intergovernmental cooperation, and exercises policy and budgetary control over several separate metropolitan commissions dealing with sewage and solid waste disposal, mass transportation, airports, and metropolitan parks and open space (see Chapter 8, pp. 106-108). The other model is exemplified in a state constitutional amendment authorizing the creation of a regional service authority for the Denver area with power to directly operate up to sixteen specific services, subject to voter approval.

As it happened, the Denver area electorate wouldn't give its consent in a 1973 referendum to set of a regional service authority involving three specific functions, so a Denver Area Study Panel in early 1977 switched to the Minnesota model (see Chapter 8, pp. 97-98). Nevertheless, the idea of a multipurpose areawide operating agency is still a valid approach. The Tri-County Local Government Study Commission in the Portland, Oregon area took a step in this direction toward the end of 1976 by proposing legislation to convert the existing Metropolitan Service District into an elected body, transfer planning to it from the council of governments, give it authority to take on new functions, and possibly later, subject to voter approval, to absorb the public transportation and port functions presently handled by independent authorities (see Chapter 8, p. 98).

Both the Portland and Denver area proposals call for an elected governing body. This is very sound. It would place the general-purpose, areawide government under the direct control of the people, a highly desirable extension of representative democracy to the whole metropolis. Moreover, both proposals call for an areawide referendum before any function can be added to areawide government. In contrast, the Minnesota legislature decides upon the powers of the metropolitan council (about half the legislators are from the Twin Cities metropolitan area, and the governor appoints the members of the metropolitan council.

Election of the areawide governing body is important not only to provide the safeguards of democratic control but also for the political process it releases. Even if members of a metropolitan council are elected by districts rather than at large (and all recent proposals require this), they are running for office on metropolitan issues. If the chairman or chief executive is elected areawide, he or she has to campaign as a metropolitan leader, and even if the council elects its own chairman and appoints the chief executive, the metropolitan prospective is dominant. This produces metropolitan politicians who participate in a metropolitan political process, and while this may frighten some people, to me it is an affirmation of American democratic principles.

Furthermore, an areawide political process makes possible metropolitan citizenship. It contributes to development of what Mathewson calls a "regional ethic" (1974:51):

> The individual citizen behaves regionally. He or she cannot exist totally within one unit of local government. And, given the rich experiences available throughout a metropolitan region, it is unlikely that any individual citizen would want to exist only within his home town. A change of attitude is needed on the part of individual citizens, to match attitude with behavior pattern.

If a regional ethic existed, such an ethic would see the citizen recognizing the results of his regional behavior, identifying the need for restructuring certain parts of the governmental mechanism, to match problem-solving ability to problem scale, and support the progress toward such regional problem solving. A citizen living that ethic would be a true regional citizen.

A general-purpose areawide government would give form to the natural polity of a people who live socially and economically interdependent in a metropolitan community. But at the same time, local federalism would provide governments in smaller areas so that the neighborhood communities, the city community, the county communities in the multicounty metropolis could all have their political expression.

Chapter 13

FUNCTIONAL DIVISION OF RESPONSIBILITY

Local federalism favors general governments for two or three sizes of areas within the metropolis. Together these governments would be responsible for providing most of the public services needed by metropolitan residents. They would share responsibilities for handling various functions. The question then arises: who should do what?

Underlying Concepts

To add clarity to the discussion, let us look for a moment at some of the underlying concepts.

FUNCTIONS AND ACTIVITIES

The term "function" is used in public administration to refer to a broad field of service. A particular function is called by the general name of the activities in that field, such as transportation, education, health, recreation, and the like.

Each function can be subdivided into parts, which are referred to as "activities" or "subfunctions." (This book calls them activities.) The solid waste management function, for instance, has two main activities: collection and disposal, with perhaps recycling coming on as a third major activity. The police function can be broken down into numerous distinct activities, such as patrolling, investigation, laboratory work, communications, training, and many more.

As American federalism features shared responsibility among all levels for the major functions of government, so local federalism is characterized by the sharing of functional responsibilities. As national, state, and local governments do different things, so areawide, city and county, neighborhood and small suburban governments handle different assignments. The differences relate to activities or subfunctions. Some activities can best be managed at a small scale while others demand a much larger service area. We can, for instance, organize small area police patrols tied into a central communications network and can train local police officers at a metropolitan academy. We can have a localized refuse collection service and a disposal facility serving a much larger area.

Assignment of activities within the various functional fields is a crucial process of local federalism. The precise division of responsibility may be different from one metropolis to another, and in any one metropolitan area assignments are likely to change over a period of time. That doesn't matter. The significant point is that activities within each function can be divided among geographic areas. This isn't all that remarkable since even departments in a unitary government will subdivide and assign certain tasks to field units working out of district offices. What distinguishes local federalism is that the activities are divided among levels of general government, each of which has a measure of independence in its ambit of power.

SERVICE SYSTEMS

Conceivably this could lead to what critiques of present metropolitan organization call fragmentation. Activities within a functional field could be so splintered that necessary interrelationships might be lost and the quality of public service would suffer. A preventative or an antidote is the concept of service systems.

A system is a group of things which regularly interact so as to form a unified whole. These things may be organs of the body, parts of a machine, specific community services, or ideas of the mind. Whatever the elements, they form a system if they are related to one another. They are interdependent. They function together. They constitute an integrated whole, or at least ought to.

Thus, a metropolis has a health service system consisting of environmental health inspection, visiting nurses, neighborhood health centers, nursing homes, general hospitals, a teaching hospital, an epidemiological laboratory and also private physicians, group practice units, and health insurance companies. It has a transportation system made up of streets, highways, expressways, public transit, taxis, parking lots, airports, bus and truck terminals, railroads, and water transportation facilities.

Some service systems have components which must be closely linked in operation. For instance, the employment-and-training system needs to provide an unbroken sequence of services to persons seeking work and who may require counseling, training, help in finding a job, and follow-up supportive services. In certain other functional fields, operational integration is less crucial but availability of a full complement of facilities and services is nevertheless important, such as neighborhood playgrounds, city parks, and metropolitan forest preserves. Although the elements of a service system need not all be administered by a single organization—indeed some will be under private auspices and others will be handled by public agencies—they do need to function together.

A variety of techniques can be utilized to achieve service integration where a number of agencies or levels of government are involved: cooperation agreements (formal and informal), contractual arrangements, planning mechanisms, information sharing, prime sponsorship, delegation of authority, and joint operations are some of the ways. Some have developed through interlocal volunteerism, others through arrangements worked out as part of intergovernmental financing. The best method depends upon the particular field, but whatever is done, the service system idea provides a conceptual basis for making local federalism work effectively.

Criteria for Assignments

What criteria might there be for assigning functional responsibilities to different levels of local federalism? This can be answered both theoretically and empirically.

THEORY

The question of size is paramount in determining what activity to assign where. On this issue, E. F. Schumacher wrote that "there is no *single* answer. For his different purposes man needs many different structures, both small ones and large ones, some exclusive and some comprehensive." For every activity there is a certain appropriate scale, he says, and "what is needed in all these matters is to discriminate, to get things sorted out" (1973:66).

Scholars and practitioners have been trying to sort out what are areawide activities and what are local ones ever since 1896 when the Boston area metropolitan study commission made its recommendation for federated government. A general set of principles emerged and were expressed in the early 1940s by Victor Jones in some recommendations on which functions should be assigned to an areawide government (1942:xxi-xxii):

(1) when co-ordination of a function over the whole area is essential to effective service in a part of the area;

(2) when it is desirable to apply the ability theory of taxation to the area as a whole, instead of allowing each part to support its own services;

(3) when the advantages of large-scale operations are desired; or

(4) when it is necessary to assure citizens of a voice in decisions which affect them at their places of work and recreation as well as their places of residence.

More recently the Advisory Commission on Intergovernmental Relations has given a lot of attention to how best to assign functional responsibility. ACIR's 1963 report, *Performance of Urban Functions: Local and Areawide,* was a landmark study on this subject. The Commission returned to the topic in its survey of substate regionalism and identified four basic characteristics which an ideal assignment system should reflect (1974A:7):

economic efficiency, fiscal equity, political accountability, and adminis- trative effectiveness. Taken together these characteristics suggest that functional assignments should be made to jurisdictions that can (1) supply a service at the lowest possible cost; (2) finance a function with the greatest possible fiscal equalization; (3) provide a service with adequate popular control; and (4) administer a function in an authorita- tive, technically proficient, and cooperative fashion.

As it developed the third and fourth characteristics, ACIR pointed toward general-purpose governments, performing in the context of shared intergov- ernmental powers with full citizen participation. "A general-purpose govern- ment," said the Commission (1974B:93-94), "not only serves to raise public awareness about functional performance but also to prevent public functions from becoming controlled by private or minority interests. Since this type of government is the focus of numerous service demands, access to the unit will increase and a system of countervailing, democratic political power will be established." This is similar to comments others have made, as reviewed in the previous chapter.

Fiscal equity, ACIR's second characteristic, is a topic reserved for the next chapter, but here let me note that it is possible to deal with fiscal equity through intergovernmental financing as well as by shifting functional assign- ments to a jurisdiction with a broader tax base. More on this later.

ECONOMIC EFFICIENCY

As to economic efficiency, economy and diseconomy of scale are major considerations in determining a particular pattern of functional assignments. This relates to unit costs of specific services, such as the cost per ton of refuse disposal, the cost per pupil enrolled in school, the cost per capita of police patrolling. The unit price might be lowered by increasing the size of operation, but there may be a point at which no more savings can be achieved by getting larger and, moreover, growing even bigger might cause costs to rise because of diseconomy of scale. Conversely, the unit price of certain services might be lowered by decreasing the size of operations, but below a certain point costs won't go down any more and might rise.

As a general observation, ACIR offered this comment about economy of scale (1974B:82-83):

> Several functions—sewage treatment, some forms of education, and hospital services—all have a large optimum population size associated with their least-cost level of output. Economies of scale tend to appear where functions benefit from specialization, lower-factor input costs, and employment of new technologies. They do not appear, however, in services that are labor-intensive and provide little opportunity for specialization, such as elementary schooling, police patrol, and basic fire protection.

After reviewing nineteen empirical studies, ACIR found evidence to suggest that economies of scale do indeed exist but that there seems to be no single optimum-size jurisdiction for service provision (1974B:83-84). This is a matter we will puzzle over later in this chapter when we look at specific functions and try to relate them to the geographic areas served by different sizes of local general government.

Many of the studies of economic efficiency concentrate upon increasing the operating size as a means of lowering costs. In my own study of the feasibility of neighborhood government, I took the opposite approach and looked at small jurisdictions and examined some standards set forth by professional organizations to determine how small a unit is practicable (though not necessarily most economical). I found (1974:50) that:

> it is possible for an urban administrative unit serving 5,000 people to conduct several kinds of activities. However, a population of approximately 10,000 might be a more desirable minimum because it would widen the range of services. For this size of population it is practicable to organize services for police protection, fire protection, street maintenance, refuse collection, creation, zoning, and general administration. As population size increases to the vicinity of 25,000, environmental sanitation, a health center, a library, and a fuller recreation program can be added.

What I was searching for was the lower population limit of practicability. In terms of economy of scale, a more favorable unit cost for many of these activities can probably be achieved by increasing the size of the small-area government to perhaps 40,000 or 50,000 people. Beyond that size, no particular cost reductions are likely to occur for such activities. Then as the population served grows beyond 150,000 and certainly by 250,000, diseconomy of scale sets in for many activities which are labor-intensive in nature. This occurs because the organization becomes loaded up with supervisors, technical specialists, and clerks (an inefficiency of hierarchical organization), and a much smaller portion of the personnel are involved in direct services. We see this, for example, in large police departments and big school systems.

To sum up, studies of economy of scale indicate that there are lower and upper limits of size for producing economic efficiency, but the broad middle ground for many urban services is within the population range of small-area units operating in the context of local federalism. This speaks of economic efficiency. Such other factors as being close to the people and building upon existing units might favor units in the ten to forty thousand range for a solid core of local service activities.

Functional Fields

Let's get more specific and explore how activities can be divided and responsibilities shared in various functional fields.

WATER, SEWAGE, AND SOLID WASTE

Water supply is one of the first functions for which areawide administrative arrangements have been devised as metropolitan areas have grown. This occurs because surface water sources can be tapped only at certain spots and many local jurisdictions aren't located where they can do so. And sometimes more distant sources must be sought, usually with the construction of a reservoir. Water treatment plants are expensive but can serve a large population. Yet at the delivery end, local water mains and connections with residential, commercial, and industrial users can be managed by fairly small units. Thus, frequently the central city or metropolitan water department sells water wholesale to small municipalities, which then distribute it to their inhabitants.

The most economical sewerage systems rely upon gravity flow, and this makes the drainage basin the natural unit. But rarely do municipal boundaries coincide with ridge lines, and anyway a number of municipalities are likely to be in the same drainage area. Sometimes an even larger area feeds into a sewage treatment plant through the use of pumping stations because the plant is located at an acceptable discharge spot. These factors and the high capital costs favor large sewerage areas, but even then it is possible to have domestic and collector sewage lines handled by small jurisdictions.

The same rationale prevails for solid waste. Disposal and recycling require expensive facilities which can serve sizable populations. But refuse collection can be organized in much smaller areas. In fact, the collection route of one truck is the basic unit to consider (the area which can be covered varies according to population density, pickup method, and distance to the disposal site).

Just this kind of division has been worked out in the Toronto area. The metropolitan government handles refuse disposal, runs the water treatment and sewage disposal plants, and takes care of trunk lines, and the municipalities manage the retail distribution of water, local sewer lines, and refuse collection.

TRANSPORTATION

A similar twofold division prevails in activities related to transportation. There are some major facilities which serve the whole metropolis: airports (the big one and smaller ones for light planes), the port, bus and truck terminals, railroad station, railyards; and even if some of these facilities are privately owned and operated, they are part of the metropolitan transportation system. Mass transit has to operate on an areawide basis, and the expressway and major highway systems are metropolitan in scope. Clearly planning for this part of the transportation system needs an areawide base. To the extent that tax dollars support these facilities, equity requires areawide financial arrangements (plus intergovernmental funding from state and federal sources). Metropolitan management of these major facilities is probably also desirable.

At the other end of the scale, local streets, alleys, and sidewalks can be maintained, kept clean, and have snow removed by fairly small administrative units. Public parking lots can be municipally operated and can be financed by fees and special assessments on benefiting properties (such as in a business district). It is even possible to run minibus service for distinct areas within the metropolis.

CULTURAL FACILITIES, PARKS, AND RECREATION

Major cultural facilities also serve the whole metropolis: art museums, science museums, concert halls, zoological garden, sports arena, stadium. Traditionally these have been built in the central city, often with city tax support, but the clientele comes from the whole metropolis and beyond. Here and there control is shifting to a metropolitan agency or special authority, and some of the new stadiums have been erected in the suburbs. Whether or not the administrative body is metropolitan, equity suggests the need for an areawide tax base.

The same is true for regional parks, forest preserves, and other major chunks of open space. Due to the foresight of nineteenth-century leaders, many central cities have large parks, such as Central Park in New York, Fairmount Park in Philadelphia, the Chicago lakefront, Swope Park in Kansas City, and Golden Gate Park in San Francisco. Some areawide agencies have provided regional parks outside the city, such as the Metropolitan District Commission in the Boston area and the Cleveland Metropolitan Park District. Today more open space needs to be set aside in growing metropolitan areas, and this is an appropriate task for a metropolitan agency, or possibly for state government to accomplish because of the spread of regional growth.

Parks of intermediate and small scale can be established and maintained by jurisdictions which are of intermediate and small size. Recreation facilities can likewise be graded into large community centers and playfields, neighborhood playgrounds, tot-lots, and miniparks for sedentary citizens, and they can be handled by administrative units of different scale. Since recreation services are personnel-intensive, they are particularly amenable to administrative and political decentralization.

PLANNING AND LAND USE CONTROL

We saw in Chapter 1 how study commissions have deplored uncontrolled metropolitan growth and lack of effective areawide planning. Chapter 8 revealed how metropolitan planning has been attempted by regional planning commissions and councils of governments, functioning as confederations but with almost no means to implement their plans. Most metropolitan planning is an empty shell because the tools to influence the pattern of development—zoning, subdivision control, expressway and highway construction, provision of water, sewers, and community facilities—are all in other hands. (An exception is where a single-county metropolis has a strong, modern county government, particularly in states without strong townships where the county is the main local government for unincorporated areas.)

The product is not only poorly planned growth but also economic and social segregation because suburban municipalities, towns, and townships have used zoning as a measure to exclude low-income groups and to permit only selective kinds of nonresidential uses. Land use control of this sort is one of the most treasured municipal powers, asserted even by the new cities of Los Angeles County which are willing to contract for police services (which seems to be the second most important power for local control). This presents one of the inevitable dilemmas of federalism: the need to reconcile general and parochial viewpoints.

The place to start in resolving this dilemma is by asserting that the metropolitan community has a right to determine its own course of development, not small enclaves which carve out areas of special privilege and not private interests which are motivated primarily by profit and aren't likely to bear the full costs of the developments they initiate. This right of the metropolitan community should be given an institutional home in an areawide, general-purpose governmental unit which is responsible to the people through elections and other democratic processes. The areawide government should have the power to produce a general plan to guide the location and timing of development and redevelopment. The plan would incorporate relevant elements of the major systems affecting the course of development, including transportation, water and sewer facilities, school construction, and other community facilities. A comprehensive capital budget and long-range capital program would be extracted from these systems, combined and interrelated so as to set the stage for coordinated implementation. The areawide plan would establish a general framework for land uses, including general location of various housing types and industrial, commercial, and institutional development.

Local plans would be developed in the context of the areawide plan but would be more specific. For example, the areawide plan might indicate the need for a new high school in a particular sector, leaving it up to the local planning body and school district to determine the precise location. The areawide plan would allocate a fair share of housing for various income groups to different localities, letting local governments determine the sites (with a few safeguards to prevent local circumvention). General location of commercial and industrial development would also be indicated. In this context, zoning would remain a local function, subject to adherence to the areawide plan, and local government would thereby fill out the details of the general plan and take care of the minutiae, such as height and setback requirements and zoning variances necessary to adjust broad regulations to specific situations.

Something like this arrangement is emerging in the Twin Cities area of Minnesota where the metropolitan council has policy control over some major areawide commissions and is now working on a metropolitan development guide which local governments will steer by; except that the metropolitan council isn't elected (see Chapter 8, pp. 106-108). Some urban counties are taking planning initiatives to get a firm hold on growth; in single-county metropolitan areas, this produces an areawide plan but even in multicounty areas any one county covers a lot of territory so that its planning efforts can be significant. Yet hardly any place has tackled the crucial issue of zoning controls and its distorted use as an instrument for social exclusion. My belief is that this is one case where the broader viewpoint should override the narrower approach because of the importance of the social equity issue, a matter the next chapter discusses in greater detail.

BUILDING REGULATIONS, HOUSING, AND COMMUNITY DEVELOPMENT

Several of the commissions reviewed in Chapter 1 lamented the jumble of building code regulations found in the diverse jurisdictions of metropolitan areas, a situation causing confusion among homebuilders preventing standardization, and thereby increasing the cost of housing. The solution is an areawide or statewide building code, adopted by an areawide government or by the state, but if that isn't possible, developed and adopted through mutual action of local governments. Building permits and inspection, though, can be handled by local jurisdictions.

High land cost is another factor driving up the price of housing in metropolitan areas, and the kind of managed growth previously recommended might make it worse because currently developable land would be scarcer. Conceivably such land reform measures as price regulation, taxes on unearned increments, and public acquisition could be instituted to counteract this trend, but this possibility is scarcely discussed and certainly not widely supported. Maybe this kind of controversial issue isn't one for a new areawide government to tackle, but it is a matter which should be addressed forthrightly.

Housing for all income groups should be dispersed throughout the metropolitan area, in my opinion. To go with an areawide fair share housing program, there needs to be one or more administrative units responsible for the construction of housing for low- and moderate-income families, and for management where the units are publicly owned. In a small metropolis this can and should be an areawide agency, preferably as part of an areawide general government. In a multicounty metropolitan area, the counties as intermediate-size governments can take on this assignment. In either case there should be a metropolitan housing assistance plan in order to direct state and federal housing aids to the kinds of housing, methods of assistance, and locations most responsive to the needs of that particular metropolis.

Housing rehabilitation is also necessary, especially in the central city, satellite cities, and the older suburbs. This can be best accomplished by municipal and neighborhood governments, working with residents and the local financial institutions which provide financing. Experience has shown that to be truly effective, housing rehabilitation should be carried out in the context of a broader community development program aimed at improving the whole neighborhood's physical environment and also directed toward solutions for various social problems, such as poverty, unemployment, inadequate education, crime, and the need for a variety of social services. This kind of community development should be neighborhood oriented and locally administered, much of it under neighborhood governments or at least advisory neighborhood councils, but the housing element should be tied to the areawide housing assistance plan.

POLICE

Police service is another crucial function. It is also one of the most controversial when talking about who should have this authority because of its role as a means of social control. Thus, Philadelphia leaders in the 1840s were disturbed by social unrest in suburban districts and the difficulties in apprehending offenders who could easily cross municipal boundaries, and they used this as an argument for consolidation (Warner, 1968:125-157). Conversely when in the late 1960s black ghetto leaders were demanding community control, resistance among the establishment was greatest for the police function. In Dade County, Florida many of the smaller municipalities have willingly transferred numerous activities to the metropolitan county, but all but one have hung on to police patrolling. This means that economic efficiency is only part of the issue of how to assign police responsibility.

On the matter of economy of scale, Juan de Torres in a study of the costs and efficiencies of many different functions indicated (1972:82): "under current standards, a neighborhood of 50,000 requires a police force of 60 to 180 men, which appears to leave ample room for whatever specialization is needed to perform efficiently the function of patrolling the neighborhood." An even larger department permits more police specialization, but there seems to be diseconomy of scale when the population served grows beyond 250,000 (ACIR, 1974B:84).

At the other end of the scale, a number of studies recommend consolidation of police units with fewer than ten to fourteen officers. This is the number of full-time persons it takes to achieve twenty-four-hour, seven-days-a-week police patrol. Many police units of smaller size are in rural areas and small towns, which is a different situation, and there part-time deputies are commonly used. Where units of ten to fourteen officers function in a suburban municipality, some police experts recommend further consolidation to produce a larger, more diverse police force.

Elinor Ostrom disagrees with recommendations for wholesale consolidation of all police services and cites evidence accumulated by the Workshop in Political Theory and Policy Analysis at Indiana University and by others. In studies comparing small suburban police departments with police services in comparable neighborhoods of Chicago, Grand Rapids, Indianapolis, and Nashville, she and her colleagues found that the smaller departments performed better in terms of resident satisfaction, victimization rates, and several other indicators, and in three out of four cases at lower costs (E. Ostrom and Parks, 1973:367-402). They compared police services in forty-four neighborhoods in the St. Louis metropolitan area, including nine neighborhoods served by ten or fewer full-time officers, twenty-four neighborhoods served by medium-size departments (eleven to seventy-six full-time officers), and eleven neighborhoods served by the large county and city police departments. On some crucial indicators of citizen assessment of performance, the medium-size departments achieved the highest ratings, but the very small units were perceived by residents to be performing better than the two largest departments (E. Ostrom and Smith, 1976:194-195). However, another research team contends that differences are more related to socio-economic characteristics than city size (Pachon and Lorrich, 1977:38-47).

These studies relate mainly to basic patrol services, but police departments engage in many other activities where specialization is required and is most economically achieved by larger units. Among these activities are police training, communications, criminal intelligence, vice investigation, homicide investigation, and crime laboratory. Small departments can't manage these and require the assistance of a larger unit, and in fact cooperative arrangements and contracting are quite common. For example, Metropolitan Dade County provides many of these special services to municipal departments.

So, a rational division of police activities is technically possible among two or three area sizes of local federalism, with perhaps also a role for state government in the more technical laboratory work. Furthermore, even without political decentralization a big city police department can administratively decentralize its service to police teams assigned to specific neighborhoods and can instruct them to work closely with residents in crime prevention and apprehension of accused offenders. A police team and a neighborhood council could maintain a very fruitful relationship and provide some of the advantages of small scale operations even if there weren't true neighborhood government with its own police force. But should the latter occur, a city police department would still be needed for specialized activities and for patrol work in the central business district and industrial areas outside the jurisdiction of the neighborhoods.

There are now and are likely always to be a number of police departments in most metropolitan areas. They can be knitted together in a police service system which achieves information exchange and mutual assistance while local control over basic police patrolling is maintained.

FIRE PROTECTION AND AMBULANCE SERVICE

"In most cases, economies of scale are quickly exhausted in fire fighting," reports de Torres (1972:110,111). "The basic operating unit is the professional 'fire company," which may vary in number of personnel from 4 to 10 men. Since a community of 100,000 requires from 75 to 100 fire fighters, it is capable of maintaining from 10 to 15 companies, or about 8 engine and/or hose companies and a few more specialized companies such as an 'aerial ladder company' needed in case of fires in high buildings."

It is possible to carve out smaller fire districts with reasonable economy, such as a combination of two pumper trucks and a ladder truck serving a population of 15,000 to 20,000 people. However, a larger jurisdiction has the advantage of being able to relocate units as the population density, commercial and industrial uses, and hazardous conditions change in particular districts.

Regardless of the administrative pattern for basic fire fighting units, mutual aid and back-up arrangements are needed among companies in the same department and in adjacent jurisdictions. For public convenience a central dispatcher is highly desirable, but it can be linked to a number of separate departments. A central training facility is also advisable.

The same considerations relate to ambulance services whether or not they are part of the fire department. In either case, they need to be tied to hospitals, and in this manner they become an adjunct to the health service system.

HEALTH SERVICES AND HOSPITALS

Health services have more specialized personnel than many other functions, and they generally need somewhat larger service areas to assemble enough kinds of specialities and be reasonably economical. A neighborhood health center, for instance, can easily handle a population of 25,000 to 30,000. De Torres feels a subunit of a health department with a staff of 20 could serve a population of 50,000 and have enough specialization to cope with most health problems (1972:62). Of course, laboratories and other highly specialized health services can serve a considerably larger population.

A hospital service area is even larger. De Torres indicates that a 400-bed hospital is considered a minimum size and that it can serve a population of 80,000 to 100,000. A teaching hospital is another matter, and it "may have to serve a population of over 250,000 in order to make it economical to provide in one hospital all, or nearly all, the services offered by modern medicine" (1972:61-62).

These are sizes for operational units. For planning the total health services delivery system, the whole metropolitan area must be considered. This permits the metropolis to locate hospitals and health centers where they are most needed and to prevent overbuilding in particular locations. It also enables personnel who deliver health services to link their efforts and provide mutual support.

HUMAN RESOURCE PROGRAMS

Similarly a metropolitan scope is desirable in planning and coordinating a system of welfare and social services. Welfare assistance is best financed by state and federal funds (preferably the latter) and not by local sources. because greater equity can be achieved through the redistributive potential of a broader tax base. Thus, there should be a single welfare system in the metropolis, though the offices where individuals come in contact with the system can be widely dispersed. As to social services, they can easily be decentralized to small-scale administrative units or delegated to independent, small-area governments, though financial support for the services can come from federal, state, and areawide sources.

The personal service end of the employment-and-training system can also be decentralized to neighborhood employment centers, adult education and training facilities, and localized job sites for public service employment as a job-creation program. However, some more specialized vocational education centers may be needed at the intermediate level. An areawide mechanism to handle labor market information is also necessary in order for all job seekers to gain access to the full range of employment opportunities within commuting range. And a metropolitan base is desirable for planning the total employment-and-training system and to link together the various components which are administered by various agencies and governments working in areas of different sizes.

EDUCATION

Operation of the education system is also amenable to subdivision. Various studies have tried to determine the optimum size of schools, and after reviewing them de Torres had this to say (1972:26): "Despite the defects of the data, however, two fairly firm conclusions with respect to economy of scale emerge: for an elementary school, economies of scale are exhausted when it contains 400 pupils; for a secondary school, when it contains 1,450 pupils." A secondary school of this size can serve an area with a population of about 30,000. Beyond that size, says de Torres (1972:30), "few advantages seem to be gained by increasing the population served—while a further loss in the 'neighborhood school' concept is likely to be incurred." Except for some special kind of schools, no particular economies will be achieved with a larger school system, and the big systems are more costly because of the layers of supervisory personnel and numerous specialities.

From a social viewpoint, though, there may be some justification for a larger jurisdiction in order to achieve a greater measure of racial integration in a metropolis where social separation is pervasive. Covering a broader area permits more options, such as prointegration attendance zones, paired schools, magnet schools, educational parks, and busing when appropriate. Perhaps a method should be developed to treat the whole metropolis as a single educational system for purposes of planning, determining attendance patterns, and raising local funds but to keep operational responsibility in the hands of smaller districts, possibly as small as districts each containing a single high school and its feeder schools. Attendance districts could be adjusted from year to year, and however drawn the supporting community would be the families of the students and other residents within the attendance zone. This could be more readily achieved if school financing were broken loose from the local property tax, a trend which is generally occurring.

Of all the service functions in the metropolis, creative local federalism is particularly needed in the field of education.

Area and Function

Clearly it is possible to divide activities within various functional fields into different sizes of operations. This is done now extensively, though areawide planning and administration isn't a widespread practice in some fields. The trouble with the present arrangement is the excessive use of special districts in many places so that each function operates on its own and interrelationships aren't well articulated, thus obscuring the general view of overall policy. But even where most functions are handled by general governmental units, the boundaries of these jurisdictions aren't necessarily the best ones to observe for the services rendered. The areas served may be too small or too large to produce the optimum economy of scale.

INTERRELATIONSHIPS

So the question arises: how to reconcile area and function? James Fesler looked at this issue as it applies to the national government and concluded that it is impossible to expect every function's most natural subarea boundaries to coincide with those of every other function because each has different needs and values to consider. But he felt that some reasonable compromises could produce some common service areas if one started "with emphasis on the interrelation of functions and the need for coordinated administration and area-based popular control of those functions as they affect a given community or group of communities" (1949:15).

Within a single government, areal coordination can be achieved through the use of generalists assigned to the field and given a role to pull together the work of field specialists. A different situation prevails when several levels of government operate within a federal system. "Each of these governmental areas," said Fesler (1949:121), "has a government that potentially can weave all its functions together so that they make a consistent pattern for the area in which they operate." Furthermore, the areas served by general government provide a common denominator about which all or many field functions of the central government can be coordinated.

If we apply these ideas to the metropolitan scene, we have to ask whether the natural service areas for various services can be made to coincide with each other and be grouped together under the authority of general governmental units. The answer is, yes, if we are willing to make some reasonable compromises. Some boundaries are clearcut, like wide rivers which separate local units and the ridgelines which determine drainage basins, but many boundaries are judgmental. Economy of scale is an inexact science, but there is almost always a broad band of economical size between too small and too large. So workable multifunctional area boundaries can be delineated.

OPTIMUM SIZE FOR SMALL-AREA UNITS

If a cluster of activities are to come together for small-area general governments as units of local federalism in a metropolis, what size should these units be? Some insights can be gained from research and speculation on optimum city size, but with caution.

Balancing the desire for economy of scale and democratic participation, Robert Dahl concluded that "the all-round optimum size for a contemporary American city is probably somewhere between 50,000 and 200,000." He found "no worthwhile evidence that there are any significant economies of scale in city governments for cities over 50,000," and he felt that the larger figure is "within the threshold for wide civic participation" (1967:965-966).

Daniel Elazar, recalling his own studies of community politics, has indicated (1975A:69): "Around the 40,000 mark, there is a radical shift upward in the availability of resources—human and economic—to provide the range of talents necessary to operate a sophisticated local government and the fiscal wherewithal to do so, without serious diminution of political communication in comparison with their small sisters." Furthermore, he feels that past 40,000 it is harder for a single group or collection of individuals to dominate while this is more possible as the population gets smaller.

These scholars are, of course, talking about free standing communities, not districts within a metropolis. And they are referring to optimum. But the size of such cities can be less, for there are many small, independent cities of 10, 20, and 30 thousand people which offer full services at reasonable cost and with satisfactory proficiency. Maybe their hospital has fewer than 400 beds and their high school has less than 1,450 pupils (optimums mentioned earlier), but in these places the functions have adjusted to the scale of the area.

Within a metropolis with governments of several sizes, the small-area units might be in the 40 to 50 thousand range. But they could be smaller, too, because local federalism features shared responsibility by different sizes of general government and the small units don't have to undertake all the activities of a free-standing city. If there is a danger of domination by a small group of people, the dynamics of local federalism offer a safeguard to the residents who are citizens of the city or county with its greater diversity as well as the more homogeneous neighborhood community.

Generally, the size of small-area government should vary with the total size of the metropolis. In the largest metropolitan areas these units should be bigger so that their total number won't exceed what is comprehensible. Thus, at one time New York City with 7.5 million inhabitants divided itself into 62 community districts and now has reduced the number to 51, averaging about 150,000 in population. In contrast, a metropolis of 300,000 might have ten small-area units of 30,000 a piece or as many as 30 units each with 10,000 citizens. Ten thousand is probably the smallest size to recommend, and it would be desirable to consolidate present suburban units which are smaller in size.

INTERMEDIATE AREAS

In multicounty metropolitan areas, the central city and urban counties are intermediate levels of government. They have become so through evolution not by original design. Their activities have accreted through the decades, but their boundaries were determined earlier by other considerations than what is the proper size for an intermediate-area government. Although the central city and urban county are likely to remain in most metropolises, some of the things they do could be better performed by small-area governments and others by an areawide government. For the city, the small-area tasks could either be turned over to neighborhoods or be administratively decentralized to little city halls and multiservice centers under district managers with an advisory role for neighborhood councils. Some of the city's major facilities, such as the art museum, zoo, and airport, are appropriate matters for areawide operation, or at least financing. The urban county which has gotten into municipal services could properly transfer many of them to small-area units, but at the same time it might take over certain functions previously handled by special districts serving a number of municipalities, such as sewerage systems. In the process, both the central city and the urban county might achieve a net reduction in the number of personnel on the payroll through transfer of greater operating responsibility to small area governments.

AREAWIDE

If we examine the major functional fields carefully, we find that the activities which unquestionably require areawide operations are not great in number. One cluster consists of facilities which serve the whole area, such as the airport, port, mass transit, regional parks, water supply, sewage treatment, and refuse disposal, though in the largest metropolitan areas the last three might be handled by intermediate-size governments. A second cluster is some specialized services, beneficial to operating agencies of the small- and intermediate-area governments, such as police and fire academies, labor market exchange, and arrangements for mutual aid in emergencies. A third cluster deals with planning for physical development, but many of the implementing measures could be carried out by smaller local governments. And a fourth cluster involves planning for major service systems, such as health, employment-and-training, and law enforcement, but almost no direct operations in these fields need to be areawide.

Taken altogether these assignments make areawide government into a major institution, but in terms of personnel it wouldn't need as many persons as the aggregate of intermediate-size governments or the total of small-area governmental employees because it wouldn't be handling many of the labor-intensive activities.

To summarize, a few activities are by nature indisputably areawide, but numerous activities can be handled in more than one manner: by small-area governments, by intermediate-size units, or with areawide government in charge of planning but with operations noncentralized. Versatility is the byword to describe the way activities can be assigned in the context of local federalism.

Chapter 14

SOCIAL AND FISCAL EQUITY

Local federalism carries into the political community the social pluralism which characterizes metropolitan areas. It divides responsibilities for various activities among different levels of local government in order to achieve effective administration and to bring government as close as possible to the people. Government so instituted aims at securing equally for all citizens the rights of life, liberty, and the pursuit of happiness, so we have been taught to believe.

The Idea of Equity

Equally for all! This gets us to the goal of equity. I perceive equity as basic fairness. In personal relationships, equity is fair dealing with one another. In society, equity is fair treatment for each and every person. In material things, equity is a fair share for everybody. In metropolitan areas, social equity for individuals and particular groups and fiscal equity for local governments are especially important.

Does equity mean equality? Yes and no. They are related concepts but not identical. Both terms derive from the same Latin word, but in our language each conveys a different concept. As stated, equity is fairness. Equality is sameness in quantity or quality: the same size, same ability, same strength, same income, same basic rights, same personal worth.

In some circumstances, equity might require full equality, such as equal citizenship rights for everyone. But in other situations, there could be equity without complete equality, such as more education for the talented. Conversely, absolute equality (quantitative sameness) might not be equitable (fair), such as identical income regardless of personal effort, social contribution, or need.

In a recent book entitled *More Equality*, Herbert J. Gans expresses a concern for three outcomes of equality: equality of opportunity, equality of treatment, equality of results (1974:63). I borrow these categories and offer my own observations.

Equality of treatment applies in the area of citizenship. Each person's vote should be equal, everyone equally entitled to run for office, and the judicial system should be motivated by the ideal of equal justice under law. Equity requires correction of any deviations from these standards for equal treatment.

Equality of opportunity has application in offering such opportunities as adequate education, satisfactory employment, a decent home in a suitable environment. If access is open to all, people can take advantage of these opportunities. But since all persons don't start on the same plane, equity demands that people be treated differently in order to truly have equal opportunity. Compensatory education for schools in poor neighborhoods is one example, and special occupational training intended to prepare low-skilled adults for available jobs is another. Equal entitlement to the aimed-for opportunity may require special treatment as an intermediate step.

Equality of results provides a test to determine whether opportunities are truly meaningful. For example, if no blacks live in supposedly open housing, the reality of that opportunity can be questioned. If women, persons of a particular color, and individuals with distinctive ethnic backgrounds don't hold executive positions in a business establishment, the validity of the "we-are-an-equal-opportunity-employer" sign is in doubt. By providing the test of fairness, a concern for equity enters into the quest for equality of results.

However, equity parts company with equality of results expressed as a desire for quantitative sameness, particularly equal income and equal wealth. Equity considers it fair for extra effort to be rewarded, for persons with heavy responsibilities to be paid more, for special social contributions to merit prestige and monetary gain. But in contrast it is inequitable for professions or businesses to use positions of dominance to extract excessively high income or for persons to live off vast inheritance while making little or no social contribution. Most importantly, it is unfair for any family to have insufficient income to obtain even a modest standard of living. It is gross income inequality which equity condemns.

In short, equity incorporates comparative measures in computing equality of results. This acknowledges that people differ in many qualities even though they are equal in worth and dignity. We shouldn't expect complete sameness, but we should strive for greater equity.

Social Equity

A concern for social justice impels us to consider social inequities found within metropolitan areas and to do something about them. By and large their origins are found in deep, underlying societal conditions and in general attitudes. Their manifestations occur where people live, and for three out of four Americans, their home is in a metropolitan area. Therefore, social equity is a metropolitan issue.

INCOME INEQUALITY

Numerous social problems arise out of the pervasive pattern of income inequality found in the United States. People of the metropolis, indeed all Americans, need money to live because in our society we must pay for most of the goods, services, and facilities we utilize. Although public agencies render many services without direct charges, these too require money because government must levy taxes to pay the costs. Yet, a sizable portion of the population lives in poverty while others are very rich and many more are quite well off.

Facts. Personal income and wealth are quite unevenly distributed within the United States. The poorest one-fifth of all families received only 5 percent of the nation's personal income in 1975 while the richest one-fifth gained 41 percent. Wealth is even more unequal, though data on its distribution are harder to come by. However, economists James Smith and Stephen D. Franklin estimate that in 1972 0.3 percent of all families were millionaires and held 15 percent of all wealth (net worth); in contrast, 55 percent of all families had less than $10,000 and 12 percent had less than $1,000 net worth (1975:14, 16). Such inequality is grossly inequitable. Worse yet, it is tragic for the poor and near-poor families which have the least.

The national government has developed a poverty index to determine how many families have less income than the amount needed to provide a minimal level of decent living conditions. In 1975 when the poverty threshold was $5,500 for a nonfarm family of four and comparable amount for other family sizes, 12.3 percent of the U.S. population lived in poverty. Inside metropolitan areas the proportion was 10.8 percent.

Current data aren't available for income distribution within specific metropolitan areas, but the wide disparities found in the nation as whole occur in every metropolis.

Solutions. What to do about income inequality goes beyond the scope of this book except for a brief hint. To a considerable extent it requires strong action by the national government, which in many different ways acts as an arbiter of income distribution within the United States. Through tax laws, it determines how much different income groups and sources of income will pay to support the government. In its spending programs, it determines what purposes and areas will benefit. In this manner, the national government achieves a certain amount of income redistribution of three varieties: between generations, between income groups, and between regions.

In fulfilling its economic mission, the first and foremost set of national actions needed are measures to bring about full employment with price stability. This requires effective national economic planning, sound fiscal and taxing policies, federal job creation programs, and from time to time selective controls over prices, wages, interest rates, and profits. Within the context of these policies there should be guaranteed employment opportunities at decent wages for all persons able to work. For people who can't work other means of income support are necessary, including social security programs to furnish income to the retired and the permanently disabled and welfare programs for others who aren't in a position to take a job because of family responsibilities or temporary disability. Unemployment insurance serves persons temporarily out of work, and supplemental cash support is needed to boost the income of workers who don't earn enough to support their families. Beyond these measures, in-kind assistance, such as food stamps and housing subsidies are useful, though my own preference is for direct cash assistance.

These kinds of programs have been developing for forty-five years, with considerable success. For example, if it weren't for social security and unemployment insurance, the poverty rate would be twice as high. Without welfare payments it would be about 23 percent higher. Moreover, according to the Congressional Budget Office (1977:vii), if the value of in-kind transfers, notably food stamps, medicare, and medicaid, were calculated (the Census Bureau considers only money income), poverty could be considered reduced by another 40 percent.

Even so, poverty remains a persistent problem in the United States, and further attention should be given to the need for more income redistribution through national action.

Yet, this task isn't only the responsibility of the national government. The states can support their own versions of some of the programs mentioned: job creation, income supplements for persons in need, special housing programs. Much can be done within metropolitan areas to see that persons in greatest need will benefit from the programs, and possibly an areawide tax can support some of the programs and in that fashion achieve a modest amount of local income redistribution.

Furthermore, a full employment plan is needed for each metropolitan area because the metropolis is a kind of little economy functioning as a labor market and as a locale for manufacturing, trade, and services. An areawide full employment plan would assess local conditions, define shortcomings, describe which people and subareas require particular assistance, and outline ways to work toward local full employment, including economic development activities, supplementary employment programs, and training and supportive services. In the context of local federalism, this plan would be carried into action by governments and agencies working in areas of different sizes, ranging from an areawide labor market exchange to neighborhood employment centers and work projects for youth. This would take advantage of one of local federalism's strongest traits, its capacity to deal with the whole while at the same time delivering individualized services.

SOCIAL SEPARATION

Income inequality in American society is given spatial expression within metropolitan areas. Poor people tend to be concentrated in slum areas and public housing projects, mostly inside the central city, while the rich occupy protected residential enclaves, mostly suburban. For the income groups in between, there is a somewhat greater mixture, but the American metropolis has a strong tendency toward social class separation.

Facts. In its 1975 population survey, the U.S. Bureau of the Census found that within metropolitan areas 15.0 percent of the central city population was poor compared to 6.2 percent in the suburbs (1976B:43). In city poverty areas, so classified because of concentration of poor people in particular neighborhoods, the poverty rate was 34.9 percent. There are also pockets of poverty in the suburbs.

However, considerable variation occurs around the nation. Richard P. Nathan and Charles Adams discerned this in a study aimed at understanding central city hardship (1976:47-62). In the process they constructed what I would call a "socio-economic disparity index," using six factors: poverty, per capita income, unemployment, dependency (population under eighteen and over sixty-four), education, and crowded housing. Then they compared fifty-five central cities with their suburbs and found that forty-three of them were worse off than the suburbs in the composite rating by the six factors, two were the same, and ten were better off. Table 14.1 lists the fourteen cities with a socio-economic disparity rating twice or more than their suburbs and also the ten better-off cities. Nathan and Adams also compared central cities to one another and suburbs to suburbs and showed that some cities, such as Hartford, have considerable disparity with their own suburbs but aren't as bad off as many other cities.

Causes. For cities with a high socio-economic disparity compared to their suburbs, no single cause explains the reasons. However, most of them are older cities located in the northeast and north central regions, their boundaries have changed little or none in many years, and they contain less than half the metropolitan population. The opposite is the case with half the cities with a lower socio-economic disparity rating than their suburbs because city

Table 14.1: Socio-Economic Disparity between Selected Central Cities and their Suburbs (1970)

Central cities with a socio-economic disparity index twice or more than their suburbs	Socio-economic disparity index*	Central cities with a socio-economic disparity index less than their suburbs	Socio-economic disparity index*
Newark	4.22	Omaha	.98
Cleveland	3.31	Dallas	.97
Hartford	3.17	Houston	.93
Baltimore	2.56	Phoenix	.85
Chicago	2.45	Norfolk	.82
St. Louis	2.31	Salt Lake City	.80
Atlanta	2.26	San Diego	.77
Rochester	2.15	Seattle	.67
Gary	2.13	Ft. Lauderdale	.64
Dayton	2.11	Greensboro	.43
New York	2.11		
Detroit	2.10		
Richmond	2.09		
Philadelphia	2.05		

*The socio-economic disparity index compares central city and suburbs for six factors: unemployment (percentage of civilian labor force unemployed); dependency (persons under 18 and over 64 as percentage of total population); education (percentage of persons 25 and older with less than a twelfth-grade education); per capita income; crowded housing (percentage of occupied housing with more than one person per room); and poverty (percentage of families below 125 percent of the low-income level).

Source: Adapted from Nathan and Adams, 1976:51-52.

expansion has absorbed a larger share of metropolitan growth including upper-income families, and the other half have other cities and low-income suburbs within the metropolitan area.

This might lead one to conclude that a governmental structure containing numerous suburban municipalities, each with zoning power, combined with rigid central city boundaries causes social separation. There is plenty of truth to that contention, but it isn't totally true because even before there was zoning, cities covering large territories had different quarters for various social groups. Nevertheless, in the last fifty years the inclination of upper- and middle-income groups to separate themselves from poorer people has been reinforced by suburban incorporation and local zoning authority and aided and abetted by federal housing policies which have provided mortgage insurance for middle-income suburban housing and subsidies for central city public housing. Out of this process has come the contemporary pattern of metropolitan settlement with increasing separation of socio-economic groups, as the commissions cited in Chapter 1 forcefully documented.

Solutions. Previously in talking abot the division of functional responsibilities for planning and housing (Chapter 13, pp. 184-185), I described some of the steps which might be undertaken in the context of local federalism. They include an areawide development plan to provide a framework for land use, including general location of housing types, and an areawide fair share housing plan to allocate housing for various income groups to different localities. Local government would handle zoning in a manner consistent with the areawide development plan and would pick the sites for their share of low- and moderate-income housing.

Several metropolitan areas have made a start toward fair share housing plans, and in 1976 seven areawide planning organizations received supplemental federal rental subsidy funds from the U.S. Department of Housing and Urban Development (HUD) to help them carry out "housing opportunity plans." The areas are Lehigh and Northampton Counties, Pennsylvania (Allentown, Bethlehem, Easton); the national capital area; Miami Valley, Ohio (Dayton); Twin Cities area, Minnesota; Southern Iowa (a town-and-country district); Puget Sound region, Washington; and Southern California. (HUD, 1976).

The Miami Valley Regional Planning Commission pioneered the fair share concept in 1970. At that time only 5 percent of the region's assisted housing was outside Dayton, and in the next six years that portion was raised to almost half through a combination of voluntary cooperation and leverage exercised in the A-95 review of housing and community development applications. The program includes housing information and referral services for lower income and minority households and a special private fund for loans and grants for housing rehabilitation.

Both Lehigh and Northampton Counties have housing authorities which are administering assisted housing programs on a countywide basis. The

Metropolitan Council in Minnesota is authorized to serve as a housing and redevelopment authority throughout the seven-county area with the consent of local governmental units, and forty-two communities have joined; among them there is no residency requirement for housing applicants, and a person may apply in one location and move to assisted housing in any other of the participating jurisdictions. The other four metropolitan areas involved in this special program have worked out their own administrative arrangements, proving that where there's a will, there's a way—and that it can be tailored to local circumstances.

In a major study of equal housing opportunity conducted for the Potomac Institute (1976), David Falk and Herbert M. Franklin endorse the idea of fair share housing plans. Indeed, they believe that HUD should allocate all of its housing subsidies to regional agencies, which would then develop regional housing market strategies; local housing assistance programs would carry out the plan, choosing the precise locations and types of assistance they want, consistent with regional standards (1976:37). These authors, both lawyers, also favor court action against local exclusionary practices which deny low- and moderate-income persons the opportunity to live in certain places (1976:93-121), and they cite some judicial decisions, particularly in New Jersey, requiring a municipality or township to take into account housing needs for the larger area extending beyond the jurisdiction's own boundaries.

Falk and Franklin advocate state initiative and discuss the Massachusetts Zoning Appeals Act of 1969 which enables developers to contest local blockage of state and federally assisted housing projects (1976:121-123). Furthermore, they insist that suburban communities themselves can and should take their own initiatives by creating housing authorities, providing zoning incentives for low-income housing, and mandating the inclusion of housing for low- and moderate-income persons in all new private housing developments (1976:126-127).

In these and many other ways the social separation of metropolitan areas could be reduced if we wanted it to. A reasonable goal might be to produce a fairly heterogeneous population for the attendance area of every high school. This would have the dual objective of offering a wider housing choice to low- and moderate-income families and of enabling all young Americans, rich, poor, and in between, to grow up in contact with people from diverse backgrounds, surely an important preparation for life in a pluralistic society. (For other ideas see Downs, 1973.)

RACIAL DISCRIMINATION

Social separation of income groups is compounded by racial discrimination. This causes blacks, and in some places Hispanics, to suffer a double liability. They are disproportionately represented in the ranks of the poor, which makes them unable to afford suburban housing, and even those with the financial means to buy a house or rent an apartment in the suburbs run into direct and subtle discriminatory practices.

Facts. Considerable progress has been made in the last twenty years to reduce the amount of racial discrimination in housing, but our society still has a long ways to go until completely open opportunity is universally practiced. Falk and Franklin cite these facts to describe the current situation (1976:3-4):

> As a percentage of the total population in the central cities, the black population increased in the 1950-1974 period from 12.3% to 20.5%.

> Blacks within central cities are increasingly concentrated in segregated neighborhoods.

> Far more blacks than whites of all income levels live in low-income areas of central cities. In 1972, 51 percent of central city blacks above the poverty level lived in low-income areas. The comparable percentage of central cities whites above the poverty level was 10.2.

> Proportionately more blacks living in suburban areas live in worse neighborhoods than whites and frequently in segragated black neighborhoods.

> The residential patterns of America's 11 million Spanish-Americans, constituting 5% of the total population, resemble those of black families. . . . Neighborhoods where Spanish-Americans live tend to be segregated, particularly in the Northeast.

Solutions. Poverty and racial discrimination are overlapping problems because blacks and Hispanics are disproportionately represented among the poor. Therefore, working toward elimination of poverty and opening more housing opportunities for low- and moderate-income households in the suburbs will help ease the plight of minority groups. But also a direct attack upon racial discrimination is needed.

The federal Civil Rights Act can be the foundation for this effort. Title VI prohibits discrimination on the grounds of race, color, or national origin under programs and activities receiving federal financial assistance. This includes most federal housing assistance programs, and while mortgage loans insured by the Federal Housing Administration and the Veterans Administration were excepted, they are covered under an executive order. Title VIII prohibits a variety of discriminatory practices in the private housing market. In addition, twenty-eight states and sixteen local governments have enacted fair housing laws substantially equivalent to Title VIII (U.S. Commission on Civil Rights, 1974:42).

The laws are there and they have helped, but full compliance lags and enforcement is often slow and cumbersome. The U.S. Civil Rights Commission surveyed the situation in 1974 and expressed considerable dissatisfaction with the results achieved. It found that the approach of the Department of Housing and Urban Development (HUD), the primary federal agency for fair housing, was largely ad hoc and based primarily upon individual complaints. As an alternative, the Commission proposed communitywide compliance review of all major institutions affecting the production, sale, and rental of housing, including state and local governments, housing authorities, builders and developers, real estate brokers. Where housing discrimination is found, HUD should use leverage, such as deferral of funds or debarment from HUD programs, in order to bring about nondiscrimination. The Commission recommended bolstering the efforts of other federal agencies, such as the Veterans Administration and the agencies regulating lending institutions. It found that state and local fair housing agencies often lacked financial and staff resources to enforce fair housing laws and suggested federal assistance for this purpose (1974:328-361; for other recommendations see Falk and Franklin, 1976:53-75).

Fiscal Equity

Social and economic disparities within the metropolis place varying service demands upon the different local governmental units. The problem is compounded by the uneven spread of revenue resources of local government. In many cases, the jurisdictions with the highest service demands are in the worst financial position. Thus, there are notable fiscal disparities in all metropolitan areas having pluralistic governments, and that's most of them.

FISCAL DISPARITIES

The existence of fiscal disparities isn't a new problem but a reversal has occurred within the older metropolitan areas. Fifty to seventy-five years ago the central cities contained most of the economic activities of the metropolis, and many of the suburbs were struggling to raise enough revenue for the public services the new, city-bred residents wanted. But in the past thirty years the outlying areas have gained shopping centers, office buildings, light industrial plants, and other economic activities while the central city's economic base has grown less rapidly and in some cases has declined. Nevertheless, some cities in newer metropolitan areas have been able to capture a good share of economic growth by expanding their boundaries, and some of them are better off than their suburbs.

The Advisory Commission on Intergovernmental Relations has performed yeoman's service for many years documenting metropolitan fiscal disparities and proposing remedies. In a major study conducted in 1966-67, ACIR outlined the glaring fiscal disparities brought about by increasing concen-

tration of "high fiscal cost" citizens in central cities accompanied by a
lessening capacity to pay for necessary public services. Relative to the
suburbs, the cities had residents with lower incomes, worse housing, and
higher unemployment. The suburbs had a much larger growth of per capita
taxable resources, and some central cities even had an absolute decline in
taxable resources. The result was a much higher per capita tax burden relative
to personal income in the central cities in comparison to the suburbs
(1967B:2-3).

Yet it wasn't simply a problem between the central city and the suburbs as
a whole, for ACIR also reported dramatic fiscal disparities among rich and
poor suburban communities. "Many of the older suburban communities are
taking on the physical, social and economic characteristics of the central city.
This type of community is especially vulnerable to fiscal distress because it
lacks the diversified tax base that has enabled the central city to absorb some
of the impact of extraordinary expenditure demands" (1967B:6).

The problem reached the crisis stage for some cities during the Great
Recession of 1974-76, forcing them to raise local taxes extremely high, cut
services, and even then teeter on the edge of insolvency. This was paradoxical
because so much of the nation's wealth is located in metropolitan areas. In
1976 ACIR puzzled over this phenomenon and supplied two reasons: "(1) a
scarcity of resources generally and a disparity in resources between central
city and suburban portions of metropolitan areas, and (2) a jurisdictional
mismatch in those areas, leaving no suitable governmental unit to apply
solutions" (1976A:3).

David T. Stanley came to similar conclusions when he reviewed a number
of studies about cities in trouble and produced a list containing Boston, New
York, Newark, Philadelphia, Buffalo, Cleveland, Detroit, and St. Louis. Why?
Because, he contended, population and economic bases in many metropolitan
areas are declining, public costs have escalated, revenue growth and federal
assistance has lagged behind the cost increase, and financial management in
some cases has been unsatisfactory (1976:iii).

This has led some public officials and scholars from the Northeast to
deplore the shift in economic resources to the "Sunbelt" states. Yet in spite
of the slowing of economic growth in the longer-settled parts of the nation
and the population decline in a few metropolitan areas, this region still has
per capita income considerably higher than the southern and southwestern
states. But in the East and Midwest the rich live mostly in the suburbs
and the poor mostly in the central cities so that socio-economic separation is a major cause of the cities' financial crisis. It's not that these
states are suddenly poverty-stricken but rather that state laws and local
practices have permitted a local governmental pattern which produces fiscal disparities.

UNIFICATION OR TRANSFER OF FUNCTIONS

This observation suggests a natural remedy: unification. And indeed, metropolises with consolidated government, such as Jacksonville, Nashville-Davidson County, Indianapolis, and Honolulu, have largely escaped severe fiscal crises, though all of them, and rich suburbs too, have had to keep a close watch on their budgets during a period of economic recession and high inflation rate.

Complete unification produces a single, areawide tax base and enables revenues to be drawn from diverse sources and expenditures to be directed where needed. This doesn't assure that poor neighborhoods will benefit the most, for we know that even in central cities the better-off neighborhoods sometimes get better services. But it at least creates a structure and a political process through which the goal of equity can be approached. Indeed, in many ways the possibility of greater fiscal equity is one of the strongest arguments favoring unification.

But as we have already explored in Chapter 7, unification is a who-will-bell-the-cat solution for most metropolitan areas. It might be politically feasible for a few single-county metropolises, but these are exceptions. Certainly for the large, multicounty areas unification is highly unlikely, and these are the ones where the central city fiscal crisis is the gravest and where metropolitan fiscal disparity is most severe.

Another remedy is to transfer operational responsibility for particular functions to jurisdictions of broader geographic coverage, thus tapping a wider tax base to pay for them. The services so financed can be rendered where necessary without regard to the amount of taxes paid by various subareas. This has happened with considerable frequency, as Chapter 5 documented, usually transference from one local unit to another but sometimes to a state agency. Even so, transfer of responsibility has limited application because of local insistence upon the right to operate many services.

Therefore, if we are to have pluralistic local government in metropolitan areas—and this seems certain for most areas, we will have to solve problems of fiscal disparity in the context of federalism, both the local variety and the broader American federal system. There are a variety of ways to accomplish this. All of them have a common characteristic: redistribution of revenue.

SHIFT OF FINANCIAL RESPONSIBILITY

Chapter 5 laid out a number of fiscal devices already in use to finance multitudinous local governments in metropolitan areas. One of them was the shifting of financial responsibility from one level to another without transferring operational responsibility.

Education. In 1969 the Advisory Commission on Intergovernmental Relations recommended that all nonfederal financing of elementary and secondary education should be shifted from the local property tax to the superior tax resources of state governments (1969:14):

> In order to create a financial environment more conducive to attainment of equality of educational opportunity and to remove the massive and growing pressure of the school tax on owners of local property, the Commission recommends that each state adopt as an objective of its long-range state-local fiscal policy the assumption by the state of substantially all fiscal responsibility for financing local schools with opportunity for financial enrichment at the local level and assurance of retention of appropriate local policy-making authority.

Seven years later ACIR reported that about two-fifths of the states have begun to increase state funding. Delaware, North Carolina, Louisiana, and New Mexico are within striking distance of the goal of state assumption of school financing. Hawaii has gone all the way not only with state financing but also operation of elementary and secondary schools, though elsewhere state operation isn't in the offing (1976A:46).

Welfare. In about three-fifths of the states local government spends little or no money on welfare because state government provides the required matching funds for federal categorical assistance and has picked up some or all of the tab for general assistance. Local governments in nine states, however, pay from 20 to 30 percent of the public welfare bill and in a dozen states local governments finance 5 to 20 percent of welfare costs.

Because welfare is clearly a redistributive measure, it should be financed from as broad a tax base as practicable. In 1972 Congress moved in this direction by wholly financing aid to the aged, blind, and disabled. Yet to come is full federal funding of public assistance for families with dependent children and Medicaid, a step ACIR and many other commissions and organizations have recommended. Also needed is a shift of general assistance to state funding in those states where local governments still pay a share. However, welfare programs can still be administered by county and city agencies, as is now the case in some but not all states.

Shifts of these kinds would reduce fiscal disparities in some metropolitan areas. Moreover, complete federal funding of public assistance would relieve state governments of this burden, and a lot of the money saved could go toward state assumption of elementary and secondary school costs.

STATE AND FEDERAL ASSISTANCE

Another way to tap a wider tax base is through state and federal assistance to local governments. Because the state economic bases vary considerably, federal sources are superior from an equity viewpoint. As ACIR has explained (1976A:3):

> The most elastic and productive governmental revenues are those of the national government, yet solutions to urban problems for the most part must be paid for by state and local governments, whose less responsive revenue systems have left them continually behind in the effort to meet expenditure demand. The Federal government collects about 90 percent of the nation's personal income taxes and about 70 percent of the rest of the nation's taxes, yet state and local governments must pay for about 70 percent of urban operating expenses. Therefore, Federal aid programs have become vital in helping state and local governments meet their service needs.

There are two principal reasons for federal aid: to meet a program need conceived to be in the national interest and to redistribute income among geographic areas and economic groups. A similar statement can be made about state aid. Unfortunately political pressures sometimes distort the redistributive objective by using factors other than relative need in the allocation formula, and this lessens the potential for relieving fiscal disparities. So we need to keep insisting that state and federal assistance programs maintain a sharp focus on reducing inequities.

Revenue sharing. Relative local fiscal capacity should be a major determinant in formulas of state and federal revenue sharing by taking into consideration local tax resources (property, retail sales, personal income) and local efforts to tap these sources. Another factor to take into account is the special demands for services which a disadvantaged population might place upon local government, and this can be approximated by the percentage of families below the poverty level, or by the number of families on welfare if poverty data aren't available. Placing an arbitrary ceiling on a city's share, as federal general revenue sharing does, reduces its effectiveness as a redistributive measure.

In the spirit of American federalism, local government should have plenty of independence in the use of shared revenues. Observance of constitutional requirements for equal protection are obviously necessary, but beyond that the localities should have considerable leeway with the money. If the state or national government wants funds spent for particular purposes, it should channel assistance through program grants. To stabilize local operations, revenue sharing needs permanence, or at least a long-term commitment.

Program grants. State and federal assistance in the form of program grants can and should focus upon needs in the particular functional fields: insufficient decent and affordable housing for housing assistance grants; factors contributing to ill health for health programs; traffic volume and miles of highways and transit lines for transportation grants; unemployment and underemployment for employment-and-training programs.

To keep state-local and federal-local relationships as simple as possible, broad block grants are preferred, allowing for considerable flexibility and local discretion in the use of funds as long as the locality keeps the program on the intended target. Categorical grants should be reserved for special needs and new activities which haven't been well tested. Of federal assistance, the present 14 percent devoted to block grants should be raised to 50 percent or more, and the 76 percent assigned to categorical programs should be reduced proportionately. The 14 percent put into revenue sharing and other general support seems a reasonable portion for this method.

Extraordinary situations. There are some extraordinary situations where special kinds of intergovernmental assistance are desirable. One of them occurs during a national economic recession which reduces local revenues and forces layoffs, thereby aggravating unemployment. Countercyclical federal revenue sharing is needed then, and it should be based upon local unemployment rates. This would be in addition to public service employment and special public works programs aimed at creating jobs for the general populace.

Even in good times some central cities and certain suburban municipalities have a shaky financial foundation because of long-term decline in the local economy or because boundary restrictions separate them from an adequate tax base. To the extent that it is the former, the national government ought to help them through a transitional period of a number of years until the local economy is revitalized or until population and services have adjusted to what the local economy can support. If it is the latter, state government has an obligation to provide regular, long-term assistance or to mandate an areawide revenue sharing program because state laws on local governmental organization have brought about the fiscally disparate situation.

LOCAL REMEDIES

Although state and federal assistance is needed to overcome fiscal disparity, a metropolitan area can do a number of things for itself short of total unification if it has the structure and authority.

Areawide taxes. Services and facilities which are metropolitan in nature can be paid for by areawide taxes rather than supported by only central city taxpayers, who are frequently saddled with the burden. Ordinarily this is accomplished by transferring responsibility to an areawide agency which has taxing authority. Among functions so financed in some places are mass transit, port, airport, hospitals, libraries, and parks. Some of them also utilize user fees as a second revenue source. If an areawide general government was established, it would have taxing authority, and it would be able to draw upon the tax base of the whole metropolis and would direct its services where necessary.

Cost sharing. The same objective can be achieved without functional transfer through cost sharing arrangements. This is now done as part of interlocal service contracts and joint facilities and services. It is easiest where the service is clearly measurable, such as the volume of water supplied or miles of streets maintained, but it is possible to devise allocation formulas even for overhead items, as Los Angeles County has done. It isn't always simple, and more than one joint operating agreement has broken up over cost disputes, but if pursued carefully and in good faith, a fair share of costs can be distributed to benefiting jurisdictions. It is even conceivable that suburban jurisdictions might contribute to the budget of a central facility, such as an art museum or a zoo which the central city can no longer afford to support by itself.

Commuter tax. An income tax on nonresidents working in the city is another way to help ease the central city's financial plight. This approach is fruitful where the city has many jobs filled by commuters, especially persons with higher incomes, but it doesn't do much for small, hard-pressed suburban municipalities lacking an employment base.

Areawide revenue sharing. The most innovative approach to metropolitan fiscal disparities this decade is the metropolitan tax-base sharing arrangement devised for Minnesota's Twin Cities area, as told in Chapter 5. It taps 40 percent of the increase in commercial and industrial property valuation in the seven-county area and allocates the money so raised to 300 local jurisdictions at an inverse ratio to their per capita valuation of all property. The governor of Michigan has proposed a similar scheme for the Detroit area, but the state legislature has shown little enthusiasm. But in spite of political resistance, it is a very appropriate measure for state government to adopt because the local governmental pattern and taxation arrangements are determined by the state and so also remedies should be fashioned at that level. Once established, they can then be administered by a local body, possibly by an areawide general government.

The case for areawide revenue sharing is deeply rooted in the quest for equity. As Julius Margolis has explained (1974:61): "If it is reasonable to argue that the tax-price an individual pays should not be effected by the wealth of his neighbors, then a fiscal redistribution scheme can be adopted within the metropolitan area that would reduce tax competitiveness and enable cities to carry on their redistributive functions with minimum risk."

In sum, a number of ways are available to redistribute revenue within metropolitan areas. They can be combined with state and federal assistance to substantially reduce fiscal disparities and thereby move toward greater equity for the people of metropolitan areas. This is not an easy objective to achieve,

Social and Fiscal Equity

for the "haves" have personal self-interest and often accompanying political influence to prevent redistribution from occurring. Yet, a sense of justice demands that we seek to achieve a fairer distribution of revenue within metropolitan areas.

PART IV

WHAT IT COULD BECOME

Chapter 15

TYPES OF METROPOLITAN AREAS

Application of local federalism, I believe, is the desired course to pursue in trying to improve the governmental structure of metropolitan areas. This can't be blind application of a single model, however, for no one form can fit the diversity among the metropolitan areas of the United States.

In order to make practice more effective, we need to comprehend this diversity. The place to begin is by realizing that there is no such thing as a "typical" metropolitan area. The range between, say, the Midland, Texas SMSA, with four governmental units for a 1974 population of 66,000, and the Chicago SMSA, with 1,172 units for a population of nearly 7 million, is enormous. Obviously the approach to governmental organization has to reflect these widely varying circumstances.

Yet, although every metropolis is unique in its own way, it is possible to identify common characteristics and to define some major types of metropolitan areas. That is the purpose of this chapter. We look at the simplest ones first—those which are contained within a single county and are physically separated from other metropolitan areas. Next we take up the smaller metropolitan areas of New England and Virginia which lack a single, strong county covering the whole metropolis. The third group consists of free-standing, multicounty metropolitan areas under one million—free-standing in the sense that they aren't part of a larger urbanized region. The fourth major group is the most complex and is composed of metropolitan regions; some of them have two or more SMSAs contiguous to one another, and all multi-county SMSAs over one million are also placed in this category.

The assignment of particular metropolises to these major categories uses OMB's delineation of SMSAs as a point of departure but doesn't adhere religiously to them, particularly by describing a number of areas as single-county even though the SMSA includes one or more fringe counties. The reader should understand that classification is intended to be illustrative rather than absolute and that many subjective factors go into the assignment. Moreover, quite a few areas are on the borderline between major types. With this caveat stated, let us proceed.

Free-Standing, Single-County Areas

The OMB delineation of SMSAs has 105 which cover only one county. My classification scheme deviates from the OMB approach in two respects. First, some of the officially defined, one-county SMSAs are packed into a larger region of continuous urbanization. Orange County, California, for example, is clearly a part of the Southern California metropolitan region and should be considered in this broader context. Secondly, the official criteria have added to SMSAs a lot of counties of small population because of a detection of commutation patterns, but these are well beyond the urbanized area, that is, the closely settled territory, and are largely outside the service area of the developed metropolis. In a broad sense of wide-scale planning they need to be considered, but for most things local government does they don't have to be integrated into the operating government of the metropolis. Therefore, I lop off some counties to come up with my own list of free-standing, single-county metropolises, but I indicate the ones which have fringe counties by the SMSA definition.

By my count, there are 142 free-standing, single-county metropolises (listed in the Appendix, Table 15). Of these 86 are one-county SMSAs and the other 56 have one or more fringe counties in the SMSA definition. Of the total, five have a consolidated city/county (Jacksonville, Lexington, Baton Rouge, Anchorage, and Honolulu). All the others have one or more central cities combined with suburbs organized under separate jurisdictions, including 117 with only one central city. Of the remainder, 13 have two central cities, such as Waterloo-Cedar Falls, Iowa and Lakeland-Winter Haven, Florida, and seven have three central cities, such as Salinas-Seaside-Monterey, California. So there are several subtypes:

Consolidated city/county (5)

One principal city and suburbs (117)

Two or more principal cities and suburbs (20)

Most of them have undeveloped rural area as well as built-up suburbs outside the central city.

More than half (55 percent) of the one-county metropolises are in the 100,000 to 250,000 range, as shown in Table 15.1, and 18 percent are less than 100,000. But two are over one million in population (San Diego and Phoenix), and seven are between 500,000 and a million. This diversity of size suggests that governmental organization might be different as well.

The governmental pattern presently varies, based primarily upon different traditions in the states and regions of the United States. This is revealed in Table 15.2. By and large, the southern states have the fewest governmental units in their metropolitan areas because they lack townships and don't make much use of special districts. For example, Buncombe County, North Carolina containing Ashville has eleven units, and Alachua County, Florida with Gainesville has sixteen units. Knox County, Tennessee where Knoxville is located has six units, but Pulaski County, Arkansas with Little Rock has twenty-seven.

The western states don't have townships either, but their greater use of special districts adds to the number of local units, such as the sixty-two in El Paso County, Colorado (Colorado Springs), the forty-three in Yellowstone County, Montana (Billings), and the one hundred twenty-eight in San Joaquin County, California (Stockton). However, not all of the West and Southwest use special districts extensively: in West Texas, for instance, such single-county metropolises as those with Lubbock, San Angelo, and Odessa don't have many units. Nor does Bernalillo County, New Mexico (Albuquerque), which has only eight units.

States with townships have many more units within the metropolis. Even though they are less significant in weak township states, they help bring the total up, such as Olmstead County, Minnesota (Rochester) with thirty-one governmental units, Allen County, Indiana (Fort Wayne) with forty-five, and

Table 15.1: Population of Free-Standing, Single-County Metropolises (1974).

Population Group	Metropolises	
	Number	Percentage
All	*14*	*100.0*
1.0 to 2.5 million	2	1.4
500,000 to 1.0 million	7	4.9
250,000 to 500,000	29	20.4
100,000 to 250,000	78	54.9
50,000 to 100,000	26	18.3

Source: U.S. Bureau of the Census, 1976A.

Table 15.2: Number of Governmental Units in Single-County Metropolises by Types of State (1972)

Type of state	Number of metropolises	Total number of governmental units					
		1-10	11-25	26-50	51-100	101 and more	NA
All	*142*	*16*	*33*	*40*	*28*	*13*	*12*
No townships—South	37	10	16	6	1	–	4
No townships—West	57	6	15	14	11	6	5
Weak townships	24	–	1	11	6	3	3
Strong townships	24	–	1	9	10	4	–

NA = not available because SMSA not delineated prior to 1972 census of governments

Source: U.S. Bureau of the Census, 1973. Table 19.

Stark County, Ohio (Canton) with fifty-eight. The strong township states
tend to have even more units in their metropolises. Saginaw County, Michigan, for example, has fifty-four, Onodaga County, New York (Syracuse) has
seventy-nine, and Lancaster County, Pennsylvania has one hundred thirty-
seven.

But if we exclude school districts and special districts from the total
number of governmental units, we find that the pattern of local general
government isn't extremely complex in these single-county metropolises.
Those in the South have a median of six municipalities, and for the West the
median is eight. A median of twenty-eight municipalities and townships is
found in weak-township states and thirty-two in strong-township states, but if
only municipalities are counted in the weak-township states, the median falls
to nine, or about the same as in the western states. An exception is Illinois,
which has weak townships but many municipalities under 2,500 in its
metropolitan areas (and also lots of special districts).

New England and Virginia Areas

The New England states have twelve metropolitan areas and Virginia four
in the size range of the bulk of single-county metropolises, but they need to
be considered separately. This is because New England lacks strong counties
and in Virginia cities are territorially separate from county government. The
sixteen metropolises in this group aren't very complex, as Table 15.3 reveals
(also see Appendix, Table 16). The seven cities and counties in the Richmond
area are the most in Virginia. The greatest number in a New England area (not
counting the metropolitan regions) is twenty-five for the Worchester, Massachusetts area, but half of the areas in New England have ten or less units of
local general government.

Table 15.3: Number of Local General Governmental Units in
Free-Standing Metropolises in New England and Virginia
(1975).

Region or State	Number of Metropolises	Number of Units		
		1-5	6-10	11-25
New England*	12	3	3	6
Virginia**	4	3	1	—

*Cities and towns
**Independent cities and counties
Source: Office of Management and Budget, 1975.

Free-Standing, Multicounty Areas

The third major type is composed of free-standing metropolitan areas where considerable urbanization has occurred in two or more counties. However, areas with these characteristics over one million are somewhat arbitrarily assigned to the next group, metropolitan regions, on the theory that a population of that magnitude produces a metropolis where several suburban or satellite centers compete with the central city, thus adding to the political complexity.

There are forty-five free-standing, multicounty metropolitan areas in this classification scheme (see Appendix, Table 17). Twenty-seven are found within a single state, and eighteen are interstate. On the whole they tend to be more populous than the single-county metropolises, and none are under 100,000, as Table 15.4 indicates. Like the single-county metropolises, the multicounty areas reflect their states in the number and kinds of local governmental units they have. The southern states are the least complicated and the strong township states the most complex. (The point has been made so such data aren't presented for this type.)

What appears in this group are different kinds of counties, depending upon their location within the metropolitan area. Of the one hundred fifty-four counties in the forty-five multicounty areas, two have a consolidated city/county (Nashville-Davidson and Columbus, Georgia), and sixty-one can be considered core counties because they contain a central city and suburbs, such as Louisville, Kentucky in Jefferson County; Augustus, Georgia in Richmond County; Grand Rapids, Michigan in Kent County; Shreveport, Louisiana in Caddo Parish, to name a few. There are more core counties than metropolitan areas because about 40 percent of the areas in this group have two or three central cities located in different counties: Duluth in St. Louis County, Minnesota and Superior in Douglas County, Wisconsin; Scranton, Pennsylvania in Lackawana County and Wilkes-Barre in Luzerne County are examples. Such duality is a complicating factor. These multicounty metropolitan areas also have forty-two suburban or satellite counties containing a

Table 15.4:   Population of Free-Standing, Multicounty Metropolitan Areas (1974).

Population Group	All	Single State	Interstate
All	*45*	*27*	*18*
500,000 to 1,000,000	16	12	4
250,000 to 500,000	16	10	6
100,000 to 250,000	13	5	8

Source: U.S. Bureau of the Census, 1976A.

substantial urban population either contiguous to the central city or in and around a satellite city, and they have forty-nine fringe counties of considerably lower density within the SMSA.

Metropolitan Regions

The fourth major type is called a metropolitan region because of great size and complexity. There are thirty-two of them (listed in the Appendix, Table 18). Twenty-eight of them are in states with large and strong counties, and the other four reflect the special circumstance of Virginia with its independent cities (the Tidewater region) and New England without strong counties (Eastern Massachusetts, Providence-Fall River, and Central Connecticut).

Twenty-three of the metropolitan regions are contained within a single state, and the other nine are interstate in character. The New York region falls within three states: New York, New Jersey, and Connecticut, with the latter introducing a distinctly different form of local government than found in the other two states. Likewise the national capital region brings together two states (Maryland and Virginia) with different approaches to local government plus the District of Columbia. Variations in local government in adjacent states also occur in the other interstate metropolitan regions (and also in the eighteen interstate, multiplex metropolitan areas discussed in the previous section).

As Table 15.5 shows, four of the metropolitan regions are over 5.0 million in population: New York (17.2 million), Southern California (10.2), Chicago-Gary (7.6), and Lower Delaware Valley (5.6). Six are in the 2.5 to 5.0 million range, and 21 are from 1.0 to 2.5 million. The remaining one is the Wasatch Front in Utah with 928,000 inhabitants, included because it takes in three metropolises (Salt Lake City, Ogden, and Provo).

A new phenomenon appearing in the metropolitan regions is the fact that seventeen of them are composed of two or more SMSAs; the champion is the New York region with eleven SMSAs followed by Southern California and

Table 15.5: Population of Metropolitan Regions (1974)

Population Group	All	Single State	Interstate
All	*32*	*23*	*9*
Over 5.0 million	4	1	3
2.5 to 5.0 million	6	5	1
1.0 to 2.5 million	21	16	5
Under 1.0 million	1	1	—

Source: U.S. Bureau of the Census, 1976A.

Eastern Massachusetts with four each. This underscores their multicentric structure. The same characteristic applies to some metropolitan regions which are a single SMSA but have a pair of large cities, such as Minneapolis and St. Paul, Dallas and Forth Worth, Tampa, and St. Petersburg. Even where a single central city is the geographic focus, submetropolitan areas can be identified, such as the Illinois portion of the St. Louis region with over half a million residents.

Amongst them the twenty-eight multicounty metropolitan regions have one hundred eighty-eight functioning counties. This figure excludes eight consolidated or separated city/counties: New York, Philadelphia, Baltimore, Indianapolis, St. Louis, New Orleans, Denver, and San Francisco. The total includes Virginia counties in the national capital region because of their size but not in the Tidewater region due to their minor character.

Of the one hundred eighty-eight counties, fifty-three can be considered core counties because they contain a central city as part, though not all, of the county. Seventy-one are suburban and satellite counties with substantial urbanization, and sixty-four are fringe counties within the commuting range but not yet heavily developed.

Of the New England metropolitan regions, Eastern Massachusetts (with Boston as the historic center) has 246 cities and towns, Providence-Fall River has 44, and Central Connecticut (Hartford) has 33. The Virginia Tidewater region consists of the two SMSAs on either side of Hampton Roads, and together they have eight independent cities and four small, fringe counties.

Types of Counties

Altogether the SMSAs outside New England contain 592 functioning counties. This total excludes fifteen consolidated or separated city/counties. Of the 592 counties, 251 are core counties with one or more central cities plus some suburbs; 117 are suburban and satellite counties, and 224 are fringe counties. This is shown in Table 15.6.

Eighteen of the functioning metropolitan counties are over one million in population, and another 41 are in the 500,000 to one million range, as indicated in Table 15.7. In a middle range of 100,000 to 500,000 are 229 counties, and 304 are less than 100,000 in population.

In the next chapter, we will explore different organizational forms local general government might take within the counties. This varies with the type of county and also in accordance with the pattern of local government within the particular state.

Table 15.6: Types of Counties in Metropolitan Areas (1976).

Type of county*	All	Free-standing Single-County Metropolises	Virginia Metropolitan Areas	Free-standing Multicounty Areas	Metropolitan Regions
All	*592*	*235*	*17*	*152*	*188*
Core	251	137	–	61	53
Suburban or satellite	117	–	4	42	71
Fringe	224	98	13	49	64

*Excludes 15 consolidated or separated city/counties.
Source: Author's analysis of census data and maps.

Table 15.7: Counties in SMSAs, by Population and Metropolitan Type (1974)

County Population	All	Free-standing Single-County Metropolises	Virginia Metropolitan Areas	Free-standing Multicounty Areas	Metropolitan Regions
All	*592*	*235*	*17*	*152*	*188*
1,000,000 and more	18	2	–	–	16
500,000 to 1,000,000	41	4	–	4	33
250,000 to 500,000	70	29	–	16	25
100,000 to 250,000	159	77	1	36	45
50,000 to 100,000	120	42	3	45	30
Less than 50,000	184	81	13	51	39

Source: U.S. Bureau of the Census, 1976A.

Chapter 16

ORGANIZATION WITHIN INDIVIDUAL COUNTIES

As Part II of this book documented, local government in metropolitan areas has found ways to cope with many of the service demands of a concentrated population, but there remain many problems to be solved. Because governmental reorganization has the potential of establishing a better institutional framework for problem-solving and improved service delivery and also for developing a greater sense of community, it is useful to consider what structural arrangements might serve best in which situation.

Not that major structural reform is needed everywhere, for some metropolitan areas haven't outgrown the governing capacity of existing arrangements and other areas have successfully reorganized or gradually adapted their structure to new challenges. But some metropolitan areas are badly in need of substantial governmental reorganization, and other areas could benefit from further evolutionary change.

The place to start in our exploration of organizational alternatives is with individual counties. For the one hundred forty-two free-standing, single-county metropolises this would encompass most of what needs to be done, leaving only the question of the metropolises' relationship to their hinterland. For the multicounty metropolitan areas and the metropolitan regions, some vexing problems of intercounty and sometimes interstate relationships arise, but even for these areas organization within individual counties can be considered first before the structure for the total area is tackled.

Among the major types of counties, the greatest challenge relates to the 251 core counties which contain the central city (or two or three) plus suburbs. (Fifteen other central counties are already part of a consolidated or separated city/county.) Thus, most of this chapter is devoted to them, but towards the end we take up organizational issues for suburban, satellite, and fringe counties. Where the urbanized area is a relatively small proportion of the core county's territory, it is appropriate to focus attention primarily upon the central city and its immediate environs, exploring what kind of a "metropolitan municipality" would be desirable and then determining its relationship to the total county. But if urbanization has become more widespread, the entire governmental organization within the county deserves fuller attention. In the following discussion, we start with the metropolitan municipality and then move to the larger county area.

Metropolitan Municipality

In many core counties, particularly those considered free-standing metropolitan areas, the urbanized area is a relatively small proportion of the county's total territory. In this situation the county, created as it was to serve mainly rural areas, lacks a strong urban orientation, isn't particularly geared to coping with metropolitan growth, and might not even have the authority to do so. In contrast, the city from its beginning has delivered urban services, has steadily expanded its community facilities in response to population increase, and may have extraterritorial power of subdivision control and zoning to regulate growth outside its borders. Or perhaps suburban municipalities or strong townships have become the primary local government for the outer parts of the urbanized area, but the county has not.

The city alone or in combination with the suburban units can be considered to be a "metropolitan municipality." Here is where the action is, so therefore this should be the primary focus for governmental reorganization. Three possibilities fall into categories we have used before: unification, federation, and confederation.

UNIFIED CITY

One approach is to keep expanding the central city through annexation and prevent or inhibit the formation of suburban municipalities. Historically this happened with many of the now large cities when they were smaller, but suburban incorporation eventually put an end to this approach for them. Yet, it is still a possibility in approximately one-third of all SMSAs in the United States. These tend to be the smaller metropolitan areas, mostly under 250,000 but there are a few in the three and four hundred thousand range where municipal unification seems to be practicable.

These are places where most of the urbanized area is already within the central city, where very few suburban municipalities exist but if present are quite small, and where the county hasn't become an urban-oriented government. They are found in states without townships or with weak ones which haven't developed an urban service capability.

A prime example of a unified, small-size metropolis is San Angelo, Texas (75,000 in 1974), which is the only municipality in Tom Green County, encompasses the entire urbanized area, but occupies less than three percent of county territory. The county as a whole has six school districts and four special districts, including two for water supply, one for flood control, and one for irrigation, basically for rural areas.

Of a large size is Wichita, Kansas with 261,000 inhabitants in 1973. The 1970 census showed the city having 91.5 percent of the urbanized population, and the proportion is probably about the same today. Although Sedgwick County has 17 municipalities, only two of them are within the urbanized area, the remainder being crossroad hamlets and small towns incorporated as "cities" under Kansas law. The city and county undertake several tasks jointly, including city/county planning, public health services, refuse disposal, and flood control. Among the civic leadership there is some talk about city/county consolidation but not much support from the two governments. Because the city has strong annexation powers, Wichita is likely to remain a fairly united metropolis through incremental expansion, but with continued city-county cooperation.

There are some cities in California's Central Valley, such as Stockton and Fresno, which appear to be naturals for unification because they are situated in very large counties and don't have numerous suburban municipalities around them. But only about two-thirds of the urbanized area is within the city in these two cases because suburban residents have been able to organize special districts and can't be annexed without their consent. It would take a change in annexation practices or a powerful incentive under existing arrangements for unification to occur. Yet for such places and others with population under 200,000 in the urbanized area, not a lot of existing local jurisdictions, and fairly large counties, consolidation into a unified city seems worthy of consideration.

Where municipal unification comes about through either incremental expansion or consolidation, special attention should be given to the governmental processes occurring within subareas of the unified metropolis. The formation of neighborhood councils would be particularly appropriate so that citizens may have a full role in matters affecting their home environment, and as the city grows beyond 200,000 some variety of neighborhood government could be considered. Wichita, for one, has divided the city into 15 areas, and voters elect a nine-member neighborhood council for each area, and each group chooses a delegate to a central council which serves as an advisory body to the board of city commissioners. Chapter 9 describes other ways neighborhood councils can be organized.

MUNICIPAL FEDERATION

In many places, though, city unification isn't likely to occur because of the existence of other municipalities and strong townships within the urbanized area. Yet, a countywide solution may not be in the offing because of the large geographic size of the county. Areas of this sort tend to be a little more populous than those where a unified city is feasible but they don't exceed half a million in population, for by the time they are that big some kind of countywide solution is needed.

Several of the smaller metropolises in Pennsylvania fall into this pattern, such as Reading, Lancaster, and York. They have half or less of the urban population and are surrounded by suburban boroughs and strong townships, but the urbanized area is a relatively small part of the total county territory. A similar pattern exists in small metropolises in other strong-township states—New York, Michigan, and Wisconsin.

Even without strong townships, quite a few metropolitan areas have fairly sizable municipalities in the suburbs, and even if their total population is less than the central city's, their existence virtually precludes municipal unification. At the same time the metropolis doesn't occupy enough of the county to contemplate countywide federation. This seems to be the case in such places as Canton, Ohio and Mobile, Alabama. Varations of this are twin cities or triplets, each with its own identity, such as Lafayette and West Lafayette, Indiana and Salinas, Seaside, and Monterey, California. In all of these cases there are some areawide concerns needing attention, suggesting the need for an instrument with a broader domain than each unit alone but perhaps smaller than the total county with its large rural stretches.

For this situation I propose a new form of local government for the United States: municipal federation. The small-area units in the federation would be the existing city, boroughs, and townships, and a new areawide unit would be formed, perhaps called the metropolitan municipality. This new government would have enumerated powers spelled out in a charter, and it would be run by governing officials elected by residents of the entire metropolis—by districts, at large, or a combination. One crucial issue would be the precise division of responsibility between the metropolitan municipality and the existing cities and towns. A second important issue would be fiscal arrangements, including the kinds of areawide taxes and the possibility of distribution of some of this revenue to the small-area units. Probably some of the personnel now working for the central city would be shifted to the areawide government, and maybe some suburban personnel, too, and this would require proper arrangements for retention of their employment and retirement rights.

Where the central city contains more than half of the urbanized population, the federation might be a little imbalanced. Conceivably in this circumstance, the central city might be divided into several smaller units, but acceptance for this wouldn't come easily. More likely, existing units would remain intact and the metropolitan municipality would start with fairly limited responsibilities, taking on only those matters on which there is a clear local consensus that areawide operation is necessary and desirable. But there should be a way to expand the powers of the areawide unit, and also to reduce them if deemed desirable. And it should be possible to expand the territory and to organize additional small-area units within an enlarged federation.

My estimate is that municipal federation is an alternative worth considering in about fifty core counties.

CONFEDERATED METROPOLIS

If federation places more power in an areawide government than is acceptable to a locality, an alternative would be the creation of a metropolitan confederation in an area smaller than the whole county. This could be done through a joint powers agreement or in articles of confederation adopted by the existing local governments. The confederation would be under the control of these units, would be run by them through a governing board of their representatives, and would perform only those activities the member units would agree to. However, it would establish an areawide structure, a staff to perform certain functions, and a focus for citizen attention in dealing with matters affecting the whole metropolis.

A confederated metropolis might be especially appropriate where twin cities or triplets constitute the principal local general governments. They want to remain in existence and federation might appear too grandiose if it were to combine only two or three small-area units. Confederation would provide the machinery for joint action without adding a lot of additional overhead.

JOINT CITY/COUNTY OPERATIONS

Altogether slightly more than half of the core counties seem to be ripe candidates to have a metropolitan municipality in some form, whether through unification, federation, or confederation. It would function within the confines of the county, which in turn would perform its traditional functions both within the city and in the rural hinterland. The county would be the main service agency for the rural area and would have a concern for its pattern of development. But the metropolis would also have an interest in the kind of development which might occur in various parts of the county.

Therefore, joint city/county activities would be useful to institute, such as for planning, subdivision control, building code, and public health services, provided to both urban and rural residents. Appropriate boards and commissions and other administrative machinery could be set up to bring this about. Such arrangements would be yet another expression of local federalism.

Consolidated City/County

The second broad choice of reorganization in core counties is to consolidate the county with the central city and possibly with all other governmental units within the county. This might consist of complete unification, but certain exclusions can occur.

COMPLETE UNIFICATION

The simplest form conceptually, but by no means the easiest to accomplish, is complete unification. In Chapter 7 we reviewed the historical experience with this approach, the arguments for and against it, and its local acceptance and rejection. Of the seven city/county consolidation efforts of metropolitan scope to succeed in the past thirty years, only two created a completely unified government: Lexington and Anchorage. But Honolulu of earlier vintage is close because only a couple of soil conservation districts keep it from being totally unified. All the others—Baton Rouge, Nashville-Davidson, Jacksonville, Columbus (Georgia), and Indianapolis—have some kind of compromise but nevertheless their consolidation is substantial. (This discussion excludes the eight nineteenth-century cases of city/county consolidation or separation because metropolitan growth has far surpassed the core counties of Boston, New York, Philadelphia, Baltimore, St. Louis, New Orleans, Denver, and San Francisco.)

Service areas. Even with unification, different levels of services are needed by subareas, varying according to the extent of urbanization. So the consolidated city/counties create service districts to reflect these differences, and each district has its own tax rate. The whole county is considered a general service district with a uniform tax rate.

Neighborhood councils. The large government produced by consolidation seems particularly capable of doing a good job in guiding development, building facilities, and running capital-intensive services. But its size makes it more remote from the average citizen. To counteract this tendency, Honolulu has set up neighborhood boards, Anchorage has community councils, and Jacksonville a neighborhood improvement mechanism. Such neighborhood councils are elected by residents, and they have an official or quasi-official role in the city/county government. Although they aren't fully developed neighborhood government, they introduce something of the spirit of local federalism into consolidated government.

EXCLUDED MUNICIPALITIES

To reduce political opposition to unification, several of the consolidated city/counties have excluded municipalities from merger. These units have their own governing bodies, provide certain services to their residents, and levy taxes to pay for them. They function as political communities, and they act as self-governing, general service districts operating in a system where most of the services are provided by the consolidated city/county.

Sometimes historical county offices are preserved and remain as elective offices, particularly if they are created by the state constitution. Countywide special districts might also be retained. In both cases the removal of controversy and reduction of opposition is a factor in keeping these offices and special districts.

Because city/county consolidation occurs in the political arena, judgments have to be made about how the anticipated change in the balance of political power will affect support for and opposition to unification. This has resulted in these various exclusions.

LIKELY CANDIDATES

Prospects are not bright for city/county consolidation in very many core counties beyond the sixteen where it has already taken place. Perhaps that number could be equalled in new unification efforts, but probably no more than that. The reason stems from local opposition to governmental centralization, or metropolitanization as opponents call it.

If we look at where city/county consolidation has been attempted during the past thirty years, we find a pattern. Except for Indianapolis (where the legislature, not the voters, brought it about), all attempts have been in the South and the West where metropolitan growth is of relatively recent origin. These regions have no townships, and most of the metropolises interested in unification have very few suburban municipalities. Therefore, it seems that future consolidation is most likely to come about in such places.

A number of defeats were attributed to the inability to gain a required majority both inside and outside the city, usually failing in the suburbs. A case arising from a county charter vote in Niagara County, New York, which lost in the suburbs, took the issue of separate majorities to the U.S. Supreme Court, which ruled that a state could require them in this situation. Whether this same reasoning carries over to voting for city/county consolidation remains untested, but it is likely to. Nevertheless, consolidation seems most probable in places where the city contains most of the county population already, such as Memphis with 89 percent in the city and El Paso with 91 percent. This doesn't mean that city/county consolidation won't come about where the city is a much lesser portion of the county, but a high percentage makes it seem more likely.

The Southwest in particular has a number of metropolises where the city has more than three-fourths of the county population, including Tulsa, Austin, San Antonio, Albuquerque, and Tucson. These are states with annexation laws favorable to city expansion and with limitations on suburban incorporation, so the cities have grown with the population. Now with the county population over 350,000 in all these cases, maybe it is timely to contemplate consolidation. And perhaps this history might be followed in smaller metropolises which are developing as unified cities but may some day grow considerably larger and then merge with the county.

Looking around for other metropolises where city/county consolidation might make sense, we notice a couple of small metropolitan counties of West Virginia sandwiched between Ohio and Pennsylvania and wonder whether governmental unification might be desirable in Weirton-Hannock County and Wheeling-Ohio County. In North Carolina the city of Winston-Salem works closely with Forsyth County, and perhaps some day city/county consolidation might be a natural step. And there are probably some other situations like that. But not very many, for opposition to centralization seems to be quite strong in most places. This means that some other organizational form must be found if the needed areawide government is to come into existence.

Countywide Federation

Where urbanization has extended over a considerable portion of the county, a major alternative to city/county consolidation is the creation of a countywide federation. The county would be adapted so as to become the areawide government, and municipalities (and strong townships where they exist) would be the small-area governments. Chapter 8 (pp. 105-106) pointed out that something like this is emerging on a de facto basis in some places, though it hasn't been formally organized as a federation. But if carefully thought through rather than just allowed to come about through happenstance, this form could be an effective instrument for combining small- and large-scale operations.

Precisely what powers the county as areawide government should assume is a key issue. Equally important is deciding what kind of small-area governments to have for each of four kinds of areas: the central city, developed suburbs, developing or potentially developable areas, and rural areas intended to remain open. The existing pattern of local government will also have its effect on reorganization, and a different pattern is likely to emerge where the whole county is organized into local units as it is in the township states compared to where unincorporated territory exists.

IN STRONG TOWNSHIP STATES

The possibility of federated government has been thoroughly explored in one metropolitan county in a strong township state: Monroe County, New

York where Rochester is located. As indicated earlier (Chapter 8, pp. 96-97), the Greater Rochester Intergovernmental Panel (GRIP) proposed strengthening the county as the areawide government, adding to its existing functions such activities as police, fire protection in specialized areas, water supply, solid waste disposal, and countywide land use planning. The existing central city and all towns and villages would remain, and some more villages would be created within the towns. The city and the larger towns would have community councils so that citizens could become involved at the neighborhood level. Residents would elect county and city or town officials, and those in villages would vote for a third set. This proposal is now being considered in Monroe County, but hasn't yet been accepted.

A similar approach would seem to make sense for other upstate counties in New York containing such cities as Syracuse, Utica and Rome, Schenectady, Albany, and Troy. In Pennsylvania the core counties with the cities of Scranton, Wilkes-Barre, Allentown, Bethlehem and Easton, and Harrisburg seem likely candidates for countywide federation, for the urbanized area takes in a lot of the county and quite a few boroughs and townships are already functioning as small-area governments. In other strong-township states, countywide federation might be appropriate for Cumberland County, New Jersey (with Vineland, Millville, and Bridgeton), Flint and Genesse County, Michigan, and Madison and Dane County, Wisconsin. In nearly all these places, considerable county modernization would have to occur in order to make this ancient institution into an effective areawide government for metropolitan areas.

IN STATES WITH WEAK OR NO TOWNSHIPS

The situation is different in states with weak townships or none at all, for the whole county isn't covered with strong small-area governments. In such places the county has been drawn into the provision of municipal-type urban services in the unincorporated territory or perhaps special districts have been organized for some of these services. Where the county government is so involved, county departments tend to give more attention to the unincorporated area than to the rest of the county, and members of the county council or board of supervisors take more interest in the day-to-day problems of such areas and provide a lot of constituency services there. This detracts somewhat from the county's areawide responsibilities. Furthermore, it creates an ambivalence in the county's relationships with the central city and the incorporated suburban municipalities, for they deal with the county as an areawide government but see it also as the municipal government for the unincorporated sections.

In order to create a true countywide federation, the county government should withdraw from municipal services in developed areas and should encourage and assist the residents to incorporate. These new municipalities would then have the option of running their own services or contracting with the county for certain services, as happens extensively in Los Angeles County (see Chapter 5, pp. 52-53). In not-yet-developed areas where incorporation would be premature, the county might set up general-purpose districts with elected governing boards, which would be half-way toward being a municipality. Or if not this approach, at a minimum, community councils should be organized to advise the county on the service needs and views of the residents on matters affecting their area. As the county gets out of most of its services to small areas, it can then give more attention to areawide issues. As it deals with these broader concerns, the county will have a federal-type relationship with the central city and the other incorporated municipalities, and together these sets of governments, functioning at different scales, can work out the most appropriate division of responsibility for the various activities they carry out.

A federated arrangement seems a desirable approach for an area such as San Diego County, which has twelve suburban municipalities in addition to the City of San Diego, a sizable developed but unincorporated area where the county serves as the municipality, and considerable tension between the city and the county derived in part from the duality of the county's role.

Maricopa County, Arizona with Phoenix is another place where county-wide federation might be a suitable form. Birmingham, Alabama and the other thirty-three municipalities in Jefferson County could federate with the county, perhaps in the process consolidating some of the smaller units and organizing some new ones to cover the entire county with small-area government. Indeed, a proposal of this sort was advanced several years ago by a Local Government Commission while another proposal bearing the title "One Great City" favored a federated, metropolitan municipality. Polk County, Florida with Lakeland, Winter Haven, and a number of smaller cities is another single-county metropolis where countywide federation would be applicable, there too forming municipalities in presently unincorporated areas.

Countywide federation seems desirable elsewhere in situations with several municipalities but no one particularly dominant and quite a bit of the county already urbanized, sometimes with part of it in unincorporated areas. This seems to be the case for a number of seacoast counties where the shore municipalities exist side-by-side and development is working its way inward. In counties where citizens have voted against city/county consolidation, federation might be an acceptable alternative.

CONSOLIDATE AND REDIVIDE

So far these examples assume that existing municipalities will remain intact as they enter into a countywide federation. A more drastic step would be to make a fresh start with municipal boundaries by consolidating all existing units, assigning certain powers to county government, redividing the county into new municipal units and giving them specific responsibilities. In effect this is what the Committee for Economic Development recommended in 1970 (see Chapter 8, pp. 94-95), and this was the idea of the "ideal" approach developed by a panel in the Greater Rochester study (Chapter 8, p. 96). However, it has never been done in the United States, though in London borough lines were redrawn in 1963 (Chapter 8, p. 100) and the old city of Berlin was divided into six districts when a larger, federated Greater Berlin was constituted in 1920 (Chapter 12, p. 169).

Forming small-area governments. To bring this about, it would be necessary to define the local communities and their boundaries so that they could serve as the basis for the small-area governmental units. For the most part these would be residential communities with a modicum of nonresidential land uses. Perhaps some predominantly commercial and industrial areas, such as the central business district, wouldn't have a small-area government at all but would be served only by the reorganized county. Similarly, outlying rural areas might be organized as general service districts of the county, but with elected governing bodies, until such time as a fuller local government is needed. Once the boundaries were defined, the governing officials of the small-area units would be elected and the governments organized. At this stage personnel who have been working for the county or previous municipalities would be reassigned to the new units. These aren't simple steps to accomplish but are within the realm of possibility.

Division of responsibility. A crucial decision would be the assignment of responsibilities to the small-area units and to the county as the areawide government. Questions of scale talked about in Chapter 13 would come into consideration and also local traditions and preferences. Because of past opposition to the centralization contained in city/county consolidation proposals, the politically wise course would be to maximize the activities of small-area units and assign to the county only those activities which clearly require areawide administration. This is a point at which bargaining can and should occur.

Fiscal distribution. Likewise the pattern for distributing fiscal resources will require some bargaining. If the locality has a sales tax or an income tax, considerations of equity favor countywide collection with some of the revenue used for areawide purposes and the remainder distributed among the small-area governments on the basis of relative need. For the property tax, areawide assessment is the most equitable approach (unless the state has taken over this task) and probably the most efficient. The small-area units could use the property tax to pay for basic services other than education, which requires a broader tax base. A county tax on the major industrial and commercial properties outside local jurisdictions could be used for county purposes and for distribution to the small units, with particular attention to

overcoming deficiencies arising from the unequal distribution of local property values.

Applicability. Consolidation and redivision could be carried out in any
county, but it would be easiest where there aren't many existing municipalities and a layer of strong townships. Those single-county metropolises
where the central city has spread over most of the urbanized area might find
this a desirable alternative to complete unification, an action voters have
rejected more often than they have accepted it.

Core Counties: Summing Up

Presently some variety of confederation or less formal type of interlocal
cooperation characterizes governmental organization in the 251 core counties
of metropolitan areas. (These are here defined as counties with one or more
central cities plus surrounding suburbs, and the total excludes the 15 cases of
city/county consolidation or separation.) The main exceptions to the pattern
of confederation are places where the city has been able to encompass all or
most of the urban growth, and some areas where a kind of de facto federation
has come into existences. In many cases, confederation is quite a workable
arrangement, but if an alternative is desired, the choice can be directed
toward unification or federation, either for the metropolitan municipality or
for the entire county.

FOUR ALTERNATIVE FORMS

This gives us, then, four forms: unified city, municipal federation,
consolidated city/county, and countywide federation. Using the rationale
previously discussed plus a lot of subjectivity, the 251 core counties are
assigned to these four forms in Table 16.1, broken down by population
groups. As this table indicates, it seems to me that the preferred course for a
majority of the smaller counties would be a unified city working coop-
eratively with county government. In contrast, countywide federation is the
most desirable form for the majority of larger counties. Municipal federation
is appropriate for small-to-medium-size counties which have quite a few
suburban municipalities and perhaps strong townships as well but where the
urbanized area isn't extensive enough to warrant a countywide federation. Of
the 17 core counties suggested for city/county consolidation, in addition to
the cities where this form already occurs, the best prospects are places where
the central city already has most of the population.

This classification is, of course, highly speculative, but it illustrates my
impressions of what forms might be most workable. All four forms would
function within an atmosphere of local federalism. This is obvious for the
federated forms but true for the others as well, for a unified city would relate

Table 16.1: Possible Organizational Forms for Core Counties of Metropolitan Areas.

County Population	Number of Core Counties				
	Total	Unified City	Municipal Federation	Consolidated City/County	Countywide Federation
Under 100,000	44	35	8	1	—
100,000 to 250,000	109	45	32	4	26
250,000 to 500,000	54	10	9	9	26
500,000 to 1.0 million	26	—	—	3	23
Over 1.0 million	18	—	—	—	18
All	251	90	49	17	95
Percentage:	100.0	35.9	19.5	6.8	37.8

Source: Author's analysis of census data and maps. See Appendix for further details.

to its county and a consolidated city/county would be part of a larger metropolitan area or a region with suburban, fringe, and perhaps some rural counties.

FREE-STANDING METROPOLISES AND THE LARGER REGION

Of these core counties, one hundred forty-two are free-standing metropolises, tending to be the ones on the smaller end of the population spectrum. For them, the organizational form within the county would take care of most matters with which local government has to deal, but there are some concerns involving a larger region of which the core county is the hub. It may, for instance, be part of a substate planning district, and governmental units within the county may be represented on a regional council.

ACIR in its study of substate regionalism observed that one of the unresolved problems is the difficulty of melding a metropolitan area into the larger district (1973A:250). For example, a single-county metropolis might be part of a district encompassing four to ten counties, or a multicounty metropolitan area might be joined with a number of rural counties. The metropolitan county or counties usually have greater population than all the other counties combined, but the one-government, one-vote mode of regional councils causes an underrepresentation of the metropolis. Yet, a switch to one person, one vote might dilute attention to rural areas, which have their own kinds of problems.

In this framework, there needs to be a sorting out of which issues can be handled solely within the metropolitan county and which ones require consideration by the broader substate district. By and large, most service delivery programs can be adequately handled within the metropolis, and not much is accomplished by placing them on the agenda of a regional clearinghouse agency. What is more appropriate for regional attention are broad issues of long-range land use planning and the closely related matters of major transportation routes and big decisions on water resources. But even for these subjects many of the detailed decisions and implementing actions can be handled within the metropolitan county.

Thus, while the free-standing metropolis itself needs an areawide government elected directly by the people—either a metropolitan municipality or a metropolitan county, the regional planning mechanism can operate satisfactorily as a confederation, as most substate districts are now organized, though greater input from citizens than is now generally the case would be highly desirable.

Suburban and Fringe Counties

In addition to the 251 core counties and 15 consolidated or separated city/counties, metropolitan areas in the United States have 117 counties which are suburban in character or contain a small satellite city and another 224 counties on the fringe but tied to the metropolis by commuting patterns and incipient development.

The suburban county is likely to contain part of the urbanized area extending outward from the central city, and maybe only a change in street signs denotes the transition across the county boundary. Further out, however, the suburbs may still be growing except for a few suburban counties which are completely urbanized. Every suburban county has some incorporated municipalities except those in Virginia and Baltimore County and Howard County in Maryland. In the strong-township states, the suburban counties are completely covered with functioning small-area governments, but in other states there is a combination of incorporated and unincorporated territory.

The existence of these small units means that unification isn't a viable alternative with the rare exceptions mentioned. Rather federation is the most likely form, and in fact already exists on a de facto basis in many places (we saw this for Nassau County, New York in Chapter 8, pp. 105-106). Three main tasks need accomplishment to get the most out of federation. First, responsibilities for various activities need to be divided between the county as an intermediate arena of action and the municipal and township units as the small-area governments. Second, if there are developed but unincorporated areas, new municipal units should be organized and the county should withdraw from its role as municipal government for unincorporated territory. Third, where municipal units are quite small (under 5,000 or even under 10,000 in the more populous counties), they should be aggregated into somewhat bigger units so that they can effectively provide a fuller range of services.

Some other counties are more like satellites because they have a small city which is somewhat removed from the central city but within the economic and social orbit of the metropolitan area. Perhaps it would be advisable for that city to expand as nearby population grows, but eventually as the satellite county becomes more urbanized and as other subcenters grow, a federated pattern will probably emerge. In both the satellite and suburban varieties, the county is an important vehicle for countywide planning and some other activities, such as creek valley parks, regional libraries, environmental sanitation, and refuse disposal, which need a base of operation of intermediate scale, wider than a single municipality but not as broad as the whole metropolitan area.

County government is equally important in the fringe area which is experiencing scattered impact of metropolitan growth, often outside the bounds of existing small cities and towns. Although it may be habitually rural oriented, the county is the logical unit to respond by managing growth and assuring that new service needs are met by some governmental unit. This could take place without any major rearrangement of governmental units and instead through expansion of county activities and perhaps some internal reorganization within county government. However, over the years as the fringe county evolves to suburban status, a fuller expression of countywide federation might be considered.

School Districts and Special Districts

This chapter has concentrated on local general government, but a word should be said about school districts and special districts. I have already indicated my preference for a sharp reduction in the number of special districts, achieving this by having general-purpose units take over their responsibilities. Better and fuller organization of suburban government would make this possible for small-area services, and strengthening county government in suburban and fringe areas would bring this about for services and facilities of an intermediate scale. And in the case of free-standing, single-county metropolises, the county would be the areawide government so that special-purpose, metropolitan authorities wouldn't be needed. Areawide general government for multicounty metropolitan areas, a subject we take up in the next chapter, would mitigate this need for special metropolitan districts.

School districts vary from state to state in their relationship to local government, as we saw in Chapter 4 (p. 39). Where they are a regular part of city and town government, school systems presumably would be consolidated if the cities and towns are unified. Where they are independent but coterminous with city boundaries, municipal unification might affect school district boundaries but might not. Where school districts aren't coterminous with local general government, a change in municipal boundaries wouldn't necessarily effect school district organization. Thus eleven separate school districts remained after Indianapolis and Marion County consolidated, but there was already a countywide school system in Duval County prior to consolidation with Jacksonville and it continued with an elected school board, though with its budget subject to review by the consolidated government. But in many places school consolidation has occurred while local general government has remained unconsolidated. There may be fiscal and social policy reasons for school reorganization at the time of restructuring of general government, but the two don't have to go hand in hand.

Chapter 17

MULTICOUNTY ORGANIZATION

When we move beyond the free-standing, single-county metropolis, we find greater complexity and considerable diversity. The majority of multicounty metropolises are contained within a single state, but quite a few are interstate in character. From state to state these multicounty areas show different configurations, and New England and Virginia without areawide county government introduce other variations. The metropolitan regions, because of their immensity and complexity, create special kinds of problems for governmental organization.

Virtually all of the multicounty areas and metropolitan regions now have some kind of confederation in operation, usually a council of governments. As we saw in Chapter 6, these organizations have facilitated communications and information-sharing among local officials but they have lacked powers necessary for follow-through, and therefore have been weak in linking areawide planning with implementation. This arrangement may be sufficient for some areas, but many places need better ways to achieve areawide decision-making and action.

This chapter explores alternatives which might be considered in various multicounty areas and metropolitan regions. Whatever is done must be tailored to local conditions and should give proper respect to the diversity which exists around the nation.

In my reckoning, there are forty-five free-standing, multicounty metropolitan areas outside of New England which aren't part of a larger metropolitan regions. (Because of their size all multicounty SMSAs over one million are here considered metropolitan regions along with multi-SMSA conglomerations.) Twenty-seven of the multicounty areas are within a single state, and the other eighteen are interstate.

Single-State, Multicounty Areas

We first take up the single-state, multicounty metropolitan areas. They have three main patterns: one main core county, an intercounty metropolis, and tandem counties.

ONE MAIN CORE COUNTY

There are many multi-county SMSAs, by the OMB definition, which have most of the urban population in the core county, and most of them I have defined as free-standing, single-county metropolises because the fringe county or counties aren't very populous. There are a few others, though, which can be considered true multicounty metropolitan areas because they have one or more suburban or satellite counties, or perhaps a fringe county or two moving toward suburban status.

The Nashville-Davidson area is one of these. With 450,000 residents the central, consolidated city/county holds about 60 percent of the population of the eight-county SMSA. There are two counties around 70,000 which have suburbs and independent municipalities of older vintage, and metropolitan growth is fanning out in all directions into five other counties. Clearly the central county is dominant, but sensible areawide planning requires a broader base. Presently a 13-county confederation, the Mid-Cumberland Council of Governments and Development District, handles this task, and it faces the challenge of what must be handled regionally and what can be best achieved within the counties of various types—metropolitan, suburban, and rural fringe.

The Charlotte, North Carolina area has Mecklenberg County at its core (374,000 in 1974), Gaston County (155,000) as a satellite, and Union County (60,000) as a fringe county. We saw in Chapter 7 (p. 89) that over the years Charlotte and Mecklenberg County have entered into numerous agreements, have transferred functions, and jointly administer a variety of services. After a vote for city/county consolidation failed in 1971, the city annexed a lot more land and now covers much of the urbanized area. City/county consolidation will probably occur eventually (though it conceivably could take the form of a freshly designed federation). This has to be worked out within Mecklenberg County while simultaneously a confederated approach is used for dealing with matters in the wider areas.

Utica and Rome, New York are both in Oneida County, and neighboring Herkimer County is added to make up the SMSA and also a substate district for a regional planning board, which serves as the A-95 clearinghouse. Oneida County has an elected executive under its adopted charter and seems to do more effective planning than the regional planning board. In fact, an ACIR study found regional planning boards in New York generally to be weak instruments (1973B:270-282). Much of the two counties is rural and urbanizing pressures aren't overwhelming, so perhaps each county functioning mainly on its own makes sense, with communications and some joint activities through a confederated body like the regional planning board.

The same reasoning applies to other areas where the core county is the principal place of metropolitan settlement but where fringe counties are being drawn into its orbit and are on the way to becoming suburban or satellite counties.

INTERCOUNTY METROPOLIS

In quite a number of multicounty metropolitan areas, the urbanized area has spread from its original site across county lines into one or more contiguous counties. This has happened, for instance, with Harrisburg, Dayton, Toledo, Grand Rapids, Peoria, Oklahoma City, Shreveport, Jackson (Mississippi), Columbia, and Orlando. The same pattern has developed in some metropolitan areas with a pair of central cities, such as Lansing and East Lansing, both in the same county with urbanization extending into an adjacent county, and Youngstown and Warren, in separate counties but connected with solid urban growth. In these situations, a metropolitan confederation might be established or an areawide federation. Another approach would be to create an intercounty municipality, either unified or federated.

Metropolitan confederation. Because county boundaries seem to have a lot of sanctity in the United States, the ordinary approach would be to work out governmental solutions in each county first, as we did in the previous chapter. Then counties would be the building blocks for arriving at some kind of an areawide structure. This is done nowadays, usually producing a confederated council of governments composed of county and municipal representatives.

Areawide federation. A second approach is federation, and there are two models to choose from, as Chapter 8 has spelled out. One is a metropolitan council with an elected governing board in charge of regional planning and also budgetary and policy oversight over separate metropolitan operating commissions. The other is an areawide body which both plans and runs facilities and services, somewhat like a city or county but without as broad a mission. In this manner the counties become the governments for intermediate areas, and municipalities and townships serve small areas within each county, thus producing three arenas for local federalism.

Intercounty municipality. Another approach deserving consideration is the creation of an intercounty municipality which would take in parts of two or more counties, but it wouldn't cover all of any county (though it might eventually spread over the entire core county). There exists some examples of this in a *unitary model*: Amarillo, Texas, which straddles a county line, and Kansas City, Missouri, which through annexation has extended out of its home county into two other counties. Both are in states where annexation is easy and suburban incorporation difficult.

However, most of the intercounty metropolises mentioned above already have quite a number of suburban municipalities. Therefore, the idea of a *federated metropolis* might be considered. Each existing municipality would remain intact (unless the central city chose to subdivide), and unincorporated urbanized areas would be shaped into new municipalities; these units would be the small-area governments. Then a new metropolitan government would be created to take in the entire area covered by the city and developed suburbs (perhaps with some expansion room not yet municipally organized), and it would carry out assigned areawide activities in the parts of the counties encompassed by the municipal federation. The counties would remain to handle their traditional functions, and their total boundaries would become the territory for broad, regional planning conducted by an areawide confederation. It might be a little awkward for a single, federated metropolis to be served by several counties, but it could be managed. At least it's a possibility for localities to explore and for state legislatures to consider authorizing.

TANDEM CORE COUNTIES

The other fairly common pattern among multicounty metropolitan areas is to have two or three core counties side by side, each with a central city. Examples are Albany-Schenectady-Troy (in three counties); Scranton-Wilkes Barre; Greensboro-Winston Salem- High Point (in two counties); Raleigh-Durham; Greenville-Spartanburg; Beaumont- Port Arthur-Orange (in two counties); Appleton-Oshkosh. In these situations, it is better to consider each county separately first and then to devise an areawide structure. It might be that both counties will have the same internal solutions, such as countywide federations for each of Lackawanna and Luzerne Counties in Pennsylvania (Scranton-Wilkes Barre). Or they might take different tacks, such as city/county consolidation for Winston-Salem and Forsyth County but a federation involving Greensboro, High Point, and Guilford County.

In these circumstances it is most likely that the areawide arrangement will be a confederation. But it is conceivable that an areawide federation might be created on top of the county-local federation. (That after all is how American federalism works.)

Interstate Metropolitan Areas

Eighteen of the multicounty metropolitan areas we are considering are interstate in character (and so are a number of the metropolitan regions we will get to later). How best to organize county and municipal government within them is no different from the examples previously considered, and the same choices are available—the several unitary, federated, and confederated models. What is more complicating is the differing laws of the adjacent states and the separate legal systems which make areawide planning and decision-making a little more difficult to achieve.

METROPOLISES ON NAVIGABLE RIVERS

One group of interstate metropolises are those on navigable rivers. We can follow some of them down the Ohio River: Steubenville, Ohio and Weirton, West Virginia; Wheeling, West Virginia and some smaller municipalities in Ohio; Parkersburg, West Virginia and Marietta, Ohio; Huntington, West Virginia, Ashland, Kentucky, and some small municipalities in Ohio; Louisville, Kentucky and New Albany, Indiana. On the Mississippi River is the Quad-City of Davenport, Iowa and Rock Island, Moline, and East Moline, Illinois. Omaha, Nebraska and Council Bluffs, Iowa face each other across the Missouri River. At the western end of Lake Superior the St. Louis River separates Duluth, Minnesota and Superior, Wisconsin. (There are also some single-county metropolises with fringe development across the river, such as Owensboro, Kentucky; Evansville, Indiana; La Crosse, Wisconsin; Dubuque, Iowa; and Sioux City, Iowa. And most of the interstate metropolitan regions are located on navigable rivers.)

The river determined the original site of settlement, and as growth has occurred on both sides, the river acts as both a uniting and a separating influence. For instance, separate water and sewerage systems are needed on opposite sides of the river, but connecting bridges must be built and maintained and a unified public transit system is desirable. The legal requirements of two different states mean that separate police forces must be maintained, but maybe only one general hospital is needed to serve people on both sides of the river, at least for the smaller metropolises. Land use controls have to be carried out under the laws of each state, but there is one metropolitan economic area and housing market which can be best comprehended and dealt with through interstate, areawide planning.

Because of the legal complexity of interstate relations, as many tasks as possible should be handled in each state. The principal city on each side of the river should work out the best possible structure with its suburbs, the core county, and surrounding counties, drawing upon the models previously discussed. Upon this foundation, interstate cooperation can be achieved, choosing from the following devices (presented in order of increased formality).

Information sharing is the first and simplest step to take, so that cities and counties on opposite sides of the river know what each other plans to do which might affect them. Written agreements can provide for mutual assistance, such as for fire fighting support and other emergency aid. Through some kind of confederation, such as an interstate council of governments, areawide planning can be conducted even though most of the implementation will be carried out separately. Joint operations can take care of mass transportation and local bridges (those which aren't part of state and interstate highway systems) and possibly other facilities, such as an airport and a solid waste disposal plant. Even a federation might be considered to produce an areawide body with authority and administrative capacity, though this wouldn't be easy to bring about.

To cite one example, many of these means of interlocal and interstate cooperation occur in the Quad-City area. H. Paul Friesma was able to identify 252 interjurisdictional agreements among the ten municipalities, touching on such matters as law enforcement, library services, transportation, planning and zoning, health, sewage disposal, and parks and recreation. The five large cities were involved in a median of 82 agreements each and the five small municipalities in a median of 16 each. Ninety-seven out of 252 agreements (38 percent) crossed the Mississippi River, which is the state boundary between Iowa and Illinois. However, only the three large cities on the Illinois side, Rock Island, Moline, and East Moline, operate the airport because Iowa law doesn't allow Davenport to be a partner in an out-of-state facility (1971:42-45).

Some other states, though, give local government strong authority for interstate cooperation, and in a few instances formal interstate compacts are adopted by the states and approved by the U.S. Congress. Perhaps there might be a master agreement between the local governments on opposite sides of the river with a number of articles spelling out mutual activities and information sharing for the main functions of government (public safety, health, transportation, et cetera).

LAND-LINKED INTERSTATE METROPOLISES

There are other interstate metropolises which are essentially a single urbanized area and aren't separated by a navigable river, though a small river might be the state boundary. Texarkana is essentially a single metropolis lying partly in Texas and partly in Arkansas. The suburbs of Chattanooga, Tennessee have spread southward into Georgia. Columbus, Georgia has the smaller Phenix City, Alabama directly across the Chattahoochee River, and across the Savannah River from Augustus, Georgia is North Augustus, South Carolina. Fargo, North Dakota and Moorhead, Minnesota have grown together, divided only by the Red River. The legal situation is the same as for the previous group of interstate areas, but the possibilities for cooperation are a little greater because physical separation isn't as great, especially for those without a dividing river.

Accordingly, the two Texarkanas have joined together to run the water and sewerage systems, the library, airport, and animal shelter. The two city councils meet together at least monthly, planning is coordinated, and a bicity commission is working on plans for a civic center. This cooperative spirit extends to the wider metropolitan area where there is an interstate council of governments and an employment-and-training consortium. Plans are underway to construct a multicounty criminal justice center on State Line Avenue, involving the police and sheriffs of the two cities, two counties, and multicounty court districts in both states, complete with concurrent jurisdiction on certain matters.

In the Chattanooga area, water supply is handled by private utilities which have interstate operations, and Chattanooga lets sewer mains from Georgia connect with its system (though the drainage basin doesn't extend very far beyond the state line). Local planners and other officials share information. The Chattanooga Area Council of Governments encompasses ten Tennessee counties and three in Georgia, but for some planning matters it defers to the overlapping Coosa Valley Area Planning and Development Commission in Georgia. For federally aided planning, the arrangement is simpler for the Section 208 water quality planning funds coming directly from the Environmental Protection Agency than for transportation planning money which goes through the two states.

MULTICENTERED INTERSTATE AREAS

The other variety of interstate metropolitan area has two or more central cities which aren't contiguous. One such area contains Johnson City and Kingsport in two separate counties of Tennessee and the dual cities of Bristol, partly in Tennessee and partly in Virginia. Areawide planning is handled by the First Tennessee-Virginia Development District which covers eight counties in Tennessee and one Virginia county and the independent city of Bristol, Virginia. The Tri-City Airport is supported by the three cities and two main counties. And the bistate cities of Bristol have their own joint planning commission.

Clarksville, Tennessee and Hopkinsville, Kentucky are joined together in a two-county SMSA. However, they are twenty-three miles apart so that the arrangement is really tandem metropolis. That means that mainly intercounty communication is needed rather than a two-county planning agency. Furthermore, each county is already in a multicounty planning district within its own state.

Metropolitan Areas in New England and Virginia

Unique in the United States are the New England states where county government is weak or nonexistent and Virginia where cities are independent from counties in territory as well as authority. This means that there is no wider unit of local general government encompassing the area served by a group of municipalities and towns. Lacking a county to make into an areawide agency, other arrangements have to be devised.

NEW ENGLAND

New England has a dozen metropolitan areas ranging from about 100,000 to 600,000 which aren't part of a large metropolitan region, as here defined. Connecticut and Massachusetts each has four such areas and New Hampshire and Maine two a piece. In all of these states, the cities and towns are strong and independent, and no general-purpose government except the state serves a wider territory. The cities and towns have worked out several varieties of interlocal cooperation, and a few special districts encompass a number of localities. All four states have regional planning commissions which serve as the A-95 clearinghouse and have a majority of local officials on the governing board. So in effect, a confederation exists for each metropolitan area, though they are weak because the cities and towns retain land use controls and other powers needed for implementation. The states are geographically small, except for Maine, and state government gets into many concerns which might just as well be handled on a substate basis.

There is talk in Maine and Massachusetts about strengthening county government, but nothing has come of it to date. A countersuggestion in Massachusetts is to broaden the powers of regional planning commissions because their boundaries are more closely related to natural social and economic areas, but this hasn't happened either. In New Hampshire there isn't much push to broaden county powers, and in Connecticut county rebirth isn't under consideration.

Nevertheless, there remains the need for areawide planning and decision-making with enough muscle to translate plans into action. Perhaps federation would be congenial to the New England tradition. A federated metropolis could be chartered directly by the state or set up through a local referendum. It would have an elected council with specified powers to deal with areawide concerns, and cities and towns would remain in place as the small-area governments of the federation. Issues of which activities to make areawide and what kind of fiscal arrangements to have would arise, and the alternatives already gone over a couple of times in this book would be available to choose from.

VIRGINIA

Virginia has counties but their exclusion of cities from county territory produces the same effect as in New England by not having an areawide general government in metropolitan areas. This is the way it is in the state's four free-standing metropolises: Richmond, Roanoke, Lynchburg, and Petersburg-Colonial Heights- Hopewell.

Virginia is divided into twenty-two planning districts, and each metropolitan area is in one slightly larger than the SMSA definition. A planning district commission is composed of a majority of local officials. The main activities are regional planning and the A-95 review-and-comment process, and they are prohibited by law from implementing plans or providing governmental services (an exception is one rural, southwestern Virginia district which has authority for small stream maintenance and solid waste disposal). However, under other legislation a separate district service commission, also with local official majority membership, can be set up if approved in each local jurisdiction, but so far this hasn't occurred because of local government opposition (ACIR, 1973B:328-336).

Since confederation into a body with both planning and implementation authority hasn't received necessary local support in Virginia, an alternative to consider would be federation with an areawide board chosen directly by the voters. This wouldn't remove the opposition of local officials and would probably increase their concern, but it would give the citizens an opportunity to vote for officials having areawide responsibilities. Thus, an optional form for Virginia might be metropolitan federation, letting the people choose between an advisory-only district planning commission, a confederated district service commission, or a federated system with an elected areawide council having specified powers and with cities and counties retained for most service activities in smaller areas.

Metropolitan Regions

The largest aggregation of population we are calling metropolitan regions. These consist of two or more adjacent and interlocked SMSAs and also free-standing, multicounty SMSAs over one million. In many respects the ones in the one to three million range are just big metropolitan areas, but as they grow this large they begin to get more complicated in their internal political relationships and the traditional central city gains rivals in the competition for power, commerce, and major cultural amenities. This is clearest where urban expansion brings more than one SMSA together within a metropolitan region.

WHAT IS REGIONAL?

In terms of governmental activities, what is regional? In practice not many of the hundreds of activities of local government have to be this broad in scope, but some highly important ones do.

Transportation systems are most clear-cut, particularly expressways, mass transit, airports, and the port for waterborne transportation. Air quality is another regional concern, at least to the extent of setting standards (if this isn't done statewide) and monitoring conditions, though some of the enforcement procedures might be localized.

Systems planning for water supply, sewage disposal, and solid waste disposal need a regional base, and in some metropolitan regions operation of one or more of these systems may be regionwide. However, it is also possible to use several subregional agencies, such as counties, for actual operations. Large parks and open space policies also need to be regional in scope. Broad development guidelines should be worked out on a regional basis, including general land use plans and the fair-share allocation of housing types. However, detailed plans and land use controls can be handled on a subregional basis within the framework of the regional plan.

It is useful to regionally organize information sharing among local governmental units and to have joint research operations for such matters as population projections, economic base studies, and labor market data.

Certain aspects of systems planning for human resource programs and services might also have a regional basis. Examples are planning for the general location of hospitals and for efforts directed toward the goal of local full employment, but the detailed plans for implementation can be handled within subregional areas. Furthermore, most direct services, such as police, fire, education, libraries, recreation, street maintenance, refuse collection, and many others clearly do not require regionwide administration. And except for the operation of transportation facilities and possibly regional water supply and sewerage systems, a regional organization or a set of regional agencies doesn't need very many personnel in comparison to the aggregate number of county and municipal employees.

SINGLE-STATE REGIONS

Like the multicounty metropolitan areas, metropolitan regions are aggregates of township, municipal, and county governments, and many of the problems of governmental structure have to be worked out within the counties. In a number of metropolitan regions this is a far more urgent need than developing an effective regional agency because so much of the service delivery is handled by small- and intermediate-size governments. But it is also desirable to create more effective regional instruments for dealing with the problems which require greater breadth of attention. Since this is easier to accomplish within a single state than for an interstate region, let us look at single-state metropolitan regions first. They tend to fall into clusters according to their internal makeup and prospective organizational solutions.

One principal city. A number of them have one principal city, but they vary in how much of the regional population is within the central city and core county. Indianapolis after consolidation with Marion County takes in about 70 percent of its region, and the surrounding seven fringe counties are only beginning to feel the impact of metropolitan growth. Franklin County, in which Columbus, Ohio is located, holds about 80 percent of the population of the five-county region; there some restructuring is needed within the core county, and at least one of the other counties is getting considerable suburban development. Harris County contains a similar proportion of the Houston-Galveston region, much of it in Houston itself; in a sense Galveston is a major satellite rather than a competing metropolitan center. Erie County, New York has 82 percent of the population of the Buffalo SMSA and the rest is in adjacent Niagara County, which has its own identity. All four regions are characterized by the dominance of the central city and core county, and any regional structure would reflect this reality.

In three other metropolitan regions—Pittsburgh, Detroit, and Milwaukee—the core county is from 55 to 65 percent of the regional population, not quite so overwhelming but clearly preeminent. Detroit has the small metropolitan area of Ann Arbor as part of the region, and Milwaukee has the Racine and Kenosha SMSAs. Presently all three regions have fairly strong regional councils functioning as confederations of local officials, and this may be a suitable approach at this time, though some people in the Detroit region favor a regional council on the model of the Metropolitan Council of Minnesota. In the Pittsburgh area restructuring of county and local government in Alleghany County with its 313 units should be a high priority.

Denver, Atlanta, New Orleans, and Baltimore have all had major reorganization in the past: city-county separation for Denver and Baltimore, city/county consolidation in New Orleans, and functional consolidation between Atlanta and Fulton County. Now regional growth has spread out so that only New Orleans has more than half of the regional population (52 percent) and Atlanta has less than one-third. In this situation an elected regional council with powers like the Minnesota model seems appropriate in order to provide a general-purpose unit directly responsible to the regional citizens. A proposal along these lines is pending for four large counties in the Denver SMSA, excluding Boulder and a couple of scarcely populated fringe counties. The Atlanta Regional Council is a strong planning vehicle and has almost as many citizen members as public officials; a next step might be to make it elective, or at least partly elective. So also elected regional councils could be established in the Baltimore and New Orleans areas.

Pair of central cities. Three single-state regions have a pair of central cities: Minneapolis-St. Paul, Tampa-St. Petersburg, and Dallas-Fort Worth. The first has its Metropolitan Council appointed by the governor. A proposal for an elected regional council has been proposed for the Tampa Bay region, but the Florida legislature hasn't yet authorized it. The North Central Texas Council of Governments is one of the stronger specimens of this species and has achieved joint planning where once rivalry between two metropolises existed;

it might properly be an elected body, but there seems not to be much local support for this idea.

Multicentered regions. Other regions are multicentered. One of them surrounds San Francisco Bay, and another goes along Puget Sound from Everett through Seattle down to Tacoma. For both of them intracounty organization needs attention and then regional structure. Bills to make the Association of Bay Area Governments an elective body, or part-elected, part-appointed have been before the California legislature but not yet enacted. Maybe something like this would be appropriate for a new Puget Sound regional council, making it directly responsible to the electorate for specified functions and bypassing the bickering of the city and county officials who now run the existing Council of Governments.

A metropolitan region stretches 75 miles along the Wasatch Front from Ogden through Salt Lake City to Provo, and because it contains about 80 percent of Utah's population, state government along with the counties and cities have a vital interest in regional problems. The three counties on the east coast of Southern Florida—Palm Beach, Broward, and Dade—constitute a region even though much of what needs doing can be managed within each one of them functioning separately in the form of countywide, metropolitan federations. Likewise the two metropolitan areas in the Virginia Tidewater region can function separately for most things, but for some planning matters regional cooperation is desirable. In these three cases from Utah, Florida, and Virginia a confederated style seems to be the most appropriate mode for regional planning at the present time.

The same is true for the Cleveland-Akron-Lorain region, which consists of three SMSAs drawn together by population expansion. Some difficult problems between Cleveland and its neighboring municipalities in Cuyahoga County need resolution within a framework of a countywide federation, and this model is valid for Summit County (Akron) and Lorain County, but confederation makes more sense for the larger region. Likewise in Southern California, a sprawling region with more than ten million inhabitants living in five huge counties, countywide federations seem logical but confederation makes sense for the whole region, bringing all regional agencies under the policy guidance of the Southern California Association of Governments.

New England. In New England, though, with its lack of functioning counties, it might be appropriate to have regional councils directly elected by the voters. This arrangement, combined with existing cities and towns, would produce a federated form, just as it was first proposed for the Boston area in 1896. Now, around Boston an elected regional council could handle regional planning and take charge of the three state-chartered metropolitan agencies (for the port, rapid transit, and water, sewers, and parks), somewhat in the same manner as the Metropolitan Council in Minnesota, with budgetary and policy control over them but allowing the metropolitan agencies to run as separate operations. Similarly an elected regional council for Central Connecticut could provide oversight to the Hartford Metropolitan District, which handles water and sewerage systems.

INTERSTATE REGIONS

Interstate regions face the same problems and have the same organizational needs as the single-state regions, but the legal obstacles of bi- and tri-state operations are greater and in some instance a navigable river makes physical separation a factor.

As Chapter 8 (p. 98) explained, the Tri-County Local Government Commission for the Portland area chose to avoid the interstate problem, concentrated only on the Oregon side of the Columbia River, and came up with a proposal for an elected Metropolitan Service Council which would get into direct operations as well as planning in a three-county area. This leaves Clark County, Washington and Vancouver to work out their own arrangements, and the interstate problems would be handled without a formal structure. In this particular region this probably can be a workable arrangement, but it might be desirable to find some kind of confederation to bring the two sides more closely together.

This is what happens in the Kansas City, St. Louis, and Cincinnati regions, where interstate councils of governments function as confederations. In the last two regions particularly, considerable attention should be given to the governmental structure on each side of the river: St. Louis and surrounding counties, a subregion in Illinois centered on East St. Louis, Cincinnati and the rest of Hamilton County, Covington and the surrounding Kentucky counties. If these subregions were better organized, implementation of regional planning would come easier.

The national capital region is a special situation because of the unique constitutional status of the District of Columbia. The Washington Area Council of Governments is a fairly effective instrument for information sharing, cooperative planning, and facilitating some joint actions, but it is completely dependent upon the member jurisdictions for most implementation. Perhaps this is one area where an elected regional council, established by interstate compact with the consent of Congress and the Maryland and Virginia legislatures, could be set up, complete with a limited taxing authority and with strong planning powers.

Rhode Island is the nearest we have to a city-state in the United States because of its small territory and extensive urbanization, and this affects the pattern of governmental services there. And now urbanization is connecting the Providence area with Fall River, Massachsetts and on to New Bedford. This requires cooperative, interstate planning, and perhaps some kind of regional confederation.

Urbanization in the Lower Delaware Valley has connected Trenton, Philadelphia, and Wilmington. But this has to be broken down into several subregions for practical action: Trenton and the rest of Mercer County; Philadelphia and the four surrounding counties in Pennsylvania; Camden and three counties in New Jersey across from Philadelphia; Wilmington and New Castle County located in something like a city-state with two rural counties attached; and finally the overflow of the Wilmington area into Salem County, New Jersey. Most of the action should concentrate upon these subregions and their counties, municipalities, and townships, but regional attention needs to be given to a few important matters in the transportation field and some broad issues of development planning.

In a similar fashion the relationships between Chicago, Cook County, and the rest of northeastern Illinois pose many problems which have to be ironed out within the state, and so also the relationships among Gary and the other cities of Lake County and other parts of northwestern Indiana. Then the interstate issues which remain can be handled on a cooperative basis without the need to organize a powerful, bistate agency.

In a way the same thing is true for the New York region with its eleven SMSAs. Newark and Essex County, Jersey City and Hudson County, and seven other counties in North Jersey completely covered with municipalities and townships contain numerous organizational problems to resolve. This is also the case for the five suburban counties in New York and the towns and cities of Connecticut which are part of the New York region. But there remain some tough, long-standing regional problems. So major are they that the states in the past have acted by creating the Port of New York Authority and the Tri-State Regional Planning Commission, neither of them controlled by the people of the region. Local officials are represented on a separate Metropolitan Regional Council, but it is so weak that it doesn't even have the A-95 clearinghouse function, which goes instead to the state-dominated Regional Planning Commission. A directly elected regional council in charge of planning and the clearinghouse function would be desirable, and it should at least have the power to approve or disapprove of projects of the Port Authority and to have budgetary control over its operations.

Concluding Remarks

This discussion of what this metropolitan region and that one ought to do is, of course, highly speculative, perhaps unrealistic, and maybe merely daydreaming. No matter. The purpose is to show that regions, along with multicounty metropolitan areas and single-county metropolises, have considerable variety, but nonetheless there are a finite number of models which can be developed and adapted to the various localities. It is the middle ground between saying that each area is unique and insisting that one solution will suffice everywhere.

If there is to be change, it will require political astuteness and perseverance. The kind of political action needed is the subject of the final chapter of this book, to which we now turn.

Chapter 18

POLITICAL ACTION

Governmental reorganization in metropolitan areas doesn't come to pass of its own accord. It is made to happen by men and women working in the context of politics and governmental processes. Therefore, it is important to know what kind of political action is required and what steps are likely to be most successful.

The Setting

BACKGROUND CONDITIONS

In the early 1960s Roscoe C. Martin conducted case studies of nine areas where some kind of metropolitan reorganization had occurred, and he came up with the following nine hypotheses of metropolitan action (1963:128-133):

(1) Metropolitan action normally results from a particular problem which requires solutions, not from considerations of doctrine.

(2) Adaptive action normally will be taken only after an extended period of incubation, including frequently a history of prior attempts and failures. It is not realistic to expect quick action even in response to demonstrated need.

(3) Without skilled and experienced political leadership a proposal for metropolitan action, no matter how meritorious, is not likely to be brought to successful issue.

(4) A campaign of civic education resulting in public acceptance is necessary to the success of an adaptive course, whether or not popular approval is required for adoption of a particular proposal.

(5) Citizens generally fail to respond to reorganization campaigns with any marked show of interest.

(6) Almost every local adaptation to changing needs results from compromises designed to satisfy the parties, and particularly the governments, affected by the action.

(7) Fortuitous developments constitute an unforeseeable but inescapable component in the metropolitan decisionmaking process.

(8) In any appraisal of metropolitan decisionmaking, the role of the State must be judged to be of fundamental importance.

(9) In recent years the Federal Government has come to play a not-unimportant role in the metropolitan decisionmaking process. It is altogether likely that it will become increasingly active in this field in the future.

Ten years later after the city/county consolidation movement had grown and led to a number of local referendums, Vincent L. Marando assessed the causes of success and failure. He found that key factors for success are a charter providing for popular election of officials, a large legislative body, an assurance to inner-city black residents of representation in the new government, and exemption of existing municipalities from consolidation. Reorganization, he discovered, isn't basically a grass roots movement but rather springs from the desires of civic groups, academics, and community leaders. Campaign efforts have difficulty reaching large numbers of people because the benefits of reorganized government are either too abstract or too long-range in their potential impact. Campaigning through mass media seems less successful than effots employing methods similar to those used by competitive political candidates. Furthermore, no reorganization plan can pass over the active opposition of the political parties, and it isn't likely to be adopted without active partisan support (1974:44-48).

After the National Academy of Public Administration had sponsored metropolitan reorganization studies in four areas, its panel concluded that unification may be feasible in smaller and jurisdictionally uncomplicated metropolitan areas but that in larger areas some variety of multitier arrangement seems more applicable. The experience of the four study areas showed that while such traditional supporters of reorganization as the chamber of commerce, league of women voters, other good government groups, and the media can form a solid base of support, they are not sufficient by themselves. In addition, there must be support from some bloc of elected officials, or at least the neutrality of most. Thus, the panel made the following observations (1977 B:Ch. VII, p. 13):

> In these four reform efforts, central city officials were likely to agree to a reorganization study at the outset, and to concur in its conclusions. This concurrence depended on how the study objectives were set forth and upon the substance and details of the final recommendations. Suburban officials were more likely to be skeptical of reform efforts at their initiation and to oppose the final plan. However, suburban reaction was not monolithic and was positive, at times, depending again upon the final proposal and its effect on individual jurisdictions.

The NAPA panel saw the mass media as useful in helping to articulate and communicate the issue of metropolitan reform, but the media cannot decide the issue. In these four studies, minority group reaction depended upon the context; since the efforts concentrated mainly on the regional level while leaving the central city intact, the minorities tended to be apathetic or neutral because their immediate needs and problems weren't addressed.

POLITICS

Some persons pushing for metropolitan reorganization like to feel that this is a strictly civic betterment endeavor, completely devoid of politics. But it isn't, for it is a very political process, and properly so.

Power is a basic commodity of politics—power to choose who will govern and power to determine who will benefit from the policies of government. The structure of government determines where the official decisionmakers will be situated and how they are to be chosen. Reorganization changes this, thereby altering the balance of power. Even action to shield governing officials from "politics," such as in a special district or authority, is a political decision because it permits certain persons to take actions affecting the public without being directly accountable to the people. Moreover, even then special district personnel are politically involved in matters affecting their particular interests. Selecting a particular mode of election, such as at large, nonpartisan contests for city council, is a political decision because it determines which segments will be most influential; in the example, the mass media and citywide civic groups rather than the citizens with a base in a neighborhood or a political party.

Politics is a means for resolving differences among competing interests. The contention arising from this process makes politics distasteful to some persons, but providing this forum for open competition is one of politics' greatest contributions to a democratic society.

Bargaining is very much part of the political process, and in working toward metropolitan reorganization it is important that all identifiable interests become involved in the bargaining which goes on. And reformers would be wise to try to gauge what the silent populace are thinking because as voters they may eventually have their chance to speak at the public referendum.

Governmental reorganization should be as objective and rational as possible, but the subjectivity and passions of politics must also be taken into account.

State-Established Framework

I'm a great believer in local initiative and action, but here I want to put the bee on state government as the place to start in producing more effective forms of metropolitan organization. Even though local governments in most states have considerable freedom of action, the state has erected the basic framework of local government, as we reviewed in Chapter 10. What the state has established, the state can change.

HOME RULE

Home rule is a cherished cause of local democracy, but to whom does this right belong? To some rich people who build homes surrounding a golf course, incorporate as a municipality, and exclude all "undesirable" uses (and people)? To a developer who owns an undeveloped tract and wants an arrangement where he determines the rules of development? To a few industries who add only enough houses to have a handful of voters in their tax haven?

Can a suburban community maintain its independence by being excluded from city/county consolidation? Can a neighborhood secede from a city, claiming home rule? Can a metropolitan community assert its right to home rule even if this results in limiting the home rule of smaller communities within the metropolis?

Our responses depend upon our values, and some of the questions are easier to answer than others. Believing as I do in local federalism, I would favor a measure of metropolitan home rule combined with assurance that smaller communities of viable size governmentally could have a degree of home rule within a federal framework. Let me here emphasize "viable" and then try to define it in a moment.

But whatever we think, it is the decision makers in state government who ultimately set the conditions for local governmental organization.

PERMISSIVE METROPOLITAN FORMS

To make possible metropolitan home rule, a state legislature could enact a law offering several alternative forms to the metropolitan areas. There could be a separate set of choices for (a) the metropolitan municipality within a larger county, (b) an entire county (core, suburban, or fringe), and (c) a multicounty metropolis.

For the metropolitan municipality, city unification would be one choice, especially in states with no townships or weak ones; this would be made possible by easy annexation, extraterritorial zoning and subdivision control, and inhibitions on suburban incorporation. Secondly, where a pattern of multiple municipalities and strong townships already exists, state legislation can make confederated action practicable by authorizing interlocal agreements and joint exercise of powers, and perhaps by providing for a general-purpose confederation, a kind of municipal council of governments with some teeth. The third choice would be a federated metropolitan municipality with an areawide unit having its own elected governing body, specified powers, and taxing authority; existing municipalities would serve as the small-area units but opportunity for internal boundary revisions should also be possible.

At the county level, the state can authorize city/county consolidation or a formal countywide federation. Issues such as exclusion of existing municipalities from consolidation and municipal boundary rearrangement in the course of federation would be left up to local decision. And the division of responsibilities in a federation could also be worked out within each county.

For multicounty metropolitan areas, the state can provide for an intercounty metropolitan municipality, either on a unified or a federated model. And it can also authorize a multicounty, areawide government with specific, though limited, responsibilities. One model is the Metropolitan Council of Minnesota (though with elections added), and another is the Metropolitan Service Council proposed for the Portland area; the first has policy control over separate operating commissions while the second would take on such operations directly. Because both the central city and the counties act as intermediate governments in a multicounty federation, in some places it might be desirable for the city to separate from its county and thus eliminate overlapping in this middle arena of action.

In New England and Virginia the options could be a formal confederation with some power to do things or a federation with an elected, areawide governing body. The cities and towns would remain in New England metropolises and the counties and independent cities in Virginia.

LOCAL GOVERNMENT COMMISSION

Beyond permitting metropolitan home rule, the states should take affirmative leadership to bring about metropolitan reorganization. Already a few states have boundary commissions, dealing mainly with annexation and proposed formation of new units, and here and there a state-created temporary local government study commission operates. But nothing as forceful as the Ontario Municipal Board, which took the initiative in producing regional federation throughout the province.

Something like this would be desirable in the American states. Through an open process of local consultation, hearings, published reports, and responses, and finally recommendations, a state commission on local government could redesign the governmental structure within a metropolitan area where the metropolitan citizens themselves haven't acted under state enabling legislation. Some broad choices could appropriately be placed on the ballot, such as unification versus federation, and ultimately a charter for an areawide government could go to a public referendum. But a local government commission should also have the authority to negotiate, and if necessary ultimately to order, the consolidation of special districts and tiny municipal units into general-purpose units of viable size. The statute could establish criteria for "viable" in terms of perceived community boundaries, economy of scale, and effective service areas for enough activities to produce a general-purpose government with an adequate tax base. There might be a statutory minimum population size for small-area governments, expressed either in numbers (such as five, ten, or twenty thousand) or as a proportion of the metropolitan or county population (such as five percent, producing a minimum size of 5,000 for a metropolis of 100,000 but 25,000 in an area of half a million).

STATE POLITICAL PROCESSES

We should recognize, though, that the political dynamics of state politics are such that state-initiated metropolitan reorganization won't come easy. There is no strong constituency for metropolitan reform but a powerful one in opposition, based upon a host of local officials in municipal, township, and county governments and special districts. They are motivated by self-preservation and are organized into statewide associations, usually with an office and staff at the state capital. Moreover, local officials often have close ties with political parties and influence the legislature through that channel, and many legislators were formerly local officials and identify with them.

The concept of local federalism has the potential for mitigating some of this opposition because it wouldn't do away with small-area, general-purpose governments (though it might bring about some consolidation of the smallest units and the abolition of special districts). Opportunity for local votes on key questions, such as through a choice of form under permissive metropolitan home rule or in response to a proposal from a state commission on local government, also offers some reassurance against arbitrary action.

Some legislators have local constituencies which would particularly benefit from reorganization because they suffer inequities under the present structure. Moreover, many members are public-spirited and are willing to seek solutions beyond the bounds of special interests. The governor is in a position to assert what seems to be best for the overall public good, and a local government commission would be in a position to go beyond narrow interests. This gives local civic leadership an opportunity to press for state action, but for this to be most successful they need to join with like-minded persons from other parts of the state in order to create a legal framework favorable to change.

It may also be possible to spur state action through law suits challenging existing arrangements which have the result of severe fiscal disparities. This is occurring with education finance and is having mixed success in modifying funding sources (but not in changing the pattern of school organization). Conceivably the courts could order state government to alter local government patterns now causing inequities, just as the courts have brought about reapportionment of state legislatures.

It will be a long haul. Governmental reorganization always is. But it has taken a long time for the accumulation of decisions by state officials to produce the present pattern. Change will have to be measured in years, not in weeks and months.

Local Initiative

If state government establishes general conditions for metropolitan reorganization, then local leaders can move into action within that framework. But if the state does nothing, people in the locality can still take the initiative and later get needed enabling acts passed by the state legislature, even a constitutional amendment if required. The challenge to local leadership is how to produce a sensible plan of organization and how to gain public acceptance.

A few persons might start the ball rolling, but as the effort proceeds a broad-based coalition is necessary. Since reorganization is likely to move toward the creation of some kind of an areawide government (this is so even with efforts carried out in the context of local federalism), public support for this action must be generated. I do believe that the metropolis is a political community searching for a suitable governmental form, as spelled out in Chapter 12, but this is a somewhat vague feeling which has to be nurtured and shaped. For this to happen, an areawide study and action organization of some sort is needed to work for establishment of a permanent areawide government.

AREAWIDE ORGANIZATIONS

Several varieties of areawide organizations are available to choose from.

Study commissions. One approach is to set up a study commission with responsibility for investigating local problems related to governmental structure and making recommendations for organizational changes. In a number of southern cities, the chamber of commerce initiated the study commission and often gained the support of the league of women voters and the newspapers (Marando, 1974:23). In a few places, city or county officials have been in on the formation of the study group, and so have members of the academic community. In the four metropolitan areas conducting studies with assistance from the National Academy of Public Administration, the study commissions were established by an informal process involving a broad band of local leadership who worked through consensus and then gained the endorsement of the governing officials of the major units of local government.

Reflecting upon this experience, NAPA has strongly emphasized that the original selection of commission membership is especially critical to eventual success or failure, both for what the individual members will contribute and for the commission's credibility with the public. Membership should be broadly representative of all segments of the community. The commission should be linked to local government either through the appointive process or by including representatives from local government. It must have strong and active leadership. NAPA also concluded that a full-time staff and a separate office are essential in order to give the commission visibility and its own identity (1977A:20-29).

As a NAPA panel member during the Denver and Portland studies, my own observation is that they were broadly representative of the various segments of the two communities, but most commission members were what might be called cosmopolitans. That is to say, they were interested in broad issues and areawide problems much more than the concerns of neighborhoods and small municipalities, and this led to much heavier consideration of areawide government than small-area government even though both were the mission of the project. Thus, if a study wants to focus on local federalism in its fullest sense, a special effort may be needed to assure that the neighborhood viewpoint is adequately represented.

Charter boards. The study process can be given a firm legal status through the appointment of a charter board, and this can lead directly to a local referendum on the study outcome. This approach is particularly relevant for a free-standing, single-county metropolis where the county is the natural areawide government. But it could also be done for a metropolitan municipality, an intercounty metropolis, and a multicounty metropolitan area if state legislation established these as areas for which charters can be drawn up. The charter board might follow a previous study commission, which has set the stage and may have even pushed for this second step, but it might also be the initial effort to devise a plan for reorganization. Generally a charter board will have fewer members than a study commission, but it needs to be as broadly representative as possible and it should work in full public view and with ample citizen input. It may be that a separate citizens body should function simultaneously as an instrument for public education and support.

Regional citizen associations. A permanent, citizens association functioning on an areawide basis can be the impetus for reform. For example, the Citizens League of the Twin Cities area in Minnesota has been the source of many of the ideas of metropolitan reform, including the metropolitan council, tax-base sharing, and neighborhood councils within the two central cities; it has promoted these ideas publicly and in the state legislature. The Metropolitan Fund of the Detroit area has been pushing for regional action in southeastern Michigan, and some of the older regional associations, organized originally to encourage areawide planning, are also interested in governmental reorganization. Because efforts of metropolitan reorganization take years to accomplish, a regional citizens association requires a long-term citizen commitment and financial support.

Regional councils. An official regional organization, such as a council of governments or a regional planning commission, already operates areawide as a confederated mechanism, and it is a focus for citizen attention to areawide issues. Potentially this can lead to consideration of further organizational change. However, since these forms of regional councils are made up of local elected officials, they tend not to be interested in building up a constituency oriented toward the areawide body, and they usually don't want to encourage a switch to direct elections. The Metropolitan Council of Minnesota is different because its members are appointed by the governor from districts not precisely aligned with local governmental units and the chairman serves at large; although they don't campaign for office, they have direct relationships with the public on areawide matters and also with local officials, and this has set in motion a regional political process and a constituency relationship with a life of its own. This could be converted to the political process of direct elections should the state legislature make this change in the selection method.

BARGAINING

Charter writing and governmental reorganization are political processes. As such, bargaining is an ever-present element. However, it isn't sitting-around-the-table bargaining involving all interested parties, but rather a more subtle process of stating opinions publicly, responding to them, anticipating reactions to possible alternative courses, trying to assuage opponents, and attempting to build countersupport. We have seen the outcome of this process in such compromises as the excluded municipalities of the consolidated city/counties and the elected county officers and certain special districts remaining intact.

What didn't happen in many of the failed unification attempts was sufficient taking into account some deep-felt opposition to centralization, a preference for government on a more intimate scale, and a desire to preserve the status quo. Because study commissions and charter boards attract people more interested in areawide action, this other viewpoint has been underrepresented and has had a weak role in the discussion, or not at all. Only at the polls when people vote "no" was this voice clearly heard.

Those who see the need for areawide government should reckon with this certain opposition by structuring the reorganization process so as to bring in more people who are hesitant about too much centralization, especially those who have institutional interests in small areas, such as officials of suburban municipalities and townships and representatives of racial and ethnic groups concentrated in geographic subareas. And reformers can go a step further by conducting surveys and anticipating what activities a majority of the populace perceives as legitimate for areawide action and what activities they prefer to handle in smaller areas.

This gets us back to the idea of the federal bargain. Each party gives up something in order to gain a union desired by both. This applies to local federalism. In light of frequent opposition to centralization, the bargain should keep areawide activities to a minimum and should clearly articulate the activities to be handled by intermediate and small areas.

INCREMENTAL CHANGE

Sweeping reorganization is rare in the history of metropolitan America. The sixteen cases of city/county consolidation or city-county separation are the prime examples occurring over a period of one hundred fifty years, and even some of them came in stages and were compromised when carried out. Gradual adaptation is the primary mode, and most structural changes have been incremental. This is not to say that major reorganization shouldn't be attempted, for it is oftentimes needed and is sometimes achievable. Rather, it is to stress what the realities are so that reformers can be guided by the possible as well as the potential.

One incremental change would be to achieve an areawide, general-purpose government by converting the existing council of governments into an elected body, or even half-elected, half-representative of local officials, as suggested in one proposal for the Association of Bay Area Governments (Jones, 1974:137-144). Depending upon state law, this might come about through local initiative or it might require state legislation.

In the beginning the elected, areawide body might have scarcely any more powers than the present councils of governments, but this could change over time. Once there is a locally elected body, it should be in charge of all areawide planning assisted with federal funds, such as transportation, water quality, land use, employment-and-training, health systems, and other functions, or should be able to choose which areawide agency it would delegate this task to. In terms of its own responsibilities the areawide government might gradually increase its mission, as the Metropolitan Council of Minnesota has done with the consent of the legislature and as is built into the proposals for Denver and Portland, to be achieved through referendum.

Where the county serves as the areawide government, its acquisition of new responsibilities can come gradually over time, which has been happening anyway through functional transfers. But simultaneously the county should examine its existing activities, determine which ones can be handled as well or better in smaller scale operations, and transfer these activities to small-area governments. This would keep county government from growing too big and unwieldy, and it would ease public acceptance of county absorption of truly areawide activities. In whatever manner the county changes, its administrative structure should be modified accordingly.

Consolidation of the tiny municipal units and special districts into more viable, small-area governments could also occur over a period of time. This could be handled by an independent local boundary commission, a special board of the areawide government, or a state commission, working primarily through negotiation but holding in reserve the power to decide upon and implement local consolidation within the framework of state guidelines.

Continuous adjustments of this sort reflect the spirit of federalism. For, federalism is a continuously changing set of relationships as well as a structure of government.

National Contribution

Even though the national government has no direct legal authority over local government, its influence is considerable, as we have seen repeatedly. Therefore, federal agencies can and should contribute to improved governmental organization in metropolitan areas.

PREFERENCE FOR GENERAL-PURPOSE UNITS

Since the national government is made up of departments and congressional committees with specific functional responsibilities, special purpose programs and organizations get much more attention than the general, overall viewpoint. Thus, each department wants its own contacts in specialized agencies of state and local government, producing what Terry Sanford has called "picket fence federalism" with specialized programs as the vertical pickets running straight to the ground and state and local general government as the connecting slats, holding the pickets in line but not bringing them together (1967:80; for a pictorial conceptualization by Deil S. Wright, see ACIR, 1976A:6). One of the most recent examples was the successful effort of the Health Resources Administration and its congressional committee allies to define health services planning areas in such a way as to preclude integration with other areawide planning.

As a counterstrategy, ACIR has advocated use of umbrella multijurisdictional organizations (UMJOs) under the control of local elected officials. Some progress has been made in this direction, but no president has yet vigorously insisted that this is his administration's policy and the Office of Management and Budget hasn't been geared to press the federal departments to support general-purpose state and local coordination. This needs doing.

However, I part company with ACIR on its preference for a confederation of local officials running an UMJO. Instead I believe that elected, areawide general-purpose governments should be encouraged, though obviously not mandated, by federal agencies. This could be done by an amendment to the Intergovernmental Cooperation Act to permit an elected areawide unit to have the right to become or to designate the local planning body for every federal program with area planning requirements. This should include the authority to waive other federal laws which lean toward functional separatism, such as the arbitrary minimum population of 500,000 for health services planning areas.

In related recommendations, the General Accounting Office has proposed that Congress establish a national policy on areawide planning in order to provide a basis for strengthening focal points at the areawide level (1977:52). The GAO has also recommended that the number of separate areawide planning programs be reduced through consolidation. Along these lines legislation was introduced in the spring of 1977 (S.892 and H.R. 4406) to require federal agencies to observe common substate district boundaries and to require an annual area development plan showing how federal assistance programs would fit together. The bills also expressed a preference for areawide planning agencies composed of elected officials (rather than directly elected as I prefer).

METROPOLITAN-ORIENTED ORGANIZATIONS

Because metropolitan areas lack areawide governments, there is no energetic advocacy of the metropolitan viewpoint in the contention among interest groups in national affairs. The functional specialities have federal agencies, congressional committees, and trade associations, and cities and counties also have powerful national organizations pressing their interests. There is a National Association of Regional Councils, but since it represents local confederations, its members are city and county officials first and regional officers second and consequently it lacks the influence of city and county associations.

Although there can't be a national association of an organizational form which doesn't exist, or has only a few specimens, that is, general-purpose areawide governments, there are other places where metropolitan-oriented units can be established. Specifically, in OMB, in HUD, and as subcommittees in Congress. The unit in OMB should deal with the national government's overall policies directed toward metropolitan areas (and toward substate town-and-country districts as well). HUD should channel financial assistance to areawide organizations and should sponsor demonstration and research dealing with general-purpose, areawide concerns (not merely housing and physical planning). The congressional subcommittees should use the influence of oversight hearings to keep the metropolitan viewpoint before the public and should make legislative recommendations favoring general-purpose planning and coordination.

In addition, a citizens lobby should be set up, bringing together people who perceive that urban America is made up of metropolitan communities which need areawide governments to cope better with a variety of urgent problems. Regional citizen associations might form the nucleus for such an organization, but citizens from other backgrounds ought to be involved, too, including persons from minority groups and others who are concerned that governmental activities in metropolitan areas don't neglect the needs of the disadvantaged population.

INTERSTATE COMPACTS

Because a significant number of metropolitan areas and regions cross state lines, the interstate metropolis should be a special concern of the national government. Accordingly, Congress might enact a general statute authorizing interstate compacts for general-purpose metropolitan and regional agencies, and this would prepare the way for later approval of specific agreements by Congress and the state legislatures. An agency within the executive branch, such as HUD or OMB, could be a facilitator of such interstate compacts.

Citizen Action

Running through all this discussion is the theme of citizen action. Ours is a representative democracy, and this applies to national, state, and local governments, and locally to municipal, township, and county governments. It could also apply to neighborhood and areawide units if we instituted them. Both the form and powers of these governments are derived from the consent of the people, and what one generation has approved the next one can change. So it is up to us citizens to decide how we want local government in metropolitan areas organized. We can express this as citizens of the metropolis and of its more localized subsections and as state and national citizens.

As citizens we aren't of a single mind, however. There are many interests within the citizenry, and even individual citizens hold diverse sets of values and desires. Thus, while citizen action needs the strong backbone of commitment, it also requires tolerance and understanding of other viewpoints. Ultimately, bargaining as part of the political process is essential in order to reconcile conflicting needs. No one gets his or her way completely, but neither should anybody lose out altogether.

Metropolitan society is pluralistic, so its governmental structure should be diversified. But not so fragmented as to be incoherent and ineffective. As metropolitan citizens we need an areawide general-purpose government responsible to us through direct elections; as neighborhood citizens we need a governmental unit closer to home; and as citizens of intermediate areas—city or county—we need this focus, too. All this is possible under local federalism, the system which brings small and large together into a sensible whole.

APPENDIX

Table 15: Free-Standing, Single-County Metropolises.

| | | | County Types | | | | | | | Governmental Units (1972) | | | | | | |
SMSA	State	1974 pop. (000)	All	CC	C	S	F	County	1974 pop. (000)	All	Co.	Muni.	Twp.	Sch. dist.	Spec. dist.	Suggested Organization
In Strong-Township States																
Rochester	NY	966	5	—	1	—	4	Monroe	707	78	1	11	19	21	26	County Fed.
Syracuse	NY	646	3	—	1	—	2	Onondaga	472	79	1	16	19	17	26	County Fed.
Binghamton	NY-PA	300	3	—	1	—	2	Broome	217	49	1	8	16	15	9	Fed. Muni.
Poughkeepsie	NY	233	1	—	1	—	—	Dutchess	233	68	1	10	20	13	24	Fed. Muni.
Elmira	NY	99	1	—	1	—	—	Chemung	99	32	1	6	11	3	11	Fed. Muni.
Atlantic City	NJ	190	1	—	1	—	—	Atlantic	190	53	1	17	6	13	16	County Fed.
Vineland-Mill-ville-Bridgeton	NJ	131	1	—	1	—	—	Cumberland	131	38	1	4	10	12	11	County Fed.
York	PA	346	2	—	1	—	—	York	284	156	1	37	35	15	68	Fed. Muni.
Lancaster	PA	338	1	—	1	—	—	Lancaster	338	137	1	20	41	16	59	Fed. Muni.
Reading	PA	305	1	—	1	—	—	Berks	305	171	1	31	44	18	77	Fed. Muni.
Erie	PA	274	1	—	1	—	—	Erie	274	89	1	18	22	13	35	Fed. Muni.
Johnstown	PA	266	2	—	1	—	1	Cambria	189	119	1	34	30	12	42	Fed. Muni.
Altoona	PA	136	1	—	1	—	—	Blair	136	54	1	5	18	29	4	Fed. Muni.
Williamsport	PA	116	1	—	1	—	—	Lycoming	116	85	1	10	42	9	23	Fed. Muni.
Flint	MI	522	2	—	1	—	1	Genesee	454	55	1	13	18	22	1	County Fed.
Kalamazoo-Portage	MI	262	2	—	1	—	1	Kalamazoo	201	36	1	9	15	10	1	Fed. Muni.
Saginaw	MI	227	1	—	1	—	—	Saginaw	227	54	1	8	27	13	5	Fed. Muni.
Battle Creek	MI	182	2	—	1	—	1	Calhoun	141	44	1	8	20	14	1	Fed. Muni.

Table 15 (Cont.)

		Standard Metropolitan Statistical Areas						Core Counties								
		1974 pop. (000)	County Types						1974 pop. (000)	Governmental Units (1972)						Suggested
SMSA	State	All	CC	C	S	F	County		All	Co.	Muni.	Twp.	Sch. dist.	Spec. dist.		Organization

In Strong-Township States (cont.)

Muskegon-Norton Shores-Muskegon

SMSA	State	All	CC	C	S	F	County	1974 pop. (000)	All	Co.	Muni.	Twp.	Sch. dist.	Spec. dist.	Suggested Organization
Heights	MI	177	2	—	1	—	1	Muskegon	157	45	1	11	16	14	3	Fed. Muni.
Jackson	MI	145	1	—	1	—	—	Jackson	145	41	1	7	19	13	1	Fed. Muni.
Bay City	MI	119	1	—	1	—	—	Bay	119	28	1	4	14	5	4	Fed. Muni.
Madison	WI	303	1	—	1	—	—	Dane	303	84	1	24	35	16	8	County Fed.
Green Bay	WI	167	1	—	1	—	—	Brown	167	36	1	6	18	7	4	Fed. Muni.
La Crosse	WI	83	1	—	1	—	—	La Crosse	83	24	1	6	12	4	1	Uni. City.

In Weak-Township States

SMSA	State	All	CC	C	S	F	County	1974 pop. (000)	All	Co.	Muni.	Twp.	Sch. dist.	Spec. dist.	Suggested Organization
Canton	OH	405	2	—	1	—	1	Stark	380	58	1	19	17	17	4	Fed. Muni.
Lima	OH	211	4	—	1	—	3	Allen	109	35	1	10	12	9	3	Fed. Muni.
Springfield	OH	189	2	—	1	—	1	Clark	155	33	1	10	10	8	4	Uni. City
Mansfield	OH	131	1	—	1	—	—	Richland	131	40	1	9	18	10	2	Fed. Muni.
Fort Wayne	IN	373	4	—	1	—	3	Allen	289	45	1	6	20	4	14	Uni. City
Evansville	IN-KY	289	5	—	1	—	4	Vanderbush	164	19	1	1	8	4	8	Uni. City
South Bend	IN	280	2	—	1	—	1	St. Joseph	242	48	1	9	13	5	20	Fed. Muni.
Terre Haute	IN	174	4	—	1	—	3	Vigo	113	26	1	4	12	1	8	Uni. City
Anderson	IN	139	1	—	1	—	—	Madison	139	51	1	16	14	5	15	Uni. City.
Muncie	IN	131	1	—	1	—	—	Delaware	131	38	1	6	12	7	12	Uni. City

Table 15 (cont.)

In Weak Township States (cont.)

Lafayette-W.Lafayette	IN	112	1	—	1	—	Tippecanoe	112	35	1	5	13	3	13	Fed. Muni.
Bloomington	IN	89	1	—	1	—	Monroe	89	NA						Uni. City
Rockford	IL	270	2	—	1	—	Winnebago	244	73	1	10	14	15	33	Uni. City
Springfield	IL	178	2	—	1	—	Sangamon	167	105	1	25	27	15	37	Fed. Muni.
Champaign-Urbana-Rantoul	IL	163	1	—	1	—	Champaign	163	163	1	23	29	20	90	Fed. Muni.
Decatur	IL	125	1	—	1	—	Macon	125	84	1	11	17	8	47	Uni. City
Bloomington-Normal	IL	114	1	—	1	—	McLean	114	114	1	21	30	13	49	Fed. Muni.
Kankakee	IL	96	1	—	1	—	Kankakee	96	NA						Uni. City
St. Cloud	MN	148	3	—	1	2	Stearns	101	NA		6	18	5		Uni. City
Rochester	MN	89	1	—	1	—	Olmstead	89	31	1				1	Uni. City
Sioux Falls	SD	98	1	—	1	—	Minnehaha	98	47	1	9	24	7	6	Uni. City
Wichita	KS	379	2	—	1	1	Sedgwick	341	78	1	17	27	10	23	Uni. City
Topeka	KS	180	3	—	1	2	Shawnee	152	44	1	5	12	6	20	Uni. City
Spokane	WA	304	1	—	1	—	Spokane	304	93	1	11	39	14	28	Uni. City.

In No-Township States—Southeast

Charleston	WV	254	2	—	1	1	Kanawha	224	35	1	13	—	1	20	County Fed.
Lexington-Fayette	KY	286	6	1	—	5	Fayette	187	7*	1	1	—	1	4	Cons. ci/co
Owensboro	KY	81	1	—	—	—	Daviess	81	9	1	2	—	2	4	Uni. City
Memphis	TN-AR-MS	853	4	—	1	3	Shelby	725	17	1	6	—	—	10	Cons. ci/co
Knoxville	TN	428	4	—	1	3	Knox	287	10	1	1	—	—	8	Cons. ci/co

* Prior to city/county consolidation

Table 15 (cont.)

| | | County Types | | | | | Core Counties | | Governmental Units (1972) | | | | | | |
SMSA	State	1974 pop (000)	All	CC	C	S	F	County	1974 pop (000)	All	Co.	Muni.	Twp.	Sch. dist.	Spec. dist.	Suggested Organization
In No-Township States—Southeast (cont.)																
Fayetteville	NC	223	1	—	1	—	—	Cumberland	223	11	1	8	—	—	2	Uni. City
Ashville	NC	166	2	—	1	—	1	Buncombe	150	11	1	6	—	—	4	Uni. City
Wilmington	NC	127	2	—	1	—	1	New Hanover	95	8	1	4	—	—	3	Uni. City
Burlington	NC	99	1	—	1	—	—	Almance	99	NA						Uni. City.
Savannah	GA	199	3	—	1	—	2	Chatham	176	14	1	7	—	1	5	County Fed.
Albany	GA	101	2	—	1	—	1	Dougherty	92	6	1	1	—	1	3	Uni. City
Jacksonville	FL	675	5	1	—	—	4	Duval	551	9	**	6	—	2	2	Cons. ci/co
Pensacola	FL	264	2	—	1	—	1	Escambia	218	8	1	6	—	2	3	County Fed.
Lakeland-Winter Haven	FL	263	1	—	1	—	—	Polk	263	29	1	17	—	2	9	County Fed.
Melbourne-Titusville	FL	229	1	—	1	—	—	Brevard	229	29	1	1	—	2	11	County Fed.
Daytona Beach	FL	200	1	—	1	—	—	Volusia	200	27	1	14	—	2	10	County Fed.
Sarasota	FL	159	1	—	1	—	—	Sarasota	159	16	1	3	—	1	11	County Fed.
Fort Meyers	FL	154	1	—	1	—	—	Lee	154	20	1	2	—	2	15	County Fed.
Tallahasee	FL	133	2	—	1	—	1	Leon	124	16	1	3	—	2	11	Uni. City
Gainesville	FL	124	1	—	1	—	—	Alachua	124	16	1	9	—	2	4	Uni. City
Birmingham	AL	785	4	—	1	—	3	Jefferson	642	52	1	34	—	9	8	County Fed.
Mobile	AL	396	2	—	1	—	1	Mobile	331	20	1	9	—	1	8	Fed. Muni.
Huntsville	AL	285	3	—	1	—	2	Madison	185	16	1	6	—	2	7	Uni. City
Montgomery	AL	248	3	—	1	—	2	Montgomery	183	7	1	1	—	1	4	Uni. City

Standard Metropolitan Statistical Areas

Table 15 (cont.)

In No-Township States—Southeast (cont.)

City	St.						County								Type
Tuscaloosa	AL	123	1	—	1	—	Tuscaloosa	123	9	1	2	—	2	4	Uni. City
Anniston	AL	106	1	—	1	—	Calhoun	106	NA	1	11	—	3	5	Uni. City
Gadsden	AL	95	1	—	1	—	Etowah	95	20	1	4	—	5	4	Fed. Muni.
Biloxi-Gulfport	MS	173	3	—	1	2	Harrison	146	14.	1	4	—			County Fed.
Pascagoula-Moss Point	MS	104	1	—	1	—	Jackson	104	NA	1	6	—			County Fed.
Little Rock-N. Little Rock	AR	356	2	—	1	1	Pulaski	313	27	1	6	—	3	17	County Fed.
Fayetteville-Springdale	AR	145	2	—	1	1	Washington	86	NA	1	6	—	6	2	Uni. City
Pine Bluff	AR	84	1	—	1	1	Jefferson	84	13	1	4	—	2	2	Uni. City
Baton Rouge	LA	407	4	—	—	3	E. Baton Rouge	309	6	1	3	—	1	28	Cons. ci/co
Lake Charles	LA	149	1	—	1	—	Calcasieu	149	36	1	6	—	1	12	Uni. City
Alexandria	LA	136	2	—	1	1	Rapides	122	23	1	9	—	2	6	Fed. Muni.
Monroe	LA	123	1	—	1	—	Ouachita	123	12	1	3	—	1	7	Fed. Muni.
Lafayette	LA	122	1	—	1	—	Lafayette	122	15	1	6	—			Uni. City

In States with No Townships—West

City	St.						County								Type
Des Moines	IA	328	2	—	1	1	Polk	298	62	1	16	—	10	35	Fed. Muni.
Cedar Rapids	IA	165	1	—	1	—	Linn	165	39	1	17	—	12	9	Uni. City
Waterloo-Cedar Falls	IA	132	1	—	1	—	Black Hawk	132	17	1	9	—	5	2	Fed. Muni.
Sioux City	IA-NE	104	2	—	1	1	Woodbury	104	27	1	15	—	7	4	Uni. City
Dubuque	IA	92	1	—	1	—	Dubuque	92	26	1	21	—	2	2	Uni. City
Springfield	MO	187	2	—	1	1	Greene	168	19	1	8	—	8	2	Uni. City
St. Joseph	MO	99	2	—	1	1	Buchanan	86	21	1	6	—	5	9	Uni. City

**Consolidated city/county enumerated as a municipality

Table 15 (Cont.)

								Core Counties		Governmental Units (1972)						
			County Types													
		Standard Metropolitan Statistical Areas														
SMSA	State	1974 pop. (000)	All	CC	C	S	F	County	1974 pop. (000)	All	Co.	Muni.	Twp.	Sch. dist.	Spec. dist.	Suggested Organization
In States with No Townships—West (cont.)																
Columbia	MO	86	1	—	1	—	—	Boone	86	25	1	8	—	11	5	Uni. City
Lincoln	NE	49	1	—	1	—	—	Lancaster	182	49	1	13	—	18	17	Uni. City
Tulsa	OK	576	6	—	1	—	5	Tulsa	416	38	1	11	—	16	10	Cons. ci/co
Lawton	OK	105	1	—	1	—	—	Comanche	105	32	1	20	—	13	8	Uni. City
San Antonio	TX	980	3	—	1	—	2	Bexar	912	56	1	20	—	16	19	Cons. ci/co
El Paso	TX	410	1	—	1	—	—	El Paso	410	20	1	2	—	9	8	Cons. ci/co
Austin	TX	389	2	—	1	—	1	Travis	354	26	1	7	—	6	12	Cons. ci/co
Corpus Christi	TX	245	2	—	1	—	1	Nueces	245	36	1	6	—	14	15	Uni. City
McAllen-Pharr-Edinburg	TX	218	1	—	1	—	—	Hidalgo	218	66	1	15	—	18	32	County Fed.
Killeen-Temple	TX	202	2	—	1	—	1	Bell	158	42	1	9	—	14	18	Fed. Muni.
Lubbock	TX	195	1	—	1	—	—	Lubbock	195	21	1	1	—	8	6	Uni. City
Brownsville-Harlingen-San Benito	TX	168	1	—	1	—	—	Cameron	168	64	1	13	—	13	37	County Fed.
Waco	TX	154	1	—	1	—	—	McLennan	154	45	1	14	—	20	10	Cons. ci/co
Abilene	TX	128	3	—	1	—	2	Taylor	103	22	1	8	—	9	4	Uni. City
Wichita Falls	TX	127	2	—	1	—	1	Wichita	119	19	1	5	—	5	8	Uni. City
Longview	TX	124	2	—	1	—	1	Gregg	81	NA	—	—	—	—	—	Uni. City
Tyler	TX	106	1	—	1	—	—	Smith	106	19	1	7	—	9	2	Uni. City
Odessa	TX	94	1	—	1	—	—	Ector	94	6	1	2	—	2	1	Uni. City
Laredo	TX	78	1	—	1	—	—	Webb	78	12	1	1	—	7	3	Uni. City

Table 15 (cont.)

In States with No Townships-West (cont.)

SMSA	State				County								Central city
Sherman-Denison	TX	78	1	—	1	Grayson	78	45	1	15	—	14	15	Fed. Muni.
San Angelo	TX	75	1	—	1	Tom Green	75	12	1	1	—	6	4	Uni. City
Bryan-College Station	TX	68	1	—	1	Brazos	68	7	1	2	—	1	3	Fed. Muni.
Midland	TX	66	1	—	1	Midland	66	NA	1	1	—	1	—	Uni. City
Albuquerque	NM	379	2	1	1	Bernalillo	357	8	1	2	—	1	4	Cons. ci/co
Phoenix	AZ	1,172	1	—	1	Maricopa	1,172	112	1	18	—	55	38	County Fed.
Tucson	AZ	434	1	—	1	Pima	434	23	1	2	—	17	3	Cons. ci/co
Colorado Springs	CO	293	2	1	1	El Paso	289	62	1	8	—	15	38	Uni. City
Pueblo	CO	124	1	—	1	Pueblo	124	24	1	1	—	2	18	Uni. City
Fort Collins	CO	115	1	—	1	Larimer	115	NA	1	—	—	—	—	Uni. City
Greeley	CO	107	1	—	1	Weld	107	NA	1	—	—	—	—	Uni. City
Billings	MT	95	1	—	1	Yellowstone	95	43	1	3	—	16	23	Uni. City
Great Falls	MT	84	1	—	1	Cascade	84	27	1	4	—	18	4	Uni. City
Boise City	ID	132	1	—	1	Ada	132	4	1	1	—	—	3	Uni. City
Las Vegas	NV	320	1	—	1	Clark	320	22	1	4	—	1	16	Cons. ci/co
Reno	NV	143	1	—	1	Washoe	143	14	1	2	—	1	10	Uni. City
San Diego	CA	1,518	1	—	1	San Diego	1,518	151	1	13	—	47	90	County Fed.
Fresno	CA	439	1	—	1	Fresno	439	200	1	15	—	56	128	Uni. City
Bakersfield	CA	338	1	—	1	Kern	338	143	1	11	—	53	78	Uni. City
Stockton	CA	299	1	—	1	San Joaquin	299	128	1	6	—	19	102	Uni. City
Santa Barbara-Santa Maria-Lompoc	CA	282	1	—	1	Santa Barbara	282	71	1	5	—	26	39	County Fed.

Table 15 (Cont.)

		Standard Metropolitan Statistical Areas							Core Counties		Governmental Units (1972)						
		1974	County Types							1974							Suggested
SMSA	State	pop. (000)	All	CC	C	S	F	County	pop. (000)	All	Co.	Muni.	Twp.	Sch. dist.	Spec. dist.	Organization
Salinas-Seaside																	
-Monterey	CA	261	1	—	1	—	—	Monterey	261	88	1	11	—	27	49	Fed. Muni.
Santa Rosa	CA	243	1	—	1	—	—	Sonoma	243	96	1	8	—	42	45	Uni. City
Modesto	CA	211	1	—	1	—	—	Stanislaus	211	107	1	8	—	29	69	Uni. City
Santa Cruz	CA	147	1	—	1	—	—	Santa Cruz	147	48	1	4	—	12	31	County Fed.
Eugene-																	
Springfield	OR	237	1	—	1	—	—	Lane	237	76	1	11	—	17	47	Fed. Muni.
Salem	OR	202	2	—	1	—	1	Marion	164	95	1	18	—	36	40	Uni. City
Yakima	WA	151	1	—	1	—	—	Yakima	151	65	1	14	—	15	35	Fed. Muni.
Richland-Konnewick	WA	97	2	—	1	—	1	Benton	71	NA						Fed. Muni.
Anchorage	AK	149	1	1	—	—	—	Anchorage	149	4*	1	3	—	—	—	Cons. ci/co
Honolulu	HI	691	1	1	—	—	—	Honolulu	691	4	**	1	—	—	3	Cons. ci/co

*Prior to consolidation
**Consolidated city/county enumerated as a municipality

County Types
CC Consolidated city/county
C Core
S Suburban or satellite
F Fringe

Governmental Units
Co. County
Muni. Municipalities
Twp. Townships
Sch. Dist. School Districts

Suggested Organization
Uni. City Unified City
Fed. Muni. Federated Municipality
Cons. ci/co Consolidated city/county
County Fed. Countywide Federation

Table 16: Free-Standing New England and Virginia Metropolitan Areas

SMSA	State	1974 pop. (000)	Governmental Units (1972)						Suggested Organization
			All	Co.	Muni	Twp.	Sch. dist.	Spec. dist.	
In New England									
Portland	ME	227	15	—	3	6	1	5	Fed. Muni.
Lewiston-Auburn	ME	95	6	—	2	1	—	3	Fed. Muni.
Manchester	NH	108	12	—	1	3	3	5	Fed. Muni.
Nashua	NH	66	4	—	1	1	1	1	Fed. Muni.
Springfield-Chicopee-Holyoke	MA-CT	590	48	—	5	16	2	25	Fed. Muni.
Worchester	MA	344	58	—	1	21	8	28	Fed. Muni.
Pittsfield	MA	150	12	—	1	4	2	5	Fed. Muni.
Fitchburg-Leominster	MA	97	12	—	2	4	2	4	Fed. Muni.
New Haven-West Haven	CT	356	28	—	3	9	1	15	Fed. Muni.
New London-Norwich	CT	240	49	—	5	11	—	33	Fed. Muni.
Waterbury	CT	209	17	—	2	8	3	4	Fed. Muni.
Meriden	CT	56	2	—	—	—	—	1	Uni. City.
In Virginia									
Richmond	VA	570	7	3	2	—	—	2	Fed. Muni.
Roanoke	VA	212	4	1	3	—	—	—	Fed. Muni.
Lynchburg	VA	142	7	2	4	—	—	1	Fed. Muni.
Petersburg-Colonial Heights-Hopewell	VA	124	8	2	4	—	—	2	Fed. Muni.

Table 17: Free-Standing, Multicounty Metropolitan Areas

	Standard Metropolitan Statistical Areas							Core Counties		Governmental Units (1972)						
		1974 pop.	County Types						1974 pop.					Sch.	Spec.	Suggested
SMSA	State	(000)	All	CC	C	S	F	County	(000)	All	Co.	Muni.	Twp.	dist.	dist.	Organization
SINGLE STATE																
In Strong-Township States																
Albany -Schenectady -Troy	NY	799	5	—	3	1	1	Albany	289	52	1	9	10	13	19	County Fed.
								Schenectady	160	37	1	3	5	7	24	County Fed.
								Rensselaer	154	59	1	7	14	13	21	County Fed.
Utica-Rome	NY	338	2		1	1	—	Oneida	270	95	1	21	26	20	27	County Fed.
Northeast	PA	633	3	—	2	—	1	Luzerne	347	130	1	38	36	12	43	County Fed.
								Lackawanna	233	67	1	19	21	10	16	County Fed.
Harrisburg	PA	426	3	—	1	1	1	Dauphin	227	86	1	17	23	11	34	County Fed.
Grand Rapids	MI	559	2	—	1	1	—	Kent	420	56	1	13	21	19	2	County Fed.
Lansing- E. Lansing	MI	441	4	—	1	1	2	Ingham	267	41	1	8	16	13	3	County Fed.
Appleton- Oshkosh	MI	282	3	—	2	—	1	Outagamie	122	46	1	11	20	7	7	Fed. Muni.
								Winnebago	131	25	1	5	16	2	1	Fed. Muni.
Eau Clare	WI	124	2	—	1	1	—	Eau Clare	75	NA						Fed. Muni.
In Weak-Township States																
Dayton	OH	845	4	—	1	2	1	Montgomery	595	56	1	18	13	17	7	County Fed.
Youngstown- Warren	OH	543	2	—	2	—	—	Mahoning	304	45	1	10	14	14	6	Fed. Muni.
								Trumbull	239	62	1	10	25	21	5	Fed. Muni.
Peoria	IL	352	3	—	1	1	1	Peoria	199	82	1	14	19	19	29	Uni. Muni.
In No-Township States																
Nashville- Davidson	TN	745	8	1	—	2	5	Davidson	450	15	**	7	—	—	8	Cons. ci/co

Table 17: (con't)

In No-Township States (cont)

City	State						County							Type
Greensboro-Winston Salem-High Point	NC	780	6	–	2	2	Guilford	299	11	1	5	–	5	County Fed.
							Forsyth	223	8	1	2	–	5	Cons. ci/co
Charlotte-Gastonia	NC	589	3	–	1	1	Mecklenberg	374	11	1	7	–	3	Cons. ci/co
Raleigh-Durham	NC	462	3	–	2	1	Wake	257	17	1	12	–	4	Uni. City
							Durham	139	5	1	1	–	3	Cons. ci/co
Greenville-Spartanburg	SC	522	3	–	2	–	Greenville	265	36	1	8	–	26	Uni. City
							Spartanburg	190	45	1	14	–	23	Uni. City
Charleston-N.Charleston	SC	362	3	–	1	1	Charleston	260	21	1	11	–	8	Cons. ci/co
Columbia	SC	361	2	–	1	–	Richland	249	17	1	7	–	7	Cons. ci/co
Macon	GA	236	4	–	1	2	Bibb	143	6	1	2	–	2	County Fed.
Orlando	FL	579	3	–	1	1	Orange	410	32	1	30	–	16	County Fed.
Florence	AL	121	2	–	1	–	Lauderdale	73	12	1	6	–	3	Uni. City
Jackson	MS	279	2	–	1	1	Hinds	224	16	1	8	–	3	Uni. City
Shreveport	LA	237	3	–	1	1	Caddo	237	19	1	11	–	6	Uni. City
Oklahoma City	OK	766	5	–	1	3	Oklahoma	551	41	1	19	–	3	County Fed.
Beaumont-Port Arthur-Orange	TX	345	3	–	2	1	Jefferson	238	33	1	9	–	16	County Fed.
							Orange	73	21	1	6	–	9	Fed. Muni.
Amarillo	TX	150	2	–	2	–	Potter	90	9	1	1	–	2	Uni. City
							Randall	60	6	1	2	–	2	Uni. City
Sacramento	CA	883	3	–	1	2	Sacramento	687	101	1	4	–	17	County Fed.

Table 17 (cont).

SMSA	State	1974 pop. (000)	County Types All	CC	C	S	F	Core Counties County	1974 pop. (000)	Gov. Units All	Co.	Muni.	Twp.	Sch. dist.	Spec. dist.	Suggested Organization
INTERSTATE																
Allentown-Bethlehem-Easton	PA-NJ	617	4	—	2	1	1	Lehigh, PA	263	67	1	9	15	10	32	County Fed.
								Northampton,PA	223	84	1	21	17	9	36	County Fed.
Steubenville-Weirton	OH-WV	167	3	—	1	1	1	Jefferson,OH	96	45	1	20	14	6	4	Uni. City
Wheeling	WV-OH	183	3	—	1	2	—	Ohio,WV	62	9	1	5	—	1	2	Cons. ci/co
Parkersburg-Marietta	WV-OH	150	3	—	2	—	1	Wood,WV	86	10	1	3	—	1	5	Uni. City
								Washington,OH	59	40	1	7	22	6	4	Uni. City
Huntington-Ashland	WV-KY-OH	290	5	—	2	1	2	Cabell, WV	106	12	1	3	—	4	7	Uni. City
								Boyd, KY	53	12	1	2	—	4	5	Fed. Muni.
Toledo	OH-MI	781	5	—	1	2	2	Lucas, OH	482	41	1	10	11	8	11	County Fed.
Davenport-Rock Island-Moline	IA-IL	364	3	—	2	1	—	Scott, IA	147	30	1	17	—	5	7	Fed. Muni.
								Rock Island, IL	163	73	1	15	24	10	34	Fed. Muni.
Duluth-Superior	MN-WI	262	2	—	1	1	—	St. Louis,MN	217	124	1	27	71	17	8	Uni. City
Fargo-Moorhead	ND-MN	126	2	—	2	—	—	Cass, ND	79	113	1	20	50	18	24	Uni. City
								Clay, MN	47	51	1	11	30	6	3	Uni. City
Omaha	NE-IA	575	3	—	1	2	—	Douglas, NE	415	135	1	7	—	16	111	Uni. City
Louisville	KY-IN	893	5	—	1	1	3	Jefferson,KY	706	120	1	65	—	3	51	County Fed.
Clarksville-Hopkinsville	KY-TN	140	2	—	2	—	—	Christian, KY	68	NA						Uni. City
								Montgomery, KY	72	NA						Uni. City

Table 17 (cont).

INTERSTATE (cont).

Area	State							County								Type
Johnson City -Kingsport -Bristol	TN-VA	392	7	—	2	—	5	Washington,TN	80	NA	1	8	—	—	11	Uni. City
								Sullivan, TN	132	NA	1	3	—	1	3	Uni. City
Chattanooga	TN-GA	390	6	—	1	2	3	Hamilton,TN	265	20	1	8	—	—	11	County Fed.
Augusta	GA-SC	274	3	—	1	1	1	Richmond,GA	154	8	1	3	—	1	3	County Fed.
Columbus	GA-AL	218	3	1	—	1	1	Muskogee,GA	157	5	**	2	—	1	2	Cons. ci/co
Fort Smith	AR-TX	173	4	—	1	1	2	Sebastian, AR	84	20	1	10	—	7	2	Uni. City
Texarkana	TX-AR	114	3	—	2	—	1	Bowie, TX	69	32	1	8	—	15	8	Uni. City
								Miller,AR	33	18	1	3	—	5	9	Uni. City

**Consolidated city/county enumerated as a municipality.

Table 18: Metropolitan Regions

Region / SMSA	State	1974 pop. (000)	County Types All	CC	C	S	F	Core County	1974 pop. (000)	Gov. Units All	Co.	Muni.	Twp.	Sch. dist.	Spec. dist.	Suggested Organization
SINGLE STATE																
Buffalo	NY	1,331	2	—	2	—	—	Erie	1,093	108	1	18	25	29	35	County Fed.
								Niagara	237	34	1	8	12	10	3	County Fed.
Pittsburgh	PA	2,334	4	—	1	3	—	Allegheny	1,532	313	1	85	42	49	136	County Fed.
Southeast Michigan		4,684														
Detroit	MI	4,434	6	—	1	3	2	Wayne	2,556	90	1	34	10	39	6	County Fed.
Ann Arbor	MI	250	1	—	1	—	—	Washtenaw	250	42	1	7	20	11	3	County Fed.
Southeast Wisconsin		1,711														
Milwaukee	WI	1,415	4	—	1	3	—	Milwaukee	1,034	37	1	19	—	13	4	County Fed.
Racine	WI	174	1	—	1	—	—	Racine	174	40	1	9	9	12	9	Muni. Fed.
Kenosha	WI	122	1	—	1	—	—	Kenosha	122	28	1	4	8	14	1	Uni. City
Northeast Ohio		2,921														
Cleveland	OH	1,984	4	—	1	1	2	Cuyahoga	1,621	100	1	56	4	33	6	County Fed.
Akron	OH	671	2	—	1	1	—	Summit	540	55	1	20	13	17	4	County Fed.
Lorain-Elyria	OH	266	1	—	1	—	—	Lorain	266	55	1	15	18	16	5	County Fed.
Columbus	OH	1,067	5	—	1	2	2	Franklin	859	65	1	27	17	17	3	County Fed.
Indianapolis	IN	1,144	8	1	—	—	7	Marion	792	52	**	5	9	11	27	Cons. ci/co
Minneapolis-St.Paul	MN-WI	2,011	10	—	2	3	5	Hennepin	925	68	1	42	1	16	8	County Fed.
								Ramsey	462	29	1	15	1	5	7	County Fed.
Baltimore	MD	2,140	6	1	—	5	—	Baltimore City	864	1	**	—	—	—	—	Cons. ci/co
Atlanta	GA	1,776	15	—	1	4	10	Fulton	580	23	1	10	—	2	10	Cons. ci/co

Table 18: (cont).

SINGLE STATE (cont)

Southern Florida		*2,667*													
Miami	FL	1,416	1	—	1	—	Dade	1,416	33	1	27	—	2	3	County Fed.
Fort Lauderdale-Hollywood	FL	807	1	—	1	—	Broward	807	46	1	29	—	2	14	County Fed.
W. Palm Beach-Boca Raton	FL	444	1	—	1	—	Palm Beach	444	75	1	37	—	2	35	County Fed.
Tampa-St. Petersburg	FL	1,333	3	—	2	1	Hillsborough	571	10	1	3	—	2	4	County Fed.
							Pinellas	640	35	1	24	—	2	8	County Fed.
New Orleans	LA	1,090	4	1	—	2	Orleans	567	4	**	1	—	1	2	Cons. ci/co
Dallas	TX	2,499	11	—	2	7	Dallas	1,376	55	1	28	—	15	11	County Fed.
Ft. Worth							Tarrant	721	61	1	33	—	17	10	County Fed.
Houston-Galveston		*2,401*													
Houston	TX	2,223	6	—	1	5	Harris	1,900	170	1	29	—	22	118	County Fed.
Galveston-Texas City	TX	179	1	—	1	—	Galveston	179	39	1	8	—	11	19	County Fed.
Denver-Boulder	CO	1,391	7	1	1	3	Denver City	502	9	**	1	—	1	7	Cons. ci/co
							Boulder	162	41	1	10	—	2	28	County Fed.
Wasatch Front		*928*													
Salt Lake City-Ogden	UT	766	4	—	2	1	Salt Lake	501	38	1	9	—	4	24	County Fed.
							Weber	132	34	1	11	—	2	20	County Fed.
Provo-Orem	UT	163	1	—	1	—	Utah	163	35	1	16	—	3	15	County Fed.
Southern California		*10,231*													
Los Angeles-Long Beach	CA	6,926	1	—	1	—	Los Angeles	6,926	232	1	77	—	94	60	County Fed.
Anaheim-Santa Ana-Garden Grove	CA	1,661	1	—	1	—	Orange	1,661	111	1	25	—	34	51	County Fed.
Riverside-San Bernardino-Ontario	CA	1,214	2	—	2	—	Riverside	511	120	1	16	—	32	71	County Fed.

Table 18: (cont).

Region / SMSA	State	1974 pop. (000) All	County Types All	CC	C	S	F	Core Counties County	1974 pop. (000)	Governmental Units (1972) All	Co.	Muni.	Twp.	Sch. dist.	Spec. dist.	Suggested Organization
SINGLE STATE (cont)																
Oxnard-Simi Valley-Ventura	CA	430	1	—	1	—	—	Ventura	430	76	1	9	—	22	44	County Fed.
San Francisco Bay		4,585														
San Francisco	CA	3,136	5	1	1	3	—	San Francisco	677	8	**	1	—	2	5	Cons. ci/co
-Oakland	CA							Alameda	1,089	62	1	13	—	22	26	County Fed.
San Jose	CA	1,182	1	—	1	—	—	Santa Clara	1,182	75	1	15	—	37	22	County Fed.
Vallejo-Fairfield-Napa	CA	268	2	—	1	—	1	Solano	180	42	1	7	—	7	27	Fed. Muni.
Puget Sound		1,794														
Seattle-Everett	WA	1,386	2	—	1	1	—	King	1,135	179	1	28	—	21	129	County Fed.
Tacoma	WA	398	1	—	1	—	—	Pierce	398	79	1	18	—	17	43	County Fed.
Eastern Massachusetts		3,918														
Boston	MA	NA								147	—	17	61	6	63	
Brockton	MA	NA								18	—	1	9	2	6	
Lawrence-Haverhill	MA-NH	NA								21	—	2	10	3	6	
Lowell	MA-NH	NA								16	—	1	6	—	9	
Central Connecticut		1,059														
Hartford	CT	NA								68	—	1	26	1	40	Federation
New Britain	CT	NA								9	—	1	3	—	5	
Bristol	CT	NA								5	—	1	1	—	3	

Table 18: (cont).

Area	State	Pop						Central area	Pop							Federation
SINGLE STATE (cont)																
Virginia Tidewater Norfolk-		*1,113*														
Virginia Beach-Portsmouth	VA	766				3	1			10	—	4	—	—	6	
Newport News-Hampton	VA	347					2			6	1	3	3	—	2	
INTERSTATE																
Greater New York		*17,181*														
New York	NY-NJ	9,634	9	5a	—	3	1	New York City	7,567	3	**	1	—	—	2	Cons. ci/co
Nassau-Suffolk	NY	2,620	2	—	2	—	—	Nassau	1,398	164	1	66	3	56	38	County Fed.
								Suffolk	1,223	202	1	29	10	75	87	County Fed.
Newark	NJ	2,019	4	—	1	3	—	Essex	897	45	1	18	4	16	6	County Fed.
Jersey City	NJ	583	1	—	1	—	—	Hudson	583	33	1	10	2	2	18	County Fed.
Paterson-Clifton-Passaic	NJ	456	1	—	1	—	—	Passaic	456	49	1	13	3	17	15	County Fed.
Long Branch-Asbury Park	NJ	486	1	—	1	—	—	Monmouth	486	129	1	38	15	51	24	County Fed.
New Brunswick-Perth Amboy-Sayerville	NJ	590	1	—	1	—	—	Middlesex	590	76	1	15	10	20	30	County Fed.
Bridgeport	CT	NA								27	—	3	5	—	19	
Stamford	CT	NA								15	—	1	3	—	11	
Norwalk	CT	NA								9	—	1	2	—	6	
Danbury	CT	NA								5	—	1	1	—	3	
Lower Delaware Valley		*5,642*														
Philadelphia	PA-NJ	4,810	8	1	—	7	—	Philadelphia	1,842	7	**	1	—	2	4	Cons. ci/co
Trenton	NJ	319	1	—	1	—	—	Mercer	319	39	1	5	8	8	17	County Fed.
Wilmington	DE-NJ-MD	513	3	—	1	—	2	New Castle	395	28	1	11	—	12	4	County Fed.

Table 18: (cont).

Metropolitan Regions and SMSAs			County Types					Core Counties		Governmental Units (1972)						
Region / SMSA	State	1974 pop. (000)	All	CC	C	S	F	County	1974 pop. (000)	All	Co.	Muni.	Twp.	Sch. dist.	Spec. dist.	Suggested Organization
INTERSTATE (cont)																
Washington	DC-MD-VA	3,015	7	—	—	5	2	(D.C.)	723	3	—	1	—	—	2	Unified
Cincinnati-Hamilton		*1,618*														
Cincinnati	OH-KY-IN	1,376	7	—	1	1	5	Hamilton	902	80	1	36	12	23	8	County Fed.
Hamilton-Middletown	OH	242	1	—	1	—	—	Butler	242	38	1	11	13	9	4	County Fed.
Chicago-Gary		*7,615*														
Chicago	IL	6,971	6	—	1	4	1	Cook	5,372	500	1	120	29	154	196	County Fed.
Gary-Hammond-E.Chicago	IN	644	2	—	1	—	1	Lake	549	84	1	17	11	16	39	County Fed.
St. Louis	MO-IL	2,371	9	1	—	5	3	St. Louis City	534	6	**	1	—	2	3	Cons. ci/co
Kansas City	MO-KS	1,302	7	—	1	3	3	Jackson	648	48	1	19	—	15	13	County Fed.
Portland	OR-WA	1,080	4	—	1	3	—	Multnomah	539	65	1	6	—	16	42	County Fed.
Providence-New Bedford		*1,318*														
Providence-Warwick-Pawtucket	RI	854								84	—	8	25	2	49	Federation
New Bedford-Fall River	MA	464								23	—	2	9	1	11	Federation

**Consolidated city/county enumerated as a municipality.

aNew York City has five counties with minor functions.

REFERENCES

ANDERSON, W. (1949) *The Units of Government in the United States.* Chicago: Public Administration Service.

Advisory Commission on Intergovernmental Relations (ACIR) (1962) *Alternative Approaches to Governmental Organization in Metropolitan Areas.* Washington: Government Printing Office.

――― (1963) *Performance of Urban Functions: Local and Areawide.*

――― (1966) *Metropolitan America: Challenge to Federalism.*

――― (1967A) *Fiscal Balance in the American Federal System.* Vol. 1.

――― (1967B) *Fiscal Balance in the American Federal System.* Vol. 2. *Metropolitan Fiscal Disparities.*

――― (1969) *State Aid to Local Government.*

――― (1970) *The Commuter and the Municipal Income Tax.*

――― *Substate Regionalism and the Federal System.*

(1973A) Vol. I. *Regional Decision Making: New Strategies for Substate.*

(1973B) Vol. II. *Regional Governance: Promise and Performance.*

(1974A) Vol. III. *The Challenge of Local Governmental Reorganization.*

(1974B) Vol. IV. *Governmental Functions and Processes: Local and Areawide.*

(1974C) Vol. V. *A Look to the North: Canadian Regional Experience.*

――― (1976A) *Improving Urban America: A Challenge to Federalism.*

――― *Significant Features of Fiscal Federalism.*

(1976B) Vol. I. *Trends.* 1976 edition.

(1977A) Vol. II. *Revenue and Debt.* 1976-77 edition.

――― (1977B) *Improving Federal Grants Management.*

BAIN, C.W. (1966) *Annexation in Virginia.* Charlottesville: University of Virginia Press.

――― (1967) *"A Body Incorporate": The Evolution of City-County Separation in Virginia.* Charlottesville: University of Virginia Press.

BALDINGER, S. (1971) *Planning and Governing the Metropolis: The Twin Cities Experience.* New York: Praeger.

BARTON, A.H. (1976) "Research report on New York experiment" in *Neighborhood, Decentralization* (January-February 1976). Washington: Center for Governmental Studies.

―――, ed. (1977) *Decentralizing City Government.* Lexington, Mass.: D.C. Heath.

BISH, R.L. (1971) *The Public Economy of Metropolitan Areas.* Chicago: Markham.

BISH, R.L. and V. OSTROM (1973) *Understanding Urban Government: Metropolitan Reform Reconsidered.* Washington: American Enterprise Institute for Public Policy Research.

BOLLENS, J.C. (1957) *Special District Governments in the United States.* Berkeley: University of California Press.

BOLLENS, J.C. and H.J. SCHMANDT (1970) *The Metropolis: Its People, Politics and Economic Life.* Second edition. New York: Harper & Row.
BOORSTIN, D.J. (1965) *The Americans: The National Experience.* New York: Random House.
BOOTH, D.A. (1963) *Metropolitics: The Nashville Consolidation.* East Lansing: Michigan State University Press.
BRADLEY, T. (1974) "Regional governments and racial and ethnic minorities" in Mathewson, *The Regionalist Papers.*
BROWN, L.J. (1975) "County administration: characteristics and managerial styles" in *The County Year Book*, 1976, Washington, D.C.: National Association of Counties.
CARPENTER, W.S. (1940) *Problems in Service Levels: The Readjustment of Services and Areas in Local Government.* Princeton, N.J.: Princeton University Press.
CASSELLA, W.N., Jr. (1975) "A century of home rule" in *National Civic Review* (October 1975) Vol. 64, No. 9.
Chamber of Commerce of the United States (1971) *City/County Government Consolidation: Columbus, Georgia.* Washington, D.C.: The Chamber.
CHI, K.S. (1975) "Lexington-Fayette attempt demerger" in *National Civic Review* (October 1975) Vol. 64, No. 9.
COMMAGER, H.S. (1950) *The American Mind.* New Haven, Conn.: Yale University Press.
Commission on Population Growth and the American Future (1972) *Population and the American Future.* Washington, D.C.: Government Printing Office.
Committee for Economic Development, Research and Policy Committee (1966). *Modernizing Local Government.* New York: The Committee.
––– (1970) *Reshaping Government in Metropolitan Areas.* New York: The Committee.
Comptroller General of the United States (1977) *Federally Assisted Areawide Planning: Need to Simplify Policies and Practices.* Washington, D.C.: General Accounting Office.
Congressional Budget Office (1977) *Poverty Status of Families Under Alternative Definitions of Income.* Washington, D.C.: The Office.
COOMER, J.C. and C.B. TYER (1974) *Nashville Metropolitan Government: The First Decade.* Knoxville: Bureau of Public Administration, University of Tennessee.
Council of State Governments (1976) *State-Growth Management.* Washington, D.C.: U.S. Department of Housing and Urban Development.
CROUCH, W.W. and B. DINNERMAN (1963) *Southern California Metropolis: A Study in Development of Government in a Metropolitan Area.* Berkeley: University of California Press.
DAHL, R. (1967) "The city in the future of democracy" in *American Political Science Review* (December 1967) Vol. 56, No. 4.
DAVIS, R. (1967) "The 'Federal Principle' reconsidered" in Wildavsky, *American Federalism.*
DEGRAZIA, A. (1962) *Politics and Government.* Vol. II. *Political Organization.* New York: Collier.
DEGROVE, J.M. (1973A) "The City of Jacksonville: consolidation in action" in ACIR, 1973A.
––– (1973B) "Southern regionalism" in ACIR, 1973B.
DE TOCQUEVILLE, A. (n.d.) *Democracy in America.* Translated by Henry Reeves. New York: A.S. Barnes.
DE TORRES J. (1972) *Governmental Services in Major Metropolitan Areas.* New York: The Conference Board.
DILLICK, S. (1953) *Community Organization for Neighborhood Development–Past and Present.* New York: Morrow.

DILLON, J.F. (1872) *Treatise on the Law of Municipal Corporations.* Chicago: James Cockcroft.

Domestic Council, Committee on Community Development (1976). *1976 Report on National Growth and Development: The Changing Issues for National Growth.* Washington, D.C.: Government Printing Office.

DOWNS, A. (1973) *Opening up the Suburbs: An Urban Strategy for America.* New Haven, Conn.: Yale University Press.

DUNCOMBE, H.S. (1966) *County Government in America.* Washington, D.C.: National Association of Counties Research Foundation.

EGGER, R. (1933) The Government of Berlin: A Study in Metropolitan Federation. Unpublished doctoral dissertation at the University of Michigan.

ELAZAR, D.J. (1961) *A Case Study of Failure in Attempted Metropolitan Integration: Nashville and Davidson County, Tennessee.* Chicago: National Opinion Research of the University of Chicago.

——— (1971) "The themes of a Journal of Federalism" in *Publius,* Vol. 1, No. 1.

——— (1975A) "Suburbanization: reviving the town on the metropolitan frontier" in *Publius* (Winter 1975) Vol. 5, No. 1.

——— (1975B) "Urbanism and federalism: twin revolutions of the modern era" in *Publius* (Spring 1975) Vol. 5, No. 2.

FALK, D. and H.J. FRANKLIN (1976) *Equal Housing Opportunity: The Unfinished Federal Agenda.* Washington, D.C.: Potomac Institute.

Federal Insurance Administration (1976) *Statutory Land Use Control Enabling Authority in the Fifty States.* Washington, D.C.: U.S. Department of Housing and Urban Development.

The Federalist (n.d.) Modern Library Edition. New York: Random House.

FESLER, J.W. (1949) *Area and Administration.* University, Ala.: University of Alabama Press.

FOLEY, D.L. (1972) *Governing the London Region: Reorganization and Planning in the 1960s.* Berkeley: University of California Press.

Ford Foundation (1973) *Community Development Corporations.* New York: The Foundation.

FORSTALL, R.L. (1972) "Changes in land area for larger cities, 1950-1970" in *The Municipal Year Book, 1972.* Washington, D.C.: International City Management Association.

——— (1975) "Annexations and corporate changes since the 1970 census: with historical data on annexation for larger cities for 1900-1970" in *The Municipal Year Book, 1975.* Washington, D.C.: International City Management Association.

FREISMA, H.P. (1971) *Metropolitan Political Structure.* Iowa City: University of Iowa Press.

FYFE, S. (1974) "Local government reform in Ontario" in ACIR, 1974C.

GANS, H.J. (1974) *More Equality.* New York: Random House.

GRANT, D.R. (1965) "A comparison of predictions and experience with Nashville 'Metro' "in *Urban Affairs Quarterly* (September 1965).

GRANT, W.R. (1975) "Detroit's experience with school decentralization" in *Neighborhood Decentralization* (May-June 1975). Washington: Center for Governmental Studies.

Greater Rochester Intergovernmental Panel (GRIP) (1975) *Two-Tiered Government in Monroe County, New York.* Rochester, N.J.: The Panel.

GRODZINS, M. (1966) *The American System.* Chicago: Rand McNalley.

GROSE, A.P. (1976) "Merger overturned in Las Vegas-Clark" in *National Civic Review* (December 1976), Vol. 65, No. 11.

GRUMM, J.G. (1959) *Metropolitan Area Government: The Toronto Experience.* Lawrence, Kansas: University of Kansas Publications.

GULICK, L. (1962) *The Metropolitan Problem and American Ideas.* New York: Alfred A. Knopf.

HALLMAN, H.W. (1967) "The Community action program—an interpretative analysis of 35 communities" in *Examination of the War on Poverty*, Staff and Consultants Reports, Vol. IV. Subcommittee on Employment, Manpower and Poverty, Committee on Labor and Public Welfare, U.S. Senate. Washington, D.C.: U.S. Government Printing Office.

——— (1970) *Neighborhood Control of Public Programs.* New York: Praeger.

——— (1973) "The neighborhood as an organizational unit: a historical perspective" in George Frederickson, ed., *Neighborhood Control in the 1970s.* New York: Chandler.

——— (1974A) *Neighborhood Government in a Metropolitan Setting.* Beverly Hills: Sage Publications. (Republished in 1977 under title of *Grass Roots Government.*)

——— (1974B) "Neighborhood power: a ten year perspective" in *Neighborhood Decentralization* (November-December 1974). Washington, D.C.: Center for Governmental Studies.

——— (1976) "Neighborhood councils: their status in 1976" in *Neighborhood Decentralization* (May-June 1976). Washington, D.C.: Center for Governmental Studies.

——— (1977) *The Organization and Operation of Neighborhood Councils: A Practical Guide.* New York: Praeger.

HANSON, R. (1966) *Metropolitan Councils of Governments. An information report of the Advisory Commission on Intergovernmental Relations.* Washington, D.C.: U.S. Government Printing Office.

HARRIGAN, J.J. (1976) *Political Change in the Metropolis.* Boston: Little, Brown.

HAVARD, W.C. and F.C. CROTY (1974) *Rural-Urban Consolidation: The Merger of Governments in Baton Rouge.* Baton Rouge: Louisiana State University Press.

HAWKINS, B. (1966) *Nashville Metro: The Politics of City-County Consolidation.* Nashville: Vanderbilt University Press.

HAWLEY, A.H. and B.G. ZIMMER (1970) *The Metropolitan Community.* Beverly Hills: Sage Publications.

HAWORTH, L. (1963) *The Good City.* Bloomington: Indiana University Press.

HOWARD, L.V. and R.S. FRIEDMAN (1959) *Government in Metropolitan New Orleans.* New Orleans: Tulane University.

Joint Center for Urban Studies (1964) *The Effectiveness of Metropolitan Planning.* Committee print of U.S. Senate, Committee on Government Operations, Subcommittee on Intergovernmental Relations. Washington, D.C.: U.S. Government Printing Office.

JONES, V. (1942) *Metropolitan Government.* Chicago: University of Chicago Press.

——— (1953) "Local government organization in metropolitan areas: its relation to urban redevelopment" in Coleman Woodbury, ed., *The Future of Cities and Urban Redevelopment.* Chicago: University of Chicago Press.

——— (1973) "Bay Area regionalism: institution, process and programs" in ACIR, 1973B.

——— (1974) "San Francisco Bay Area regionalism" in Mathewson, *The Regionalist Papers.*

JONES, V., J. GANSEL, and G. HOWE (1972) "County government organization and services" in *The Municipal Year Book, 1972.* Washington, D.C.: International City Management Association.

KANDEL, I.L. (1955) "History of education—United States" in *Encyclopaedia Britannica*, Vol. 7. Chicago: Encyclopaedia Britannica.

KAPLAN, H. (1967) *Urban Political Systems: A Functional Analysis of Metro Toronto.* New York: Columbia University Press.

KAUFMAN, H. (1969) "Administrative decentralization and political power" in *Public Administration Review* 29 (January-February 1969).

KELLER, S. (1968) *The Urban Neighborhood: A Sociological Perspective.* New York: Random House.

KOLDERIE, T. (1973) "Governance in the Twin Cities Area of Minnesota" in ACIR, 1973B.

KOTLER, M. (1969) *Neighborhood Government: The Local Foundations of Political Life.* Indianapolis: Bobbs-Merrill.

——— (1976) Statement before the Committee on Banking, Currency and Housing, U.S. House of Representatives, 94th Congress, 2nd Session. *The Rebirth of the American City,* Part 1. Washington, D.C.: Government Pringting Office.

KRAMER, R.M. (1969) *Participation of the Poor.* Englewood Cliffs, N.J.: Prentice-Hall.

LAWRENCE, C.B. and J.M. DeGrove (1976) "County government service" in *The County Year Book, 1976.* Washington, D.C.: National Association of Counties.

LEACH, R.H. (1970) *American Federalism.* New York: W.W. Norton.

League of Women Voters of the United States Education Fund (1974) *Supercity/ Hometown, U.S.A.: Prospects for Two-Tier Government.* New York: Praeger.

LETWIN, W. (1974) "A British approach to the reform of metropolitan governance: the Redcliffe-Maud Report, 1966-1969" in Wingo, *Reform as Organization.*

LIVINGSTON, W.S. (1967) "A note on the nature of federalism" in Wildavsky, *American Federalism.*

LONG, N. (1962) *The Polity.* Chicago: Rand McNally.

——— (1976) "The three citizenships" in *Publius,* (Spring 1976) Vol. 6., No. 2.

LOTZ, A. (1973) "Metropolitan Dade County" in ACIR, 1973B.

LYONS, W.E. (1973) "Lexington charter approval analyzed" in *National Civic Review* (March 1973) Vol. 62, No. 3.

MCARTHUR, R.E. (1973A) "The Atlanta Regional Commission" in ACIR, 1973B.

MCKENSIE, R.D. (1933) *The Metropolitan Community.* New York: McGraw-Hill.

MARANDO, V.L. (1974) "An overview of the political feasibility of local governmental reorganization" in Murphy and Warren, *Organizing Public Services in Metropolitan America.*

MARGOLIS, J. (1974) "Fiscal issues in the reform of metropolitan governance" in Wingo, *Reform as Reorganization.*

Marshal Kaplan, Gans and Kahn (1970) *The Model Cities Program: A Comparative Analysis of the Planning Process in Eleven Cities.* Washington, D.C.: U.S. Department of Housing and Urban Development.

MARSHALL, D.R. (1972) "Metropolitan government: view of minorities" in Wingo, *Minority Perspectives.*

MARTIN, R.C. (1963) *Metropolis in Transition: Local Government Adaptation to Changing Urban Needs.* Washington, D.C.: U.S. Housing and Home Finance Agency.

——— (1965) *The Cities and the Federal System.* New York: Atherton.

MARTIN, R. (1968) *Consolidation: Jacksonville-Duval County.* Jacksonville: Convention Press.

MATHEWSON, K., ed. (1974) *The Regionalist Papers.* Detroit: Metropolitan Fund.

MOGULOF, M. (1971) *Government Metropolitan Areas.* Washington, D.C.: The Urban Institute.

——— (1972) *Five Metropolitan Governments.* Washington, D.C.: The Urban Institute.

——— (1973) *A Modest Proposal for the Governance of America's Metropolitan Areas.* Washington, D.C.: The Urban Institute.

MURPHY, T.P. (1970) *Metropolitics and the Urban County*. Washington, D.C.: Washington National Press.

MURPHY, T.P. and C.R. WARREN, eds. (1974) *Organizing Public Services in Metropolitan America*. Lexington, Mass. D.C. Heath.

MUDD, J. (1976) "District manager cabinets in New York City" in *Neighborhood Decentralization* (January-February 1976). Washington, D.C.: Center for Governmental Studies.

NATHAN, R.P. and C. ADAMS (1976) "Understanding central city hardship" in *Political Science Quarterly* (Spring 1976) Vol. 91, No. 1.

National Academy for Public Administration (1977A) *Guidelines and Strategies for Local Government Modernization*. Washington, D.C.: The Academy.

––– (1977B) *Four U.S. Reform Efforts: Multi-Tiered Metropolitan Government*. Washington, D.C.: The Academy.

National Advisory Commission on Civil Disorder (1968) *Report of the,–––*. Washington, D.C.: U.S. Government Printing Office.

National Association of Regional Councils (1976) *Directory '77*. Washington, D.C.: The Association.

National Commission on Urban Problems (1968) *Building the American City*. Washington, D.C.: U.S. Government Printing Office.

National League of Cities (1966) *Adjusting Municipal Boundaries: Law and Practice*. Washington, D.C.: The League.

National Research Council, Social Science Panel on the Significance of Community in the Metropolitan Environment (1974) *Toward an Understanding of Metropolitan America*. San Francisco: Canfield.

National Urban League, Urban Renewal Demonstration Project (1973) *Toward Effective Citizen Participation in Urban Renewal*. New York: The League.

NEIMAN, M. (1975) *Metropology: Toward a More Constructive Research Agenda*. Beverly Hills: Sage Publications.

NISBET, R. (1966) *The Sociological Tradition*. New York: Basic Books.

Office of Management and Budget (1975) *Standard Metropolitan Statistical Areas*. Revised Edition, 1975. Washington, D.C.: U.S. Government Printing Office.

––– (1976) A-95: *What It Is—How It Works*. Washington, D.C.: U.S. Government Printing Office.

––– (1977) *Special Analysis: Budget of the United States Government, Fiscal Year 1978*. Washington, D.C.: U.S. Government Printing Office.

OSTROM, E., R.B. PARKS, and G.P. WHITAKER (1973) "Do we really want to consolidate urban police forces? A reappraisal of some old assumptions" in *Public Administration Review* (September/October 1973) Vol. 33, No. 5.

OSTROM, E. and R.B. PARKS (1973) "Suburban police departments: too many and too small?" in L.H. Masotti and J.K. Haden, eds., *The Urbanization of the Suburbs*, Urban Affairs Annual Review, Vol. 7. Beverly Hills: Sage Publications.

OSTROM, E. and D.C. SMITH (1976) "On the fate of 'lilliputs' in metropolitan policing" in *Public Administration Reveiw* (March/April 1976) Vol. 36, No. 2.

OSTROM, V., C.M. TIEBOUT, and R. WARREN (1961) "The organization of government in metropolitan areas: a theoretical inquiry" in *American Political Science Review* (December 1961) Vol. 55.

OSTROM, V. and E. OSTROM (1971) "Public choice: a different approach to the study of public administration" in *Public Administration Review* (March/April 1971) Vol. 31.

PACHON, H.P. and N.P. LORRICH, Jr. (1977) "The consolidation of urban services: a focus on the police" in *Public Administration Review* (January/February 1977) Vol. 37, No. 1.

PADOVER, S.K. (1943) *The Complete Jefferson.* New York: Duell, Sloan & Pearce.
––– (1963) *The Meaning of Democracy.* New York: Praeger.
PRICE, E.K. (1873) *The History of the Consolidation of the City of Philadelphia.* Philadelphia: J.P. Lippincott.
RAVITCH, D. (1975) "School decentralization in New York City: 1975" in *Neighborhood Decentralization* (May-June 1975). Washington, D.C.: Center for Governmental Studies.
RHODES, G. (1970) *The Government of London: The Struggle for Reform.* Toronto: University of Toronto Press.
––– ed. (1972) *The New Government of London: The First Five Years.* White Plains, N.Y.: International Arts and Science Press.
RIKER, W.H. (1967) "Federalism, origins, operation, significance" in Wildavsky, *American Federalism.*
ROBSON, W.A. (1974) "The reform of local government in England and Wales" in *National Civic Review* (November 1974) Vol. 63, No. 10.
RODGERS, B.D. and C. McLIPSEY (1974) Metropolitan reform: citizen evaluation of performance in Nashville-Davidson County, Tennessee" in *Publius* (Fall 1974) Vol. 4, No. 4.
ROSE, A. (1972) *Governing Metropolitan Toronto: A Social and Political Analysis, 1953-1971.* Berkeley: University of California Press.
––– (1974) "Too decades of metropolitan government in Toronto: 1953-1973" in ACIR, 1974C.
SANFORD, T. (1967) *Storm Over the States.* New York: McGraw-Hill.
SCHMANDT, H.J. (1973) "Decentralization: a structural imperative" in G. Frederickson, ed., *Neighborhood Control in the 1970s.* New York: Chandler.
––– (1974) "Intergovernmental volunteerism pro and con" in Mathewson, *The Regional Papers.*
SCHUMACHER, E.F. (1973) *Small is Beautiful: Economics as if People Mattered.* New York: Harper and Row.
SCOTT, M. (1969) *American City Planning Since 1809.* Berkeley: University of California Press.
SENGSTOK, F.S. (1960) *Annexation: A Solution to the Metropolitan Area Problem.* Ann Arbor: Legislative Research Center, University of Michigan Law School.
SMALLWOOD, F. (1963) *Metro Toronto: A Decade Later.* Toronto: Bureau of Municipal Research.
––– (1965) *Greater London: The Politics of Metropolitan Reform.* New York: Bobbs-Merrill.
SMITH, J. and S.D. Franklin (1975) The Distribution of Wealth among Families and Individuals, 1972. Unpublished paper.
SOFEN, E. (1963) *Miami Metropolitan Experiment.* Bloomington: Indiana University Press.
SONEBLUM, S., J.J. KIRLIN, and J.C. RIES (1975) *Providing Municipal Services: The Effects of Alternative Structures.* Los Angeles: University of California; Institute of Government and Public Affairs.
STANELY, D.T. (1976) *Cities in Trouble.* Columbus, Ohio: Academy for Contemporary Problems.
STENBERG, C.W. (1972) *The New Grass Roots Governments? Decentralization and Citizen Participation in Urban Areas.* Washington, D.C.: Advisory Commission on Intergovernmental Relations.
––– (1972) "Decentralization and the city" in *The Municipal Year Book, 1972.* Washington, D.C.: International City Management Association.

STONER, J.E. (1967) *Interlocal Governmental Cooperation: A Study of Five States.* Agriculture Report No. 118. Washington, D.C.: U.S. Department of Agriculture.

STUDENSKI, P. (1930) *The Government of Metropolitan Areas in the United States.* New York: National Municipal League.

Suncoast Study Panel (1974) *Report to the Region.* St. Petersburg: The Panel.

TEMPLE, D.G. (1972) *Merger Politics: Local Government Politics in Tidewater Virginia.* Charlottesville: University of Virginia Press.

THOMAS, S.F. (1960) *Nassau County: Its Governments and Their Expenditure and Revenue Patterns.* New York: City College Press.

TIEBOUT, C.M. (1956) "A pure theory of local expenditures" in *Journal of Political Economy* (October 1956) Vol. 64.

Twentieth Century Fund, Task Force on Community Development Corporations (1971) *CDCs: New Hope for the Inner City.* New York: The Fund.

UPSON, L.D. (1931) *The Growth of a City Government.* Detroit: Detroit Bureau of Governmental Research.

U.S. Bureau of the Census (1960) *Historical Statistics of the United States, Colonial Times to 1957.* Washington, D.C.: U.S. Government Printing Office.

——— (1971) *U.S. Census of Population: 1970.* Number of Inhabitants. United States Summary. Final Report PC(1)-A1.

——— (1973) *1972 Census of Governments.* Vol. 1. Governmental Organizations.

——— (1975) *1972 Census of Governments.* Vol. 5. Local Government in Metropolitan Areas.

——— (1976A) *Estimates of the Population of Metropolitan Areas, 1973 and 1974, and Components of Change Since 1970.* Current Population Reports. Series P-25, No. 618.

——— (1976B) *Money Income and Poverty Status of Families and Persons in the United States: 1975 and 1974 Revisions.* Current Population Reports, Series P-60, No. 103.

U.S. Commission on Civil Rights (1974) *The Federal Civil Rights Enforcement Effort— 1974.* Vol. II. to Provide . . . For Fair Housing. Washington, D.C.: The Commission.

U.S. Department of Housing and Urban Development (1976) Seven "Opportunity Housing Plans." News Release of August 30, 1976.

U.S. Housing and Home Finance Agency (1965) *1964 National Survey of Metropolitan Planning.* Prepared for the Subcommittee on Intergovernmental Relations, Committee on Governmental Operations, U.S. Senate, 89th Congress, 1st Session. Washington, D.C.: U.S. Government Printing Office.

WAGER, P., ed, (1950) *County Government Across the Nation.* Chapel Hill: University of North Carolina Press.

WALKER, D.R. (1977) Correspondence, March 29. (Walker is assistant director of the Advisory Commission on Intergovernmental Relations.)

WARNER, S.B. Jr. (1968) *The Private City: Philadelphia in Three Periods of Growth.* Philadelphia: University of Pennsylvania Press.

WARREN, R.O. (1966) *Government in Metropolitan Regions: A Reappraisal of Fractionated Political Organization.* Davis, Calif.: University of California Institute of Governmental Affairs.

WASHNIS, G.J. (1972) *Municipal Decentralization and Neighborhood Resources.* New York: Praeger.

——— (1974 *Community Development Strategies: Case Studies of Major Model Cities.* New York: Praeger.

WEILER, C.J. Jr. (1971) Community Control in West German Cities. Unpublished paper at Temple University.

WHERE, K.C. (1964) *Federal Government.* 4th Edition. New York: Oxford University Press.

WILDAVSKY, A., ed. (1967) *American Federalism in Perspective.* Boston: Little, Brown.

WILLBERN, Y. (1964) *The Withering Away of the City.* Birmingham: University of Alabama Press.

——— (1973) "Unigov: local government reorganization in Indianapolis" in ACIR, 1973B.

WILLIAMS, O.P. (1971) *Metropolitan Political Analysis: A Social Access Approach.* New York: Free Press.

WINGO, L., ed., *The Governance of Metropolitan Regions.* Washington, D.C.: Resources for the Future.

    (1972A) No. 1. *Reform of Metropolitan Governments.*

    (1972B) No. 2.*Minority Perspectives.*

    (1972C) No. 3. *Metropolitanization and the Public Services.*

    (1974) No. 4. *Reform as Reorganization.*

YATES, D. (1973) *Neighborhood Democracy.* Lexington, Mass.: D.C. Heath.

YLVISAKER, P. (1959) "Some criteria for a 'proper' areal division of governmental powers" in A. Maass, ed., *Area and Power.* New York: Free Press.

ZELLER, F. (1975) "Forms of county government" in *The County Year Book, 1975.* Washington, D.C.: National Association of Counties.

ZIMMERMAN, J.F. (1974) "Intergovernmental service agreements and transfer of functions" in ACIR, 1974A.

——— (1976) *Pragmatic Federalism: The Reassignment of Functional Responsibility.* An information report of the Advisory Commission on Intergovernmental Relations. Washington, D.C.: U.S. Government Printing Office.

INDEX

ABOUT THE AUTHOR

HOWARD W. HALLMAN received his Master's Degree in Political Science from the University of Kansas. He has worked as a volunteer in a New York settlement house, and in urban improvement programs in Philadelphia and New Haven. In the late 1960s he directed a study of the poverty program for a Senate subcommittee, and organized the Center for Governmental Studies in Washington, D.C., for which he currently serves as president. He is author of *Neighborhood Control of Public Programs* (1970), *Neighborhood Government in a Metropolitan Setting* (1974), *The Organization and Operation of Neighborhood Councils: A Practical Guide* (1977); and *Emergency Employment: A Study in Federalism* (1977). He also is editor of *Neighborhood Ideas*, an information-exchange bulletin and served on the panel of the multi-tiered metropolitan government project of the National Academy of Public Administration, of which he is a member.